Education
in the Two Germanies

This book has already been published in Germany and has been praised for its objectivity, authenticity and originality. It is the first book in English to attempt a comparison between the two States: the West, with its desire for pre-1933 values, and the East with its wish to transform the traditional culture through the school system. There is an historical introduction, an analysis of contrasting objectives and the partial retreat from entrenched ideological positions.

Arthur Hearnden is a graduate of Cambridge and spent 14 years teaching modern languages in schools in Northern Ireland, England, France and Germany before becoming interested in the study of Comparative Education. He has been a Research Officer for the Schools Council at Oxford University Department of Educational Studies and is at present a Lecturer in the Department of Comparative Education at London University Institute of Education.

Education
in the Two Germanies

ARTHUR HEARNDEN

WESTVIEW PRESS
BOULDER · COLORADO

Printed and bound in Great Britain

Library of Congress Cataloging in Publication Data

Hearnden, Arthur.
  Education in the two Germanies.

  Condensation and translation of Bildungspolitik in der BRD und
DDR.
  Based on the author's thesis, Oxford, 1972.
  Bibliography: p.
  Includes index.
  1. Education—Germany.   2.   Education and state—
Germany.   I.   Title.
LA721.82.H3813   1976   370'.943   75-46557
ISBN 0-89158-539-7

Contents

Preface

This book is based on a doctoral thesis presented at Oxford in 1972. The opening chapter was added later and is designed to give a broad outline of the history of German education for the benefit of the general reader. I hope that the specialist will be tolerant of this addition which is likely to appear grotesquely superficial by comparison with the remainder of the text. For the rest, the original has been condensed somewhat and the notes greatly reduced in number. The full version is available in German under the title *Bildungspolitik in der BRD und DDR*, Schwann Verlag, Düsseldorf 1973.

Parts of the text have been adapted for an article in *Comparative Education* and I am grateful to the editors for permission to reproduce in the present volume both these passages and the diagrams in Appendices VII and VIII. Other Appendices have been kept to a minimum by giving only sufficient school curricula to illustrate the historical development. More up-to-date curricula are however discussed in some detail in Chapter 6.

My thanks are due above all to Dr. W. D. Halls, under whose supervision the work was carried out and without whose generous support it could not have been completed. In the course of the research, I benefited from discussions with many colleagues in East and West Germany and in England. I owe a particular debt of gratitude to Dr. C. Führ of Frankfurt, Dr. M. Klewitz of Berlin and Dr. J. L. Henderson of London who have subsequently read parts of the manuscript and given valuable advice.

Arthur Hearnden

Introduction

Since the Second World War there has been a remarkable universality about some of the factors which compel the introduction of changes in the educational systems of developed countries. Similar social and economic pressures, occurring in diverse national contexts, have given rise to what are now ubiquitous phenomena, the increase in demand for education, the broadening of the social base from which the most highly qualified cadres are drawn, the reduced readiness to accept a traditional hierarchy of disciplines. In many respects such resemblances transcend the cardinal ideological barrier between communist and non-communist societies. Western European countries are cautiously adopting comprehensive school systems that are structurally little different from those that have long been established in Eastern Europe. And in Eastern Europe the early uncompromising aversion to differentiation of any kind has in recent years been patently modified. This global picture prompts speculation as to whether educational development has been characterized by a diminishing significance of ideological differences. If the social and economic pressures are increasingly similar, and if it is primarily in response to them that educational policy is formulated and school systems evolve, then it may be that past differences are being correspondingly reduced.

A proposition of this nature is difficult to explore. The peculiar historical, political, religious and ideological factors must be taken into account in any analysis of the nature and aims of a country's educational policy. Evaluation of the balance stuck between these indigenous forces on the one hand, and the increasingly supra-national social and economic pressures on the other, cannot but underline the unique character of each case. The educational systems of Europe, while they have influenced one another in a number of ways and mostly follow one of several dominant models, are none the less basically expressions of dissimilar national cultures. Comparisons are therefore difficult.

However in the case of the two German States, the Federal and Democratic Republics, the most daunting problems are obviated. Common in origin and culture until 1945, they have since undergone separate processes of development from opposed ideological points of departure. Consequently they provide a rare opportunity to examine and compare the conditions for educational development in communist and non-communist societies. To some extent the validity of the comparison must be limited to the two countries under scrutiny. The mutual hostility that has marked East-West relations in Europe as a whole has, in the case of Germany, carried emotional overtones that have caused certain trends to be exaggerated. But though these exaggerations are in some respects peculiar to Germany, it may also be that they illustrate with unusual clarity basic general premises which underline educational policy in communist and non-communist States. If this is in fact so, then a more general validity may be claimed for the comparison.

In view of the common historical origin, such explanation as can be given of the divergence of policy will derive from factors that are the product of the post-war situation. In the Federal Republic, West Germany, the desire remained strong throughout the period under review to retain the values that had traditionally impregnated the system, to preserve the traditional culture. In the Democratic Republic, the *DDR*, the purpose was systematically to transform it through radical change in the educational system. The school was seen as an instrument for the achievement of new social, economic and political objectives. This stands in marked contrast to the traditionalist view that education should be an 'autonomous province' concerned purely with the cultivation of the individual and unaffected by the economic requirements of the State or by any theory of how society should be ordered. Since the latter view remained strongly held in West Germany after the war, it contrasted vividly with the concept of the consciously socializing role of education which was subscribed to in the *DDR*.

More recently in the West, however, the claim that education either can be in theory or is ever in practice impervious to social and economic pressures has appeared as increasingly unfounded. With the growing awareness that the development of the educational system inevitably implies social change and equally inevitably must be used to serve economic ends, education has come to the fore as a political issue, revealing new and marked affinities with the approach in the *DDR*. In order to explore the pattern of divergence and convergence which is being adumbrated, it is proposed to present, after a brief historical introduction, a chronological survey of the course of educational policy—as conveyed by the term *Schulpolitik*—in the two States throughout their post-war existence. The major emphasis is placed on curricular developments and on the structure of the school system since the view is taken that it is in these areas that the effects of changing social, economic and political factors are most clearly to be seen. It is however readily acknowledged that there are other areas which also lend themselves to comparative study of this kind and it is to be hoped that new research will subsequently throw further light on the course of educational development in the two Germanies.

CHAPTER 1

The Educational Heritage

The Medieval Tradition

The medieval tradition in education owed its origins to the institutional needs of the Church.[1] The fulfilment of the Christian mission was dependent on a priesthood sufficiently educated to carry out its professional duties, above all reading and interpreting the scriptures. It was to meet this need that there grew up in the course of the Middle Ages an extensive network of institutions in which the requisite instruction in Latin could be given. For the laity, on the other hand, education was of much lesser importance. The peasantry need hardly be considered in such a context; as for the sons of merchants and artisans, they learnt their business or trade on the job, as apprentices; and even among the aristocracy such accomplishments as were required were for the most part learnt informally at home or at court. Where instruction of a more formal kind involving reading, writing and arithmetic was considered necessary or desirable among these lay social categories, it was acquired in the clerical schools and did not differ from that which was provided for the future clergy. The Church had in fact appropriated a monopoly of education which survived unimpaired until near the end of the Middle

[1] The major sources for this chapter are: F. Paulsen, *Geschichte des gelehrten Unterrichts*, 3rd ed., Vols. I and II, Leipzig, 1919, also the abridged version in English: *German Education, Past and Present*, London, 1908. F. Blättner, *Das Gymnasium*, Heidelberg, 1960. T. Wilhelm, *Pädagogik der Gegenwart*, Stuttgart, 1967.

Ages. Even then, when the growing demands of municipal life gave rise to the establishment of new institutions which were technically speaking secular, these were in practice little different from their clerical counterparts. Thus even after the monopoly of Church control was broken medieval education remained strongly clerical in character.

The genesis of this ecclesiastical provision of education in the German-speaking territories must be viewed against the background of the instability that followed the fall of the Roman Empire. Under Roman direction there had developed an effective system of schools designed to furnish municipality and state with practitioners of the various kinds required in order to exercise authority and guarantee efficient administration. The disintegration of this system of education left behind it a nullibiety following which the rebirth of education as an organized activity can be attributed to the work of the Benedictine monks. It was they who established the early monasteries at such places as St. Gallen, Reichenau and Fulda where from 822 to 842 the Abbot was Hrabanus Maurus, who had been a pupil of Alcuin at Tours and whose scholarship brought him the unofficial designation *praeceptor Germaniae*. Monastery schools therefore form the earliest category of institution in the medieval period. To begin with they were *scholae internae* existing exclusively for the training of future members of the order, but from the ninth century on some of them acquired *scholae externae* for future members of the secular clergy and of the laity too. A later category comprised the cathedral schools set up by individual bishoprics for the training of the clergy of the diocese. Thirdly the secular clergy of the collegiate churches followed suit by establishing the 'college schools' with the similar object of training their successors.

As befitted an education for the priesthood, the acquisition of the skills of literacy was accompanied by a strong devotional emphasis. As well as learning to read and write Latin the pupils committed to memory catechisms, psalms and liturgies in order to participate daily in formal worship. After this elementary stage the curriculum was based on the Roman classification of the *trivium* and the *quadrivium* which together comprised the 'seven liberal arts'. The *trivium*, originally aimed at fostering the eloquence which had been an indispensable skill in Roman political life, comprised grammar, rhetoric (the art of expression, both spoken and written) and dialectic (logic). The *quadrivium* was made up of arithmetic, geometry, music and astronomy. Three of these four had particular relevance for an ecclesiastical training: arithmetic and astronomy were both important for calculating the Christian calendar while music occupied a central place in worship. The monastery, cathedral and college schools therefore drew on the seven liberal arts in such a way as to provide the preliminary training appropriate for the eventual study of theology, of which the supreme importance was unchallenged.

From the thirteenth century onwards the need for schools made itself felt in a new context. In the cities which were major centres for trade the better-off inhabitants who were increasingly requiring schooling for their children began to find the existing clerical schools inadequate, not as regards the instruction they provided but rather because they were not always conveniently situated for easy access. Consequently as the demand for education spread, the municipal authorities took the initiative in setting up 'city schools' (*Stadtschulen*) to meet it. By the fifteenth century there was widespread provision of this kind, further supplemented by a number of private schools for elementary instruction in the reading and writing of German. In the city schools the programme did not greatly differ from that of the clerical schools, being primarily concerned with the study of Latin—both groups were sometimes comprehended within the term *Lateinschulen*—but there were some cases where the curriculum overlapped with that of the universities.

The earliest German universities were founded in the fourteenth century though in several cases such as those of Cologne and Erfurt the new institutions were in fact carrying on an

B

older tradition of philosophical and theological scholarship among the local clergy. The role of the medieval university was very largely to complete the ecclesiastical education begun in the schools. The teachers were clerics, the instruction, given in Latin, was based on the doctrine of the Church and successful students would generally expect to enter the ranks of the clergy. Despite the widespread development of educational institutions in the late Middle Ages it would be misleading to suggest the existence of an articulated system with clearly defined points of transition. True enough a school was a different kind of establishment from a university but there was no clear dividing line in terms of what was taught. While the most common age for the transition was probably about fifteen it was not uncommon to be enrolled at a university at a younger age. The initial stage of study was in the faculty of arts, leading first to a bachelor's, then to a master's degree at the age of twenty or so. The minority who reached this level successfully, then undertook teaching in the faculty and could also go on to further study in the higher faculties of law, theology or medicine. This could lead to a doctorate after seven or eight years.

The overriding significance of the growth of the universities lies in their potential intellectual independence. While it is true that they had the closest connections with the Church and acknowledged the authority of Rome, the medieval universities were also places where scholars gradually began to throw off intellectual inhibitions in a spirit of independent and critical inquiry.

Renaissance and Reformation

The flowering of this spirit of inquiry in the humanism of the Renaissance, the 'New Learning', had far-reaching consequences for German education. The predominance of philosophical and theological disputation in medieval scholarship had been accompanied by a certain disdain for creative literature.

The humanist scholars reversed the trend towards the ever more linguistically meticulous, ergotizing discourse dubbed scholasticism by reviving interest in a much wider range of classical writings than had hitherto been studied. Poetry and oratory came into their own and, correspondingly, medieval Latin was replaced by classical Latin. Interest in Greek literature grew in the universities. The new simplified manuals of classical Latin which began to appear at the turn of the fifteenth and sixteenth centuries bear witness to the gradual dissemination of the new approach to education.

The forerunners of the new development were the *fratres collationarii* (Brethren of the Common Life) who established themselves as teachers in the late fourteenth century at Deventer in Holland and later carried their activities and influence to various parts of Northern Europe including Germany where they set up some of the city schools in such places as Münster and Hildesheim. Their particular mode of reaction against scholasticism lay in their emphasis on the simple Christian virtues, but they did comparatively little to change the curriculum and improve teaching methods. Indeed Erasmus, one of the most illustrious pupils of the school at Deventer, later described it as 'barbarous'.[2] His own interest in education was marked by a concern to ease the task of learning Latin for school pupils by making it an attractive pastime pursued for enjoyment. For the corporal punishment which had been conspicuous among the incentives resorted to by the medieval schoolmaster he sought to substitute more positive motivation through praise which he described as the 'foster-mother of all the arts'. This element was necessary if the humanist desire to return to the sources of antiquity and scour them for new insights was to be fulfilled on a wide scale.

Renaissance influences in Germany were eventually overshadowed by the Reformation which also had a profound effect on educational developments. For Luther, as for Erasmus,

[2] D. Hay, *Europe in the Fourteenth and Fifteenth Centuries*, London, 1966, p. 335.

it was important that education should promote independent thinking. In this very general sense, the liberating drive of the Renaissance was reinforced by the Reformation. The new and significant element in the latter lay in its popularist implications. For Luther, learning was not to be valued primarily for the possibilities of aesthetic gratification which it opened up to communities of scholars, its function was rather to give every individual direct access to the scriptures and thereby to make possible a religious experience which was personal and not transmitted solely through the intermediacy of the priesthood. His German translation of the Bible was of foremost significance for this objective. But the extent to which the Bible was to be read by the mass of the people depended very largely on the fortunes of the elementary schools. It has already been noted that in the later Middle Ages private schools had begun to appear, providing rudimentary instruction in the German language. From the point of view of the Reformers these 'German schools' were valuable in that they could be entrusted with the teaching of the catechism to many children who would not subsequently be candidates for a classical education. But in the event they only developed as a genre in their own right in a makeshift way in the less populous areas. Elsewhere they were greatly overshadowed by the Latin schools, of which they were as often as not adjuncts of inappreciable significance. The initial boost given to the expansion of elementary education by the Reformation was limited in this way.

The 'secondary' schools remained very much *Lateinschulen*, viewed pre-eminently as constituting a preparation for the theological studies ultimately to be pursued at the University where Latin was the lingua franca of scholarship. Apart from doctrinal matters the new characteristics that can be attributed to the Reformation are firstly that there was perhaps a more conscious effort to inculcate a spirit of piety among pupils and secondly that the reformed church desired a more universally high standard of education among its clergy. Such blending of the humanist and reformist interests as came about can be perceived at its most efficacious in the person and work of Melanchthon who exerted the dominant influence on the development of schools in the first half of the sixteenth century. Not only was he himself active as a teacher and author of textbooks, first in Tübingen and later in Wittenberg, he was also instrumental in encouraging and promoting the foundation of new institutions in which the twin aims of piety and classical scholarship could be pursued. Like Hrabanus in an earlier age Melanchthon acquired the unofficial title of *praeceptor Germaniae*.

Much of the impetus for the growth in number of secondary, or, to use a more appropriate term, grammar schools along the lines of Melanchthon's model derived from the new self-consciousness of individual territories that followed the schism in the Church. Where the universities had formerly had no specially local character but had attracted teachers and students from all parts of Europe, various cities and states now began to aspire to the status and prestige which possession of such institutions could bestow. A recognizably separate ecclesiastical and educational unity had become one of the symbols of independence, a trend reflected in the appearance of grammar schools of a new kind founded by Protestant rulers. Variously known as *Fürstenschulen, Landesschulen,* or *Klosterschulen* in cases where they were installed in secularized monasteries, these schools were designed to train the most able young people for future service as officials of Church and State. Among the most famous examples were the three *Fürstenschulen* established in Saxony at Pforta, Meissen and Grimma. In the following century this somewhat utilitarian interest in education on the part of the State authorities was to grow substantially. The corresponding expansion which took place in the Catholic territories was primarily the work of the Society of Jesus. Although the Jesuits were not necessarily responsible for the foundation and endowment of the new grammar schools they generally succeeded in exercising effective control over them and indeed dominated education at this time in Catholic

States throughout Europe. Here too the spirit of classical learning was all-pervasive as in the Protestant domain.

The least satisfactory outcome of the triumph of classical learning in the schools of the sixteenth century was that the vernacular lapsed into desuetude as a vehicle for literary culture. German was stigmatized as the language of the uneducated; major writers wrote in Latin. This rejection of the vernacular prepared the way for the subsequent widespread adoption of French as the language of educated society, a trend that was only reversed through the efforts of leading figures of the German Enlightenment such as Lessing in the eighteenth century.

The Rise of the States and Reform Impulses

The closeness of the relationship between the Church and education continued into the seventeenth century. The grammar school (*Gelehrtenschule*, now beginning to be termed *Gymnasium*) was thoroughly permeated by the spirit of Christianity. The orthodoxy that this spirit engendered was, however, out of keeping with newer demands made on it. The desire to bring the activity of such schools up to date can be seen in the work of reformers like Comenius and Ratke who insisted that the real aim of education was not 'eloquens', liguistic facility in the service of theological debate, but rather 'sapiens', knowledge of external phenomena derived from the study of the sciences. Thus their preoccupation was with content, with the discoveries of the present rather than the heritage of the past. A natural corollary of this more realistic approach was a more utilitarian view of the role of languages in the curriculum. Some doubt was cast on the value of Latin teaching as generally practised, that is, with a strong emphasis on the mastery of grammar. In the new view the teaching of language should aim at skill in communication as well as being a means of access to the writings of scholars. These were still very largely in Latin of which the dominant place in the curriculum was difficult to challenge. But there was a new concern with the method of teaching foreign languages, on the analogy of the inductive method of the physical sciences, and, more significant for the longer term, a new concern for the mother tongue. In this development are reflected the beginnings of the movement to cultivate the German language as a competitor with Latin and French which were the established media in intellectual life. The response to the movement was however lukewarm, its impact piecemeal.

A more insistent call for a realistic approach to education derived from political sources rather than from the efforts of pioneer practitioners. An edict in Weimar in 1733 stated that henceforth the *Gymnasium* was to turn out not merely future theologians, physicians and lawyers but men 'who wish to serve God and the fatherland in other political offices, especially in military service, in economic, administrative, commercial and other affairs but especially as choir-masters and schoolmasters in country districts'.[3] This illustrates the kind of demands that the States were beginning to make on the schools. In Prussia the authorities were increasingly at pains to regulate their output, in particular in order to provide the educated cadres required for a civilian service which is sometimes regarded as having set the pattern for modern bureaucracies.

But the secondary schools did not always respond to calls for reform and adapt themselves to meet contemporary demands. More often than not they remained preparatory schools for theological studies, offering a curriculum with the traditional content taught in the traditional way. Consequently in a number of States they were supplemented by other forms of education among the nobility. The secular requirements of court diplomacy, internal administration and military leadership were growing steadily in importance and since the existing schools were mostly unable to meet them, those in court circles either employed private tutors or patronized the

[3] Blättner, op. cit., p. 38.

'*Ritterakademien*' which flourished from the mid-seventeenth to the end of the eighteenth century and in which worldly accomplishments, 'galantiora', were valued at least as highly as the more narrowly intellectual studies constituted by 'humaniora'. The grammar schools were thus by-passed by the ruling class largely because their curriculum was inappropriate for the secular needs of the State.

These secular needs also influenced the development of primary education. In the seventeenth century one or two of the smaller States, notably Gotha and Weimar, considered it worthwhile to compel parents to send their children to school. During the eighteenth century, interest in education spread northwards and the principle of compulsory schooling gained widespread acceptance. In Prussia which gradually emerged as the most powerul unit, Frederick William I issued edicts to this effect in 1716–17 partly out of Christian motives but partly for the economic benefits of training his subjects in general and his soldiers in particular. Enforcement of the edicts was not easy but succeeding Prussian governments built on this foundation and in 1763 the famous *Landschulreglement* of Frederick the Great went so far as to lay down that compulsory school attendance should span the age range of five to thirteen or fourteen and prescribed the curriculum. In Prussian elementary education a premium was placed on loyalty and obedience. A century later, a well-known anecdote ascribed the victory over Austria at Königgratz in 1866 to the qualities instilled into their pupils by Prussian schoolmasters. Whatever the element of caricature about this, it does serve to illustrate a view of the schools as the servants of the State which originated in the eighteenth century.

The rise of the German States was strongly influenced by the example of France whose stability and power had reached a high point under Louis XIV. It was on this absolute monarch that the German princes tended to model themselves. In so doing they emphasized their independence and created a particularistic tradition that hindered the development of aspirations towards unity of the German-speaking peoples. Indeed, by importing French culture they created an international atmosphere in which the German language carried the stigma of barbarism referred to earlier. It was the French character of the court in State capitals such as Berlin, Hanover, Dresden and Karlsruhe that was instrumental in injecting the strong element of 'galantiora' into the education of the aristocracy that has already been mentioned. But as the statesmanship of Frederick the Great gradually established Prussia as a power that could rival France in a military sense, the French cultural dominance came more and more to be resented. Out of this resentment grew the consciousness of being German, the interest in the traditions of the Germanic peoples and the autonomy of German literature established by men like Herder and Lessing.

The French influence had not been confined to the establishment of court conventions and activities. It ensured that the ferment of thought about education that was stirred up above all by Rousseau extended to Germany. Indeed Rousseau's ideas probably made a greater practical impact in Germany than in France. Following these ideas, educational pioneers tried to bring school into touch with real life by taking more account of the study of nature. Here was yet another strand to the reaction against the academic orthodoxy of the grammar schools. One of the leading figures in this trend was Basedow who, at Dessau in 1774, founded the 'Philanthropinum', a kind of middle-class counterpart of the *Ritterakademien*. Another practical exponent of Rousseau's views was the Swiss, Pestalozzi, whose teaching methods, devised in terms of their appropriateness for the developing capacities of the child, were for a time influential in Prussian schools. Froebel later went further than Pestalozzi in his concentration on the creative qualities inherent in a child's natural self-expression.

A second trend which also had its origins in the latter half of the eighteenth century was the growth of a new spirit in the teaching of the classics. In this the emphasis shifted from

linguistic exercises towards the study of the real spirit of antiquity as it emerged from the art and literature of the ancients,
with Greece replacing Rome as the primary source of inspiration. Winckelmann's famous evocation of the harmony of
Greek art appeared in 1755. The growing enthusiasm for
Greece was reflected in Wolf's theory of the Homeric origins of
the German nation which was advanced about this time. These
were the beginnings of the neoclassical movement and for its
adherents the natural science of the Basedow school of thought
with its utilitarian implications was of minor significance.

The early nineteenth century was to see the total inundation
of the *Gymnasium* with neoclassical values but in the eighteenth
century aspects of both neoclassicism and 'philanthropinism'
found a place alongside one another in the discovery of a new
cultural identity for Germany. Herder, prominent both as a
literary contributor to this new cultural dynamism and as a
theorist of education proposed a school programme in which
the classics were to be taught as living languages but with their
time allocations reduced to make way for natural science,
mathematics, physics, history and geography—subjects regarded as corresponding to the natural impulses and interests
of youth and useful to the individual in fulfilling his role in the
community. Subsequently the philosopher Schleiermacher was
another who saw separate and equally valid justifications for
both the classics and the more modern subjects. It was at the
failure to retain a balance between these two domains that he
directed his criticism of the *Gymnasium* in its neoclassical phase.

Neoclassicism and the New Nationalism

For all the novelty of the educational ideas thrown up during
the period of the German Enlightenment (*Aufklärung*) and
earlier, much of the actual practice in schools remained un-
changed. At the end of the eighteenth century there was still
a remarkable degree of harmony between the churches and the

grammar schools but, as already indicated, the latter had lost ground on account of their failure to adapt to contemporary needs. The *Aufklärung* therefore failed to bring about any radical innovation in the school system as a whole: this came only with the thoroughgoing application of the neoclassical ideas to the *Gymnasium* in the early nineteenth century.

The new impetus derived in large measure from the setback to German political and cultural pride suffered through the defeat by the French at Jena in 1806. In education its effect was to accelerate the tendencies which had been developing during the earlier period. In Prussia in particular the course of secularization was speeded up by virtue of the gradual extension of the State's powers through the central educational authority. Secondly there was a markedly reduced tendency to recoil from the pagan implications of the new cult of antiquity. Above all, the urge to build up the German nation independently of the French influence associated with cosmopolitanism asserted itself with renewed vigour. It found articulate expression among philosophers, notably Fichte who in his 'Addresses to the German Nation' advanced the thesis that it was through education that the way to the realization of Germany's greatness was to be found.

This passionate desire for strong, independent nationhood coincided with the diffusion of the new enthusiasm for antiquity. The attempts to trace the origins of the Germanic peoples to ancient Greece and to establish a linguistic link between them epitomizes the extravagance with which the break with the former cultural dominance of Romance languages was advocated. It was in Greek culture, so ran the theory, that the key to true 'Germanness' would be found; young people were to be educated to strive towards the Greek ideal of humanity and the ability to do so came to be regarded as the mark of the future leader. For though inherent in this movement was the urge to build up German political and military superiority in Europe, this superiority was regarded more or less as a German birthright by virtue of the superior civilization which, it was claimed, made Germany the new Athens. Hence the paradox that one educational manifestation of this violent nationalism was the education of scholars towards self-fulfilment, the all-round development of the powers of the individual and the corresponding disdain for the utilitarian considerations of the *Aufklärung*, the learning of skills for specific ends, such as for example the political expertise supposedly imparted in the *Ritterakademien*. The new objective was to foster, not specific accomplishments of this kind with direct application, but idealized qualities of character such as the civic virtues of the Athenians.

An educational manifestation of the new nationalism which was more in keeping with the political ambitions inherent in it was the gymnastic movement founded by '*Turnvater*' Jahn on whom Fichte's Addresses made a powerful impression. Physical education as Jahn interpreted it fell little short of a deliberate exercise in military discipline. If the ideals of Athens were frequently proclaimed in the neoclassical argument, those of Sparta featured prominently through the influence of Jahn's *Turnerschaft*. The violence of its nationalism was strongly Prussian in inspiration but came to be subsumed under the general cause of German nationhood, of which the common German language was regarded as the criterion. Many of the attitudes associated with the *Turnerschaft* were at odds with the humanism of the scholars but the common denominator of nationalism effected some sort of reconciliation between them.

The conversion of these new trends into practical measures affecting the *Gymnasium* began during Wilhelm von Humboldt's brief period of office as head of the newly formed *Section des Cultus und öffentlichen Unterrichts* in the Prussian administration. The strong tradition of *Allgemeinbildung*, general education unaffected by vocational considerations, can be traced to this time. According to Humboldt 'the concern in teaching is not with the practical requirements of life but purely with the pupil himself, with knowledge for its own sake, with the cultivation of the feelings and in the longer term with the study of academic disciplines'. The end product of *Gymnasium* education was thus defined, not narrowly as the useful servant of the State but broadly as the cultivated individual. It was assumed that this kind of aim would in any case be a guarantee of social progress in the widest sense and promote the superiority of German civilization. The *Ritterakademien* gradually died out in the face of the dynamic momentum generated by the ethos given to this new humanistic *Gymnasium*. Its general education became established as the accepted training for the future leaders of society and therefore as the basis for the new criteria for university entry, the concept of a unitary norm of fitness for higher education denoted by the term *Hochschulreife*, whereby holders of the *Abitur* were regarded as qualified to enter any faculty of the university.

The Rise of 'Realien'

So demanding was this conception of general education that it inevitably lost some of its momentum after a decade or two. Humanist education remained the objective, the classics remained the cornerstone of the curriculum but the commitment to the ideal waned. It was subsequently weakened still further by the challenge to the claims of classical languages to be the cardinal medium for propaedeutic training of the intellect which was presented by the modern subjects, *'Realien'*, during the latter half of the century. The rise of the new subjects accelerated in response to gradually increasing public demand for a more modern brand of education, a demand that was generated above all by rapidly growing vocational opportunities in industry, commerce, the civil service and elsewhere. The great advances in industries such as electricity, chemicals and light engineering, the so-called second phase of the industrial revolution, depended on the technological skill of highly trained people. The demand was met, not in the classical *Gymnasium* but in the different grades of modern secondary school (*Realschule*). These schools were denied the high prestige

of their classical counterparts and some of them made strenuous efforts to counteract this by building up their Latin. By the
new Prussian curriculum regulations of 1882 the amount of
Latin taught in the top category of these schools, the *Realschule
I Ordnung*, was substantially increased while in the classical
Gymnasium there was a reduction in the time allocation for both
Greek and Latin, allowing more for French, mathematics,
physics and natural science. There was a corresponding rapprochement of nomenclature whereby the *Realschule I Ordnung*
was officially renamed *Realgymnasium*.

The regulations of 1882 were regarded as unsatisfactory in
both camps, inevitably so for they were attempting to reconcile
the irreconcilable. The humanists argued that the concessions
to *Realien* undermined the classical education they themselves
offered. The protagonists of the *Realgymnasium* cause resented
the fact that their leaving certificate was not recognized as the
equivalent of the traditional *Abitur* and therefore did not confer
the right to university entry. No solution was possible so long as
the propaedeutic function continued to be the exclusive prerogative of the classical *Gymnasium*. The rivalry was intense and
bitter. Added pressure was put on the humanists when the
young Emperor William II made a personal intervention at an
education conference in 1890 expressing dissatisfaction with the
sterile teaching of the classics, on the basis of his own experience
as a pupil at the *Gymnasium* in Kassel. This criticism was in tune
with the thinking of a new post-unification generation, fired
with a new version of nationalism strongly identified with the
idea of scientific and technical advance. The resistance, largely
on the part of *Gymnasium* teachers, to the kind of development
advocated, was vigorous and obdurate.

The classical *Gymnasium* held on to its monopoly of university
entrance for some years more. Its defenders reserved their most
vituperative attacks for the *Realgymnasium* from which the
strongest challenge to their privileged position came. The other
category of modern secondary school, the *Oberrealschule*, had
no Latin in the curriculum and hence was a rival to a much

lesser extent. Eventually the monopoly was broken in 1901 when the right of entry to university was officially recognized for holders of the leaving certificate of all three kinds of school. This 'Gleichberechtigung' can be regarded as the symbol of the final victory of the cause of the Realschulen which had increased steadily in number and importance in the course of the century. Modern languages, mathematics and natural sciences had been placed on an equal footing with classics as appropriate disciplines in which to concentrate the major component of the propaedeutic training which gave school leavers the cachet of a general, liberal education and ensured that they were intellectually fitted to undertake university study.

Thus in the course of the nineteenth century the Gymnasium tradition was established on the basis of rigorous and uncompromising classicism and then became diversified to allow greater scope for modern languages and scientific subjects. But the supreme prestige of the classical Gymnasium survived well into the twentieth century and its ideal of disinterested scholarship exerted a powerful influence on its semi-classical and non-classical counterparts.

Twentieth-century Developments

The broadening of the curriculum that resulted from the rise of 'Realien' however placed a heavy burden on pupils who were expected to follow the entire range of subjects up to Abitur level. Moreover their teachers were trained in the thorough, intensive scholarship of the German universities and inevitably strove to promote a high level of achievement. The result was a strong emphasis on factual content, reinforced through the issue of exhaustive regulations and syllabuses. This encyclopaedism, pejoratively referred to as Vielwisserei, provoked a critical reaction among a number of teachers and administrators. The Gymnasium was accused of being a 'Lernschule', characterized by highly formalized teaching methods, and by the artificial incentive of passing examinations, a provision notably absent from Humboldt's conception; education towards independent thinking was declared to have been neglected. Furthermore this severe approach was alleged to have permeated the entire school system. The role of the teacher at all levels was to transmit knowledge in an authoritarian manner and the role of the pupil was to absorb it passively.

At the heart of the reaction was a line of thinking that sought to lay the emphasis on first-hand experience, to make education 'child-centred'. A manifesto published by some Leipzig teachers in 1909 stated:

The development of the child is the law and the rule for all education. The school should concern itself with the pupil's life now rather than in the future. . . . The school of today is failing because its teaching is based upon subject matter that a child will need when he becomes a man and not upon what he needs today while he is still a child. . . . We see the goal but not the child.[4]

In the experimental situation created by this group, teachers were free to devise their own curricula in the early elementary classes using whatever methods they thought appropriate. Hamburg and Dresden were other notable centres of new thinking about education.

In the vanguard of the *Reform* movement that was growing up three strands deserve particular mention. The first is the revival of art as a school subject, pioneered primarily by Alfred Lichtwark, the director of the Hamburg Art gallery and publicized through Art Teaching Conferences held in 1901, 1903 and 1905. The aim was to restore the creativity which, it was declared, had been sacrificed to the demands of the intellect.

The second strand is the emphasis on the educative value of practical activity. Particularly notable here was the contribution of Georg Kerschensteiner, Director of Education in Munich.[5]

[4] Quoted in T. Alexander and B. Parker, *The New Education in the German Republic*, New York, 1929, p. 125.
[5] For a full account of Kerschensteiner's work see D. Simons, *Georg Kerschensteiner*, London, 1966.

His objection to the long-established expository approach to teaching was on the grounds that it led to excessively passive attitudes on the part of the pupil. To replace this with genuine activity he considered it necessary to synthesize the intellectual and theoretical aspects of learning with the physical and practical ones. Kerschensteiner also justified his approach on the social grounds that the great majority of children would eventually earn their livelihood by the exercise of practical, manual skills and that it was therefore wrong to give them the impression that such skills were barely related to academic education. He was thus concerned to remove the barriers which separated general from vocational education. A further development of the theory was that if the value of practical activity were given due recognition it would infuse a genuine element of vocation into the work of all sections of the community: and the individual contribution to the whole would lead to the perception of a similar relationship between the individual and the community.

This preoccupation with the creation of a school community that would simulate the social situation of the adult world was the third major element of reformist thinking. This impulse, somewhat pent up during the pre-war years, was released with the establishment of the Weimar Republic in 1918 and the number and scope of experiments in the field of elementary education increased. Where teachers had previously had to confine themselves to isolated ventures in the face of official disapproval, they now had in some areas opportunities to establish systematic experiments which were designed to pioneer the new democratic social order that was hoped for. The most obvious examples of this approach were the 'community schools' (*Gemeinschaftsschulen*) which sprang up in various cities such as Berlin, Leipzig, Dresden, Chemnitz, frequently against a background of bitter controversy. They were attacked as irreligious, as denying the German cultural heritage and their approval of coeducation was denounced as immoral. There was, too, a very obvious political aspect to the criticisms,

C

Many of the teachers in these schools had social democratic or communist affiliations and consequently the *Reformpädagogik* theories came to be identified with strong left-wing views. At the extreme end of the scale was the group known as the League of Radical School Reformers (*Bund entschiedener Schulreformer*) founded by a Berlin teacher Paul Oestreich. This group was strongly influenced by the ideas about polytechnical education which were being explored in the Soviet Union and which constitute the most obvious antecedent of the developments of the later 1950s in the *DDR*. The limits to the influence of the *Reform* movement are partly to be explained by the steady progression to the political right of large sections of German society during the 1920s.

None of the various elements of the *Reform* movement made any great impact on the *Gymnasium* sector which continued to be characterized by its fervid pursuit of erudition. The less traditionally minded among the better-off middle classes had an alternative in the private boarding schools, notably the boarding schools (*Landerziehungsheime*) founded by Hermann Lietz who had been inspired by the experience of teaching at Abbotsholme in England. But the major reaction against the excessive formalism and intellectualism of the *Gymnasium* was expressed in the *Wandervogel* youth movement.[6] This dated back to an informal banding together of young people, mostly *Gymnasium* pupils, in a middle-class suburb of Berlin in 1901 and developed into a powerful movement much given to communion with nature in the course of lengthy rambles and to a neo-romantic reverence for the folk music and customs of an earlier and, as they saw it, more genuine German culture.

Though the *Reform* ideas failed to take root on anything approaching a nationwide scale, there were significant developments during the Weimar period which laid the foundation for the present-day structure of the West German educational system. A major difficulty has always been that of establishing

[6] For a comprehensive treatment of the *Wandervogel* movement see W. Z. Laqueur, *Young Germany*, London, 1962.

a clear distinction between the primary and secondary phases. During the period up to the First World War transfer from the elementary school (*Volksschule*) to the *Gymnasium* took place at the age of nine. After this small group had been hived off the remainder continued in the senior classes of the *Volksschule*. The exclusiveness of the *Gymnasium* was partly intellectual, partly social: intellectual in that entrance was by competitive examination, social in that a good proportion of the middle class sent their children to private preparatory schools (*Vorschulen*) where the instruction was more specifically aimed at ensuring access to the *Gymnasium* than was the case in the *Volksschule*.

One of the measures introduced early in the Weimar period was to raise the age of transfer to the *Gymnasium* to ten and to attempt to make greater provision for late transfers. At the same time the exclusive preparatory schools were abolished and a four-year common elementary schooling for all children was established as the primary stage. Although various steps were taken to expand the secondary stage the overlapping of primary and secondary schools continued, with most children receiving their entire full-time education in one school. The community schools, for example, embraced both primary and secondary phases. Weimar educational policy did envisage a reorganization that would ultimately provide separate and consecutive primary and secondary education for all but it was impossible to achieve agreement among the constituent States in little more than a decade and in the face of mounting opposition to radical change of this kind.

The major interest in education at this time lay rather in restoring German cultural pride after the defeat of 1918 and in the course of the 1920s in Prussia in particular, the main thrust of new thinking came in the attempt to achieve some sort of unified conception to embrace the different types of secondary education that had developed historically. According to Hans Richert, senior official with responsibility for secondary education in the Prussian Ministry, the unifying factor should be a new emphasis on those subjects that were or could be made to be concerned with specifically German culture—the mother tongue, religious instruction, history, geography and civics—and which were common to the curriculum of all types of school. By means of this core of '*Kulturkunde*' the German cultural heritage was to be absorbed and this was regarded as the fundamental task of the schools. It was forcefully pointed out that schools were not preparatory institutions for specific professions or university faculties and that neither of these spheres was to influence what happened in them. The core curriculum was therefore not merely common to all types of school, it was to stand 'at the centre of school activity' in the belief that it would unify the system despite the other differences in curriculum as between the *Gymnasium*, the *Realgymnasium*, the *Oberrealschule* and the recently created genre, the *Deutsche Oberschule*, of which German language and literature was the particular specialism.

Though this group of subjects was held to constitute the very stuff of German culture, other sources which were, so to speak, at one remove from it could not be neglected: these so-called '*Quellbezirke*' were the individual responsibilities of the different types of school. Thus the *Gymnasium* was concerned with antiquity, the *Realgymnasium* with modern Europe and the *Oberrealschule* with the fields of mathematics and science. The aim of studying such specialisms was to gain insight into German culture through close acquaintance with the soil in which it had its deepest roots. In the case of the *Gymnasium*, for example, the study of the classics was expected to reveal the relationship of antiquity to modern German culture so that the intervening evolution could be followed through the great epochs of cultural history, early Christianity, the Middle Ages, Renaissance and Reformation, modern Europeanism and German idealism. Modern Europeanism was the specific field for the *Realgymnasium* and took its place alongside antiquity and Christianity as a major source of the dominant ideas that have shaped modern thinking and without which an understanding of the peculiar spirit of German culture was held to be impossible. The mathematics and natural science of the *Oberreal-schule* were regarded as a further important source, the role of which had in the past been somewhat neglected. But this study, as much as the classics or modern Europeanism, it was pointed out, had deep roots in the great epoch of German idealism. This period of German intellectual greatness, the era of Kant and Goethe, had by the 1920s become something of a legend. As the model to be emulated, Greek civilization yielded pride of place to the age of German civilization that it had inspired. Thus all the elements in the total conception contributed to the funda-mental 'Germanness' of the education system.

The implications of this development for the subsequent rise of National Socialism are obvious enough: for the Nazis the *Deutsche Oberschule* was the most important type of school. Apart from this innovation, however, the work of Richert illustrates the evolution of the post-war pattern of three major types of *Gymnasium*, biased towards classics, modern languages and mathematics/natural science respectively. But it was only the beginning of the process of imposing some order on the prolifera-tion of types of school that were to be found throughout the German States at this time.

The order that did come to be imposed after the Nazis came to power in 1933 was one of a more sinister kind, namely the enforcement of uniformity on all institutions as regards educa-tional aims. It was the intention to manipulate the entire educational system to serve the purposes of aggressive national-ism, to force it to turn its back on all that Germany owed to the earlier inspirations of its culture represented by antiquity and Christianity. Though the classical *Gymnasium* continued to exist young people were actively discouraged from entering this type of school whereas, as already noted, the full support of the authorities was given to the *Deutsche Oberschule*. While religious instruction continued to be given in schools, its influence was systematically undermined by such measures as the pro-scription of the activities of church youth organizations. Intellectual capacity and achievement came to be of secondary importance, as compared with character and physical fitness. Character was assessed in terms of orderliness, obedience, comradeship, leadership and above all receptivity to the National Socialist *Weltanschauung* which permeated the entire teaching. Physical fitness was the fundamental requisite of the future soldier. The lack of concern for academic education can be seen in the measures taken in 1936 which curtailed the period of secondary schooling by one year to allow for activities of the Hitler youth and proposed curtailment by a further year at a later date.

The priorities just enumerated were also applied to the criteria employed in the matter of university entrance. Written examinations were abolished in favour of oral tests and interviews. Those who were successful were then required to spend six months in a labour camp and two years in military service. Enrolments to the universities fell substantially. They were halved between 1933 and 1936 as a result of various kinds of pressure to remain in military service rather than return to take up a university place. The propaedeutic issue of what constituted appropriate preparation for university studies and professional careers was utterly compromised by the assumption that the function of education was to produce good Nazis. The Hitler era represents at best a standstill in the development of German education. After the war it was from the pre-1933 period that the threads had to be picked up.

CHAPTER 2

Four-Power Control: 1945–49

The importance of the role of education in the period immediately following the liquidation of the Third Reich was widely recognized. The National Socialist regime had provided a telling illustration of how effective an agency the school system could be in the pursuit of political ends. The resulting damage awaiting repair created an awareness that what could be manipulated in this sinister way could also be harnessed to the task of bringing about a change of heart. In the early post-war period policy was concerned not merely with education but with 're-education'.

At Potsdam the Allied Powers undertook responsibility for the post-war development of the German educational system with the formal statement that 'German education shall be so controlled as completely to eliminate Nazi and militarist doctrines and to make possible the successful development of democratic ideas'.[1] But it subsequently became clear that a variety of meanings could be attached to this pronouncement. Moreover by the time it was made, a number of steps had already been taken in the formulation of educational policy by the individual powers concerned so that it cannot be said that the efforts to rebuild the system started from a common position over the crucial issues, arrived at jointly at the conference table. Much of the variegation in the pattern that subsequently emerged is attributable to the differences in policy

[1] Berlin Conference, Protocol of Proceedings. In U.S. Department of State, *Germany 1947–49, the Story in Documents*, Washington D.C., 1950, p. 49.

and strategy of the four powers concerned, above all the sharp distinction that eventually arose between the Soviet zone and the others.

The immediate and pressing problems of material reconstruction were similar for all concerned. Many school buildings had been destroyed or damaged, textbooks were in short supply, in particular because those that had survived from the Nationalist Socialist era were unacceptable, and there were difficulties in providing sufficient stationery for the basic requirements of instruction. The textbook question was a fundamental one, for much of the re-education programme hinged on the content of the syllabuses, particularly in history. Equally important for re-education was the 'denazification' of the teaching profession. In these two spheres which vitally affected the delicate process of fostering a new ideological outlook the initiatives taken by the zonal organizations differed markedly. A similar individuality can be seen in the approaches to the structural reform of the educational system. The occupying powers were influenced, consciously or unconsciously, by their own educational traditions which differed widely from one another. In each case the nature of the programme adopted depended very much on the relationship between the zonal authority and those Germans in whom responsibility for educational reconstruction was invested.

Before examining developments in the individual zones of occupation, however, it is useful to look briefly at what in fact emerged as the *status quo* in the early months of the school year of 1945-46 (Diagram in Appendix VII). Largely for reasons of expediency the school system began functioning in the form established during the Weimar Republic. After four years of common primary schooling covering the age range from six to ten, a minority, comprising the most able children, under 10 per cent of the relevant age group, were selected by examination for one of the various forms of grammar school (*Gymnasium*). Traditionally the highly academic course had lasted nine years but, as noted earlier, had been reduced to eight under Hitler. After the war it remained at eight years to begin with, but the ninth year was gradually restored in the British, American and French zones during the Occupation period or shortly after it. The *Gymnasium* leaving certificate, the *Abitur*, was simultaneously regarded as proof of '*Hochschulreife*', fitness for higher education, and conferred the right of entry to any faculty of the university. At the other end of the scale the great majority of children continued their education in the upper classes of the elementary school (*Volksschule*) until the school-leaving age which was then fourteen, after which they were obliged to continue with part-time education at a vocational school (*Berufsschule*) till the age of eighteen. An intermediate alternative was provided by the *Mittelschule*, which was also selective but less highly so than the *Gymnasium*, and which generally offered a six-year semi-academic course, preparing its pupils not for university like the *Gymnasium*, but mainly for the kind of further education which would qualify them for employment in the intermediate administrative echelons of the civil service, industry and commerce. However, schools of this kind were not highly developed in all *Länder* of the country.

The Four Powers and Educational Policy

As a first step towards an analysis of how the modifications of this inherited system came about, leading ultimately to the sharp divergence of educational policy in the separate Republics that subsequently came into being, it is helpful to examine briefly the point of departure of each of the occupying powers in turn.

THE UNITED KINGDOM: THE INFORMAL APPROACH

Perhaps the most marked feature of the British approach was its informal, pragmatic nature. It was deliberate policy on the

Germany 1937—1945—

	Federal Republic: West Germany	Democratic Re East Germa
Surface area:		
(a) in sq. miles (approx.)	95,900	41,700
(b) as proportion of 1937 Reich	53%	23%
Population in millions (approx.)		
(a) 1946	44	17
(b) 1969	61	17
Population density: inhabitants per sq. mile	622	158

Kaliningrad
(Königsberg)

U.S.S.R.

zecin
ettin)

POLAND

Wroclaw
(Breslaú)

A

▬▬▬	Frontier of the German Reich in 1937
─────	Administrative boundaries in 1945
▤	Territories placed under Polish administration in 1945
▨	Territory placed under Soviet administration in 1945
▥	Soviet Zone 1945-1949; territory of Democratic Republic (DDR) after 1949
▨	British, U.S. and French Zones 1945-1949; territory of Federal Republic after 1949 (including the Saar, incorporated after a plebiscite in 1957)

part of the Education Branch to deploy its members as widely as possible in order to influence German education through personal contact with individuals.[2] In this respect a certain amount of preparatory work had been done towards the end of the war, notably by an organization called German Educational Reconstruction whose members, together with other voluntary workers in the field, supplemented the work of the education officers. The practical benefits of the large network of contacts built up between the two countries were evident both at official and unofficial level in the large numbers of cultural exchanges and visits that took place during the Occupation period. As regards the workings of the school system, the thinking of the British was strongly influenced by their own 1944 Education Act, and it is hardly surprising that in the *Länder* which they occupied (Hamburg, Schleswig-Holstein, Lower Saxony and North Rhine-Westphalia) the tripartite structure had been consolidated by the time control was handed over to the German authorities in January 1947. But the precise form which this structure took had by no means been imposed by the Occupation authorities and after the handover the latter, while continuing to support various reform measures, left the ultimate decisions to the Germans.

There were three main issues on which the British took up a position. They wished to see fees abolished for secondary schools so that this sector would cease to be so markedly the preserve of the middle class. The main opposition to this came from the German right-wing parties on grounds of cost and the need to safeguard parents' right of choice. Though it was not immediately practicable it would clearly be achieved eventually, as there was by the end of the Occupation period some degree of consensus about the need for greater equality of opportunity. Secondly, in the controversy over whether or not the schools should be mono-confessional, the British had in 1946 based their policy on the wishes of the communities concerned by means of

[2] R. Birley, 'Education in the British Zone of Germany, RIIA, *International Affairs*, Vol. XXVI No. 1, January 1950, p. 42.

a plebiscite at the level of the smaller administrative divisions. The resulting state of affairs continued throughout the remainder of the Occupation period. Finally, there was the duration of primary schooling which was to continue a burning issue throughout the first two decades of the existence of the Federal Republic. The British authorities gave guarded support to the lengthening of primary school attendance from four to six years, but in each of the *Länder* under their control it was the internal political situation which was decisive in determining the policy actually adopted.[3]

THE UNITED STATES: EQUALITY OF OPPORTUNITY

In the United States there was, towards the end of the war, a good deal of public debate on the subject of 're-education' but such a variety of attitudes among the authorities that by the time of the Potsdam Conference no clear conception of aims had been arrived at, let alone agreement reached on specific plans for the development of the school system.[4] This serves to emphasize the fact that the Potsdam statement was no more than the formal expression of a minimum consensus. Apart from the immediate needs of restoring buildings and providing textbooks, in the first year of occupation American energies in the field of 're-education' were concentrated primarily on the denazification programme. This resulted in a more active purge of the teaching profession than in the British zone. In more general respects the Americans exercised a closer control and were more prepared to intervene directly in administrative matters than their partners.[5] The rather negative character of American policy reflected at this point the predominantly

[3] Birley, op. cit., pp. 33–9
[4] K.-E. Bungenstab, *Umerziehung zur Demokratie? Re-education Politik im Bildungswesen der U.S. Zone 1945–49*, Düsseldorf, 1970, p. 42.
[5] H. Liddell (ed.), *Education in Occupied Germany*, Paris, 1949, p. 119. M. Knappen, *And Call it Peace*, Chicago, 1947, p. 120.

punitive spirit of the 1945 Policy Directive[6] and was further accentuated by the low status of the Education and Religious Affairs Section and its consequent inability to influence policy to any great extent.[7] A year of occupation elapsed before there was any indication of the more positive approach on which the seal was set in September 1946.[8] In specifically educational policy the new orientation was reflected in the dispatch of an official mission to study the school system in the U.S. zone at about this time.

The report of this commission gave clear expression to American ideas of educational reform. In place of the existing system a comprehensively organized one was recommended in which a six-year primary school was to be followed by a six-year secondary institution which would incorporate the *Berufsschule* into the hitherto exclusively academic sphere. Thus where primary and secondary schools had previously overlapped with one another, and were regarded as providing fundamentally different types of education, the suggestion now was that they should be consecutive levels catering for all children. This, together with the demand for abolition of fee-paying, was designed to guarantee equal opportunity for all, regardless of social origin, and thereby to expand the secondary sector drawing into it a more representative cross-section of the community. Among further recommendations were the introduction of social studies into the curricula, the encouragement of teaching methods that promoted free discussion, and provision to involve pupils and parents in decisions regarding the internal organization of schools.[9] This report became the basis for U.S. policy in education: using its recommendations as guidelines the personnel of the Education and Religious Affairs Section

[6] 1945 Directive to the Commander in Chief, U.S. Forces of Occupation (JCS 1067), Text in Dept. of State, *Germany 1947–49* . . . op. cit., pp. 21–33.

[7] Knappen, op. cit., pp. 75–81.

[8] *Restatement of U.S. Policy in Germany.* Address by Secretary James F. Byrnes. *Germany 1947–49* . . . op. cit., pp. 3–8.

[9] U.S. Department of State, *Report of the United States Education Mission to Germany*, Washington D.C., 1946, esp. pp. 14–23.

brought immense energy to the task of infusing American democratic ideals into the institutions under their control.[10] None the less they were obliged to accept that reconstruction was fundamentally a task for the Germans themselves and in the end their plans for restructuring the system made very little impact, except in Bremen where the Social Democratic Party which was dominant in the City Assembly favoured consecutive primary and secondary education for all.[11]

FRANCE: 'MISSION CIVILISATRICE'

Of the three Western allies it was the French who approached the 're-education' issue with the greatest precision. The drawing up of plans had begun in Algiers before the end of the war and these began to be put into effect from August 1945 onwards.[12] The emphasis on purging the system of personnel with Nazi affiliations was less pronounced than in the British and American zones and the day to day administration of the system was handed back to the Germans almost directly. It remained however under very close surveillance.[13] As with the Americans, policies were adopted somewhat in the spirit of a *mission civilisatrice*, designed in this case to awaken in the Germans a love of freedom and individualism as revealed in French cultural traditions. However, due perhaps to their greater first-hand knowledge of German education, the majority of their officials being *germanistes*, the French were able to arrive at a clearer conception of what they wanted to achieve in the reform of the system. And since the territory allotted to them was smaller and more homogeneous than the others the policies were less difficult to implement.[14]

[10] Cf. R. F. Lawson, *Reform of the West German School System 1945-62*, Ann Arbor, Michigan, 1965, pp. 39, 79.
[11] *Arbeitsgemeinschaft Deutscher Lehrerverbände, Material- und Nachrichten-Dienst*, 8/1951, pp. 9-11.   [12] Liddell, op. cit., p. 112.
[13] Cf. R. H. Samuel and R. Hinton Thomas, *Education and Society in Modern Germany*, London, 1949, p. 165.   [14] Liddell, op. cit., p. 112.

Like the Americans the French were particularly concerned at the undemocratic nature of a system in which the selection which took place at the age of ten was virtually irrevocable. In the event they were not, any more than the British or the Americans, able to extend the duration of common primary education but they were more determined than their Western partners to intervene directly in the drawing up of the curriculum. Thus the study of Latin was abolished in the first three years of the *Gymnasium* in order that during this period pupils could be transferred to it from the *Volksschule* without undue disadvantage. From the sixth year of the *Gymnasium*, four options were offered which allowed opportunities for specialization in the humanities and sciences, in addition to the basic curriculum common to all.[15] A compulsory daily period of French was regarded as the appropriate medium for fostering independence of mind and clarity of judgement.[16] These measures added up to a major rationalization whereby the former variety of types of secondary school, differentiated according to the curriculum followed, were replaced by one type with four sections in its upper stage.

A further measure taken in the French zone concerned the school-leaving examination, the *Abitur*. This had been left as it was by the British and Americans and had remained a largely internal matter within the schools. The only external moderation was by the school inspectors but in the early years, like all other members of the teaching profession, these were in short supply. Consequently standards varied considerably and with the shortage of places at the universities it was difficult to ensure that the best qualified applicants gained admission. In the British zone where the problem was particularly acute, many were made to retake the examination, the standard of which had fallen during the Hitler regime. The operation of the rough and ready *numerus clausus* that was applied was further

[15] F. R. Willis, *The French in Germany 1945-49*, Stanford, 1962, p. 170.
[16] E. Vermeil, *Notes sur la Rééducation en Zone Française*. In Liddell, op. cit., pp. 65, 66,

complicated by the need to take former political affiliations into account.[17] The French authorities regarded the system of internal assessment traditionally used in the *Abitur* as too haphazard, and created a centralized one whereby written papers were set which were the same throughout the zone and which were marked centrally by external examiners. By this means it was also possible to make the examination more selective by increasing its difficulty and thereby reduce the pressure for university entrance. The authorities justified the measure on the grounds both of this necessity and of the need for strict impartiality.[18] This action illustrates the French concern to standardize the operation of the German educational system throughout their zone. The resistance which it met with is a measure of the German aversion to central control of this kind.

THE SOVIET UNION: PLANNED INITIATIVES

It was in the Soviet Union that the most comprehensive planning for the reorganization of the German educational system took place before the end of the war and it was the Soviet policy which had the most far-reaching effects. Within the organization known as the National Committee for Free Germany (*Nationalkomitee Freies Deutschland*) which aimed at drawing support from the widest possible range of anti-fascist opinion in order to establish a united popular front against Hitler, a commission was set up in February 1945 consisting largely of German émigré teachers with instructions to study the reform of the educational system. There was a strong Marxist influence in this group, and the policy advocated in its report emphasized the raising of the general level of education of the people and the 'removal of the monopoly of the ruling classes' through the creation of an educational system that

[17] *British Zone Review*, I, 22, 20 July 1946, p. 6.
[18] Vermeil, op. cit., pp. 66, 67.

D

would be entirely secular and comprehensive in structure.[19] The main practical work of the commission was, however, devoted to the immediate priorities as laid down in a document prepared by a special committee of the *Politbüro* of the German Communist Party under the chairmanship of Walter Ulbricht. These were denazification, the establishment of reliable local administrative bodies and the provision of new textbooks. This last item required the most preparation and priority was given to the teaching of history for which guidelines appear to have been drawn up and new textbooks completed by the summer of 1945.[20]

The Soviet policy was to support wholeheartedly these initiatives. Like the French they put the administration of the educational system under German control as soon as it was possible to do so. But clearly they were at pains to ensure that the key posts were held by Communists or Social Democrats who were prepared to liaise closely with their own education officers.[21] It seems likely that from the outset the democratic reconstruction of Germany was regarded by the Soviets as corresponding precisely to the demands of the German Communist Party and the development of the educational system was considered a vital, integral part of these demands.[22]

In the event, this was one area in which agreement between the two German left-wing parties was not difficult to achieve. In October 1945 they combined to issue their Joint Appeal for Democratic School Reform which repeated earlier demands for a secular, non-fee-paying system, organized along comprehensive lines.[23] With strong support from the Soviet authorities these demands, which in the meantime had become part of the

[19] F. Rücker, *Die Arbeit der Lehrer in Nationalkomitee Freies Deutschland*. In *Quellen zur Geschichte der Erziehung*, Berlin, 1968, p. 483.

[20] Cf. W. Leonhard, *Child of the Revolution*, London, 1957, p. 247.

[21] Ibid., p. 358. See also E. Weinert, *Das Nationalkomitee 'Freies Deutschland'*, Berlin, 1957, pp. 99–101.

[22] Cf. L. Gläser, *Die deutsch-sowjetischen Beziehungen auf schulpolitischem und pädagogischem Gebiet in den ersten Nachkriegsjahren. Vergleichende Pädagogik*, 2/1970, p. 120.

[23] *Gemeinsamer Aufruf zur demokratischen Schulreform.* See K.-H. Günther and G. Uhlig, *Geschichte der Schule in der DDR 1945 bis 1968*, Berlin, 1969, p. 11.

policy adopted at the first congress of the new Socialist Unity Party (*SED*), were incorporated in the 'Law for the Democratization of the German School System' (*Gesetz zur Demokratisierung der deutschen Schule*) which was adopted in all *Länder* of the Soviet zone during May and June 1946.[24]

The kind of structural changes made in the Soviet zone under the 1946 Law were in many respects not greatly different from those advocated by the Western allies and indeed there were some favourable American reactions on the grounds that they were contributing to the breaking down of the 'caste system of German society'.[25] The Soviets maintained that their Law constituted the only measures taken at that time that were genuinely in the spirit of the Postdam Agreement and subsequently that it corresponded very closely to the Four Power directive on education.[26] Since there is a good deal of justification for this latter claim, it is pertinent to explore the question of how and why major changes were made in the Soviet zone while similar initiatives on the part of the British and Americans met with no success. It is here that the views of the Germans who were concerned with education in the post-war period—administrators, educationists, teachers and politicians—are of the foremost relevance, for the policies adopted were the outcome of their interaction with the Occupation authorities.

German Reactions in the Western Zones

The British and Americans were clearly taken aback by the resistance to the reforms they advocated. In the words of a revealing statement on policy in the British zone:

[24] Ibid., p. 37.

[25] *School Reform in the Soviet Zone.* In Information Control. *Intelligence Summary No. 61* (23.9.46), p. 6.

[26] *Control Council Directive No. 54* on the 'basic principles for the democratisation of education in Germany'. Text in B. Ruhm von Oppen (ed.), *Documents on Germany under Occupation* (RIIA), London, New York, Toronto, 1955, pp. 233-4.

the power of routine justified as efficiency, of inertia glorified as loyalty to tradition, particularly in regard to education, is surprising in Germany. The political and social revolutions that have been going on uninterruptedly since the First World War have left remarkably little trace. Even Hitler did little to alter the outer form, though the Nazi influence on the *content* of education, more especially in the schools, was strong. Today both in schools and universities the same dislike of change, the same unwillingness to reassess the whole situation and modify past practice to meet it is very marked.[27]

American efforts also met with strong resistance, particularly in Bavaria where there was protracted wrangling between the two sides over plans for reorganization of the school system. In the end, American demands for democratization were met by inclusion of pupil responsibility for internal school organization, rather than by any radical change in the structure.[28] The French went further than either the British or the Americans to impose their ideas, and in consequence aroused much resentment and the determination to revoke the measures they had introduced when the opportunity came.[29]

It would be wrong to imply that there was no German support for Allied policy. A call for democratization had been a marked feature of the pre-Nazi *Reform* movement of which the practical expression was the consistent demand for a lengthening of the duration of primary schooling and hence postponement of selection. This, it had been felt, would open up secondary and university education to a more representative cross-section of society. The residue of such reformist thinking lay chiefly in the Social Democratic Party (*SPD*) and among *Volksschule* teachers. In such circles, especially in the city states, Schleswig-Holstein and to a lesser degree Lower Saxony and Hesse, there was agreement with the verdict of the American mission that the traditional educational system had furthered

[27] *Control Commission for Germany (British Element) Report*, Sept. 1947, p. 18.
[28] Fully documented in I. Huelsz, *Schulpolitik in Bayern zwischen Demokratisierung und Restauration in den Jahren 1945–50*, Hamburg, 1970.
[29] Lawson, op. cit., p. 101.

the growth of authoritarianism, and there was a widespread feeling that somehow the educational system must play a constructive role in the rebuilding of German democracy. A number of the plans put forward by German educationists and politicians laid great emphasis on democratic and social objectives.[30] But there was not nearly such widespread agreement that a radical restructuring of the system was the best way to achieve them. The urge to realize the objectives of the *Reform* movement was only one of the sources from which German educational thought drew its inspiration in the immediate post-war years.

A major preoccupation which ran counter to the desire to lengthen primary education was the high value placed on classical humanism. This is particularly well illustrated in the plan devised by Josef Schnippenkötter for North Rhine province.[31] At the heart of this lay the restoration of the classical *Gymnasium* with its full nine-year course. Apart from this form, there were to be at most two other types of *Gymnasium*, but common to all was to be the teaching of Latin as the first foreign language. The conviction as to the importance of Latin as one of the fundamental components of secondary education was deep-rooted, and it was accompanied by the firm belief that it was highly undesirable to leave the starting age for the study of it any later than ten. Thus the plan was dominated by the internal requirements of the *Gymnasium* which took precedence over any consideration of how it could be integrated more fully into the remainder of the system. Other plans were less resolute about Latin, recommending English as the first foreign language. In general they showed, even that of Schnippenkötter, a desire to make late transfer from one kind of school to another possible, but none of them seriously contemplated interfering with the long-established character of the

---

[30] Cf. L. Kerstiens, *Die Höhere Schule in den Reformplänen der Nachkriegszeit.* *Zeitschrift für Pädagogik Jg.*, 11 (1965), pp. 538–61.

[31] J. Schnippenkötter, *Rede zur Eröffnung der Höheren Schulen in der Nordrheinprovinz. Bildungsfragen der Gegenwart*, Bonn, 1945.

Gymnasium. This strength of tradition ensured that in the early post-war years selection at ten plus was more or less taken for granted.[32]

These attitudes to the rebuilding of the system had become firmly entrenched by the time the debate about six-year primary education, stimulated by Allied pressure, was fully launched. As far as incorporating this into actual policy was concerned, the prospects turned on the fortunes of the Social Democratic Party. Schleswig-Holstein was the first *Land* in which they were in a position to legislate accordingly. But it was not a straightforward matter. There was a significant absence of public discussion of the issue and this impression of secrecy was deplored by the British authorities, who felt that there should be as much agreement as possible between government and opposition in educational matters. There were grounds for maintaining that the measure was premature since very little thought had been given to the educational problems of lengthening primary education in this way, above all in a *Land* which had had to absorb an immense number of refugees and in which financial resources were strained to the utmost. These and other considerations affected the British attitude to reform measures. However much they wished to see the introduction of six-year primary education, they had three main provisos. The first was that the necessary resources should be available and the neccessary preparations carried out to ensure the success of the venture. The second was that it should be a consensus decision and not a controversial party one. This was in turn linked to the third consideration that wide divergences in practice between *Länder* should be avoided. It was felt that strongly partisan legislation in one *Land* might lead to strong reaction in another.[33]

In the Western zones, apart from Schleswig-Holstein only Hamburg and Bremen introduced significant changes. The Hamburg system provided for a six-year *Grundschule* with instruction in a foreign language from the fifth year onwards,

[32] Kerstiens, op. cit., p. 550.   [33] Birley, op. cit., pp. 35, 36.

followed by three types of '*Oberschule*', one with a practical bias lasting three years, one with a technical bias lasting four years and one with the traditional academic programme lasting seven years and comprising classical, modern languages and mathematics/natural science streams. The tripartite division into practical, technical and academic suggests the influence of the British model of the 1944 Education Act.[34] The system introduced in Bremen was similar but reflected American rather than English influence. After the six primary years there was, in addition to the three divisions made for the Hamburg *Oberschule*, a fourth sector which was to provide a further three years of full-time education for those successfully completing the practical and technical streams and aiming at entrance to institutions of tertiary education specializing in such fields as economics and business studies. The academic sector corresponded to the former *Gymnasium* but included a stream with a bias towards music and art which was not provided for in the Hamburg counterpart.[35]

It is however significant that elsewhere in the Western zones there was no serious attempt to change the traditional pattern. The policies adopted by the left-wing governments in the city states were along the lines that were broadly favoured by the British and Americans. But however much the two occupying powers might themselves wish to see the adoption of similar measures in the large *Länder* in their zones, they considered that they must stop short of imposing them, for they were convinced that policy had to be formulated in accordance with the wishes of the Germans. And there is no doubt that the general view, in by far the greatest part of what was to become the Federal Republic, was that the system should be restored in its traditional form.

But though there was broad agreement among most of the *Länder* about this restoration, there were all kinds of minor variations of practice that reflected disparate regional traditions. Educational policy had always been a jealously guarded

[34] *Material- und Nachrichten-Dienst*, 8/1951, pp. 7-9.   [35] Ibid., pp. 9-11.

prerogative of the individual *Länder*, but at the same time it was clear that cooperation was necessary in order to find solutions to the problems created by such a variegated inheritance. For this purpose informal meetings of Ministers of Education began to be held in 1946 and two years later these were formalized through the creation of the Standing Conference of Ministers of Education (*Ständige Konferenz der Kultusminister* or *Kultusministerkonferenz*) with a permanent secretariat in Bonn. It is interesting to note in passing that, also in 1948, a meeting of the *Kultusminister* of all zones, including the Soviet, took place, a venture that was not repeated. Subsequently, with its activities confined to the territory of the Federal Republic, the *Kultusministerkonferenz* became the agency through which a degree of rationalization of the policies of the individual *Länder* was effected.

German Reactions in the Soviet Zone

The attitude of the Soviets was different to that of the major Western powers. From the very beginning of the Occupation it was their view that radical changes in the educational system were desirable. Their success in bringing these about was based on the effective mobilization of the support of those groups— left-wing political parties and teachers associated with the pre-Nazi *Reform* movement—which in the Western zones were only able to exert a minority influence. By contrast in the Soviet zone membership of such groups was an advantage. As it happened, the somewhat anti-establishment tradition of the schools which were identified with the *Reform* movement during the Weimar Republic was particularly strong in the territories which became the Soviet zone; a good many of the more important posts were filled with former teachers from these schools, the great majority of whom were favourably disposed to the reorganization proposed by the 1946 Law.[36] As might be

[36] Cf. M.-G. Lange, *Totalitäre Erziehung*, Frankfurt/M., 1954, pp. 36–8.

expected, the *Gymnasium* teachers on the whole were opposed to the proposed changes, but whereas in the Western zones it was from among their ranks that the key administrative positions tended to be filled, in the Soviet zone they were likely to be denied similar access to the positions of influence. Thus within the education service as a whole the balance of power between what can broadly be characterized as the traditional and the radical factions was different from that which was to be found in the Western zones.

Yet in the wider political context the situation was potentially delicate for the Soviets. The policy of which the 1946 Law was the culmination was strongly contested by the Liberals and the Christian Democrats. These two parties disputed the monopoly of anti-fascist initiative that was constantly claimed by the left, and they provided a focus for the defence of the traditional *Gymnasium* beginning after the four years of primary schooling. The *CDU* in particular, basing its policy of democratic re-construction on Christian principles, was a strong advocate of the confessional and private schools which it was official policy to abolish. However, it never became possible for the 'bour-geois' parties to mobilize opposition. The Law was adopted by the provisional administrations of the various *Länder* somewhat in advance of the first elections. Educational policy therefore did not become an issue on which public opinion was directly consulted. This is in marked contrast to the Western zones where great emphasis was laid on such consultation.

The 1946 Law met the demand for a comprehensive school which would cut across the established divisions into *Gymnasium*, *Mittelschule* and *Volksschule*. So sweeping a change was only feasible in terms of exclusive State control of the system and this was therefore a major starting-point for the legislation. Private schools were forbidden, whatever the purposes for which they existed, and the relationship between the Churches and the schools was severed, although religious instruction was tolera-ted on a voluntary basis. The new State comprehensive system (*Einheitsschule*) comprised a *Grundschule* which took all children for the first eight years of their education, after which there was a choice between three years of part-time study at a *Berufsschule* in conjunction with an apprenticeship and four years full time at the *Oberschule* within which were three divisions specializing in classics, modern languages and mathematics/natural science respectively (Diagram in Appendix VIII). The structural changes were accompanied by various other measures. The curriculum was reorganized so that a start could be made in providing modern language instruction for all pupils from their fifth year of school, and the revision of syllabuses and the preparation of new textbooks were put in hand. In addition a massive programme for the emergency training of new teachers was begun, an important provision in view of the fact that, in the course of the denazification of the profession, little over 20 per cent of those who had been qualified before 1945 were reinstated.[37] It was possible to demand of the new teachers recruited in this way evidence of commitment to the comprehensive system.

In the struggle between the various factions which strove to exert an influence on the development of the system, the introduction of the *Einheitsschule* represents a victory for those for whom the overriding consideration was the abolition of the privileged access to secondary education which the middle class was alleged to enjoy. For this group, which can broadly speaking be identified with the Communist and Social Democratic parties, it was important that there should be common schooling throughout the duration of compulsory education.[38] It was their view that only in this way could the children of the urban and rural working class overcome their long-established disadvantage, and find the way open to them to upper secon-

[37] Estimates vary between 20 per cent (E. Säuberlich, *Vom Humanismus zum demokratischen Patriotismus*, Köln, 1954, p. 8) and 25 per cent (E. Wendt, *Die Entwicklung der Lehrerbildung in der Sowjetischen Besatzungszone seit 1945*, Bonn/Berlin, 1959, p. 6).

[38] K.-D. Mende, *Schulreform und Gesellschaft in der Deutschen Demokratischen Republik 1945-65*. In S. B. Robinsohn, *Schulreform in gesellschaftlichen Prozess* I, Stuttgart, 1970, pp. 2/14-15.

dary and higher education. The policy was therefore inspired primarily by considerations of social justice. At the same time, however, there was concern to develop individual abilities to the full. This had been a strong feature of the radical tradition, and many of the plans advocated, and experimental programmes entered upon, during the Weimar Republic had involved a differentiated system of instruction, with a 'core' curriculum comprising subjects taught to all pupils in mixed ability groups, supplemented by various courses which would take into account individual abilities and preferences. Following this tradition special course instruction was made available in classes 7 and 8.

No doubt the flexibility of this arrangment allayed the fears of many teachers that standards of achievement would be sacrificed for the sake of doctrinaire social considerations, and represented for them an acceptable degree of compromise with the old vertically structured system. In one *Land*, Thuringia, where the innovative traditions built up in the Weimar period remained strong, there was even provision for differentiation on grounds of ability and inclination from class 5 onwards.[39] It eventually became clear, however, that the more academically oriented courses in years 7 and 8 were, in practice, preparatory classes for the *Oberschule*, and were largely the preserve of the middle class in much the same way as the old *Gymnasium* had been.[40] This was a contributory factor to the disrepute into which the entire *Reformpädagogik* tradition fell at the time of the transition from Soviet occupation to the formation of the Democratic Republic. During the school year 1948-49 the 'core and course' system was suppressed in favour of total mixed ability grouping, and a common curriculum was introduced throughout the entire eight years of the *Grundschule*.[41] This development reflects the adoption by the *SED* of a Marxist-

[39] Ibid., p. 2/22.
[40] Monumenta Paedagogica III, *Zur Entwicklung des Volksbildungswesens auf dem Gebiet der Deutschen Demokratischen Republik 1946-49*, Berlin, 1968, p. 33.
[41] K. Ellrich, *Die Entwicklung des Grundschulwesens in der Sowjetischen Besatzungszone seit 1945. Pädagogik*, 6/1950, pp. 284-5.

Leninist political line and the accompanying increased determination to change forcibly the existing social order. It was the starting-point for an entirely new orientation in educational policy in which there was to be no further trace of compromise with the desire to preserve the old *Gymnasium* tradition in some form or other.

Berlin: East-West Confrontation in Microcosm

The contrasts in methods of operating of the Soviets on the one hand, and the British and Americans on the other, is shown clearly in the case of Berlin under the Four Power Kommandatura. It is a special case, characteristic neither of East nor West, and by that token it provides an illuminating concentration of the various standpoints taken up on both sides and an apt illustration of what was considered to be at stake in the major issues. The early initiative in the city belonged to the Soviets who were able to use the two months before the arrival of the Western allies to establish a situation favourable to their policy. This was to set up a German administration as soon as possible, consisting of prominent citizens with an acceptable anti-fascist record. Following the 'block politics' of the period this comprised a broad coalition of all parties but with a majority of former Communist and Social Democratic Party members. As in the Soviet zone proper, care was taken to ensure that the key positions of power were occupied by individuals who sympathized with their views. The education service was one of the areas to which this particularly applied.[42] In the course of the academic year 1945-46 the administrators pushed ahead with plans for a reorganization of the school system along similar lines to those being worked out in the Soviet zone.

The task was made easier by the fact that the political

[42] All details of the situation in Berlin are based on M. Klewitz, *Berliner Einheitsschule 1945-51*, Berlin, 1971.

atmosphere in general was favourable to reform. The unity of
the reconstituted political parties was promoted by the overriding desire to wipe out all traces of Nazism: indeed this had
been a necessary condition for their foundation. Cooperation
was particularly close between the left-wing parties, and many
leading Social Democrats were at pains to iron out former
differences with the Communists. An important factor in this
early unity was the common fear of a resurgence of the right
wing, and the memories of the opportunity to block Hitler in
1933 that was lost through the disunity of the forces of the left.
The former ideological differences were further pushed into the
background by the fact that the Communist Party was at some
pains to point out its independence of the Soviet programme,
its desire to find a German road to socialism.[43] In the middle-
class circles, too, there was a generally favourable disposition
towards the democratic reform programme as an immediate
reaction against the stunting of educational development that
had taken place under National Socialism.

The unity forged in the common condemnation of fascism,
however, did not last. The differences that had remained in the
background in the early months came to the fore as policy
began to be formulated in an unambiguous way. In some
circles there began to be suspicion of the abuse of power by the
Soviet sympathizers in the education department of the city
administration, and as the evidence mounted that a radical
reorganization was being prepared for, so education became
an increasingly important issue in the middle-class parties whose
independence had been steadily growing. More significant than
the opposition of the Christian Democrats and the Liberals
was the split in the ranks of the Social Democrats, which came
to a head over their merger with the Communists to form the
SED. These events affected the development of a Western
Allied policy. It has already been pointed out that the British
and Americans had been far less precipitate than the Soviets as
regards implementing a policy for German education, largely

[43] Cf. D. Childs, *East Germany*, London, 1969, pp. 19–20.

from lack of understanding of what was at stake. But the purposeful initiatives of the Soviet-oriented administrators in Berlin caused them to develop a counter-strategy which supported the rights of other groups to have a say in policy. Paradoxically the British, and to an even greater degree the Americans, were broadly in favour of the kind of reforms that were being planned, but they were only prepared to countenance them if they were convinced that they were genuinely endorsed by a cross-section of German opinion. The fact that the British and the Americans had very few supporters inside the administration, and a good deal of contact with German circles outside it which were opposed to the changes being mooted, made its leaders suspect that the education department was not representative in this way, and they insisted as early as September 1945 that any major changes in policy would have to be referred to the Kommandatura.

Amid the protracted disputes among various political alliances in the period which preceded the passing of the Berlin School Law in 1948, three issues predominated. The first was the separation of Church and State in educational matters. The reformers had begun by taking the strong line that religion had no place in the educational system. The opposing case was put by the Catholic Church on the familiar grounds that the education of children was the responsibility of the family, and that in consequence the State's role was the subsidiary one of providing for the material needs of the system, guaranteeing a minimum period of education for all and making good the deficiencies where the parental interest had been inadequate; the Church, on the other hand, as the supreme authority in educational matters was the source to which parents turned for guidance, and it was considered part of its pastoral role to impose on them the duty of bringing up children in accordance with Christian beliefs. On this basis the Catholics argued for mono-confessional schools.

The attitude of the Protestants was more flexible than that of the Catholics in the early stages, when they made no de-

mands for confessional schools and accepted a compromise
between the two extreme positions. This gave parents the right
to opt for religious instruction, which was to be the responsibility of the Churches, and could be given in school in an extra
period which was not considered an integral part of the normal
curriculum. But as various steps were taken to impede the
implementation of this, the Protestants and Catholics became
increasingly united in their opposition to the administrators.
The campaign found its main political expression by way of the
CDU but the case for religious instruction was also supported
by many Liberals and Social Democrats. In the end a decisive
consensus emerged according to which religious instruction
was neither to be grudgingly tolerated nor indiscriminately
imposed. The earlier attempts to encourage its suppression, by
defining it as an extra item to be fitted in at the school's convenience, were combated by obliging schools to set aside two
periods per week either at the beginning or the end of the day
for the purpose.[44] The strength of the consensus in favour of
this compromise can be judged by the fact that even in 1951
when the Berlin School Law was substantially modified, and
when the Churches had a much increased political influence,
this section of the Law was not amended and has remained in
force up to the present day.

The second major centre of controversy, the problem of
private schools, overlaps to a considerable extent with the first
in that religious interests were strongly affected. On the socialist
side private schools were regarded by the *SED* and by many in
the *SPD* as undermining the principle of a unified comprehensive State system and in the early stages of the democratic
reform movement there was general agreement among Communists, Social Democrats and Liberals that the principle
should be interpreted in a thoroughgoing way which excluded
denominational private schools. However through the intervention of the Americans and the British to whom the Churches

[44] *Schulgesetz für Groß-Berlin*, para. 13. *Verordnungsblatt für Groß-Berlin*,
1 July 1948, p. 358.

had made representations, existing private schools were authorized to continue, though new schools could not be set up without the prior consent of the administrative authorities and the Kommandatura.[45] The wrangling however continued over a series of test cases. When in 1951 the political situation changed so that the Christian Democrats and the Liberals, who had in the meantime moved to the right of this issue, together outnumbered the socialists in the City Assembly, a new dispensation was promised. This came eventually in 1954 when a special law was passed guaranteeing the unconditional right to set up private schools in accordance with Article 7(4) of the Constitution of the Federal Republic.[46]

Of all the controversial questions raised by the Berlin School Law the one with the widest implications was that of the new comprehensive school. Whereas the problems of religious instruction and private schools were generally settled one way or the other by the time of the creation of the two Republics, the question of structure has remained in the Federal Republic a burning issue up to the present day. The case of Berlin illustrates the tussle between the extreme left-wing advocacy of an eight-year common school, similar to the model adopted in the Soviet zone, and the extreme right-wing determination to retain the selective *Gymnasium* unimpaired as in the Western zones. Many of the *SPD* favoured a compromise in the form generally endorsed by the Western Allies, namely a six-year common primary school, followed by a six-year secondary stage. The *CDU* opposition was however obdurate, and in a climate of increasing acerbity and mutual suspicion the left-wing alliance of the *SPD* and the *SED* became determined to push through a radical reorganization undiluted by compromise. This was finally incorporated in the Law passed in 1947 and ratified after certain changes by the Allies in 1948. However, when the political situation changed, it was amended to

[45] Ibid., para. 2.
[46] *Gesetz über die Privatschulen und den Privatunterricht vom 13 Mai 1954. Gesetz und Verordnungsblatt*, Berlin, p. 286.

give a six-year primary school followed by three types of *Oberschule*, academic, technical and practical, a parallel to the system which had been introduced in Hamburg.

The Nub: Consultation of Public Opinion

The controversies in Berlin reflect the major issues that came to divide Soviet policy from that of the Western Allies. In every case the crucial factor was the interaction between the authorities of the occupying power and the Germans themselves. The case of Berlin shows how from the outset the Soviets encouraged those factions which were in favour of the far-reaching changes which were incorporated in the 1946 Law introducing the comprehensive *Einheitsschule*. But it also shows the opposition to this law emanating from Christian Democratic and Liberal sources. This opposition was in evidence in the Soviet Zone too, but it was unable to mobilize itself sufficiently to prevent legislation in any of the *Länder*. In Berlin, however, the right wing and liberal factions could appeal for support to the British and Americans on two issues in particular, namely religious instruction and private schools. The support was forthcoming because the British and Americans were at pains to ensure that minority interests were represented in these matters. On the question of the comprehensive school, however, the Western Allies were not prepared to intervene, but agreed to ratify the plan for reorganization which had been passed by the City Assembly.

Thus although the British and Americans were inevitably forced to align themselves with the Christian Democrats and Liberals in Berlin there were limits to their readiness to override the wishes of the City Assembly. It was fundamental to their viewpoint that educational policy should develop in accordance with the wishes of the electorate as a whole, as their acceptance of an eight-year comprehensive school as the basis of the system showed. It was as a result of this principle that no clear pattern

E

emerged in the Western zones in contrast to the East. Thus Schleswig-Holstein and the city states of Hamburg and Bremen showed a strong degree of similarity to Berlin in their readiness for reorganization. Elsewhere in the Federal Republic, however, the weight of public opinion was behind a policy of restoration. The U.S. authorities devoted immense energy to the task of altering this opinion but without conspicuous success. Ultimately, and with the consent of the occupying powers, the course of educational policy was decided by the Germans themselves.

The crucial factor was therefore the mechanics of the consultation of public opinion. The case to be made out for the kind of action taken by the Soviets rested on the assumption that the traditional structure of the educational system had contributed in some way to the growth of authoritarianism and militarism. It followed from this that its reform was an indispensable element in any active policy. It was therefore considered vital to seize the initiative before opposition could be mobilized, and the question of eliciting German majority opinion was not regarded as relevant. The only hope for German regeneration was held to reside in the encouragement of what had historically been a minority tradition in educational affairs. In the West, on the other hand, the regenerative power of this minority tradition was successfully disputed, and the view prevailed that established practices associated with the pre-1933 selective system provided a sound basis on which to rebuild.

There has been acrimonious argument over the question of whether the respective policies pursued were or were not 'in the spirit of' Potsdam: there can never be agreement on the letter according to which they are to be judged. But behind the striking contrast between the two different systems that had emerged by 1949 can be perceived the survival of many attitudes to education common to both sides. The 1946 Law in the Soviet Zone for example did not banish from the educational system the deeply rooted inclination to accord the highest priority to the requirements of the academically gifted. It will be the task of the chapters that follow to explore the similarities as well as the differences revealed in the policy of the two new States that were created in 1949, the Federal and Democratic Republics.

CHAPTER 3

Two New Germanies: 1949–55

Ideological Points of Departure

In the new Federal Republic, set up in 1949 to replace the administrations of the three Western occupying powers, the general principles which it was intended should underline educational legislation were incorporated in the constitution or 'Basic Law', the *Grundgesetz*. The major theme affecting education was freedom from coercion—the right of the individual to 'the free development of his personality provided he does not harm the rights of others or offend against the constitutional order or the moral code'—and it was developed in two main respects. Firstly, while the entire school system was declared to be under the surveillance of the State which was to be the normal source of provision, there was specific recognition of the freedom to deviate from the State pattern. Private schools were to be authorized provided that their standards did not fall behind those of their State counterparts. The principle of freedom was invoked secondly in the approach to the long-standing tension between Church and State. In the controversial question of whether State schools should be mono-confessional or not, the deciding factor was stated to be the wishes of the parents concerned. This resulted in a diversified pattern whereby in some *Länder* confessional schools became the prevailing type, in others they existed side by side with inter-denominational ones while in a third group only the latter were provided.[1] The resulting confused pattern of practices that

[1] Cf. E. C. Helmreich, *Religious Education in German Schools*, Harvard, 1959, pp. 227–30.

diverged, even within *Land* boundaries, met with criticism which was a reflection of a more fundamental disagreement over the role that the Churches should play in education. The *Elternrecht*, the principle of the parents' right to choose the kind of education their children should receive, was attacked as an oblique way of perpetuating Church control of schools and of fostering divisiveness in the community.[2] The constitutional preoccupation with the rights of various segments of society can, however, equally be regarded as evidence of the determination to guarantee a democratic development in the new State and to preclude the possibility of the kind of centralized tyranny that had existed under National Socialism. In this interpretation the inconvenience caused by lack of uniformity was merely the price of the safeguards of freedom.

In the Democratic Republic set up in the former Soviet occupation zone, the constitution laid down principles which placed particular emphasis on democratic rights and on the illegality of any attempt to infringe them. In education these rights were regarded as being incorporated in the 1946 Law, the provisions of which were confirmed. Thus in contrast to the Federal Republic private schools were not permitted since they were regarded as seedbeds of privilege, representing a denial of democratic principles. Confessional schools had likewise been abolished in 1946 but the constitution guaranteed the right of the Churches to give religious instruction in schools. The only overt intimation of future socialist policies was contained in a statement to the effect that educational opportunity should not be dependent on social and economic circumstances. Rather was special attention to be devoted to children who were at a disadvantage in this respect. But in general the document was couched in comparatively neutral terms, in marked contrast to the explicitly socialist version which was to supersede it in 1968.

Though the two constitutions have superficial similarities by

[2] W. Ebert, *Elternrecht, Volksschule und Lehrerbildung. Material- und Nachrichten-Dienst*, 57/1954, p. 5.

Länder *of the Federal Republic after 1949 (Saarland added in 1957)*

virtue of their generalized statements on such matters as equality before the law and freedom of worship, the grandiloquent wording does not conceal differences of approach which were fundamental and which became steadily more marked during the 1950s.

It was a basic assumption of the constitution of the Federal Republic that responsibility for educational policy should be distributed as widely as possible. Following this, legislation was left to the individual *Länder* and the federal constitution merely laid down certain general principles which were themselves designed primarily to guarantee the distribution of responsibility throughout the community. The constitution of the *DDR* also gave considerable responsibility to the *Länder* in the administration of the educational system, but the fundamental legislation was declared to be a matter for the central government whose decisions were binding on the entire country. This predilection for central control contrasts with the lack of any provision for the Federal government in the West to interfere with the legislative activities of the *Länder*. The position taken up on this issue was reinforced by the sharp awareness of the harmful effects of centralized control under National Socialism when a central ministry had been created in order to facilitate the manipulation of the educational system for political ends. But cultural federalism was more than merely a device to encourage democratic development. In education there was a pre-National Socialist tradition of *Land* autonomy, and it was felt that a *Land* ministry was better qualified to assess and meet the needs of its own region than a central one. Moreover, a federal structure appeared to offer the advantage that in those *Länder* where the urge to re-think the structure of the system was strong and where changes had already been introduced before 1949, new directions in policy could be pursued with the minimum of friction.

The distinction between the legislative patterns in the two States became quite sharply defined in 1952 when the dissolution of the *Land* parliaments in the *DDR* marked the final

centralization of responsibility for educational policy. Following
the principle of democratic centralism, the regional assemblies
which replaced the *Land* parliaments were conceived of as
organs of the central administration, and in consequence
policy decisions emanated from the highest levels of the
hierarchy of the dominant Socialist Unity Party. By contrast
the federalism of the West had created a situation where
conflicting policies of opposed political parties could and did
exist side by side. Consequently the Federal Republic inherited
the full multiplicity of educational practice that had accumula-
ted by the end of the period of the Weimar Republic. The
variety of types of school reflected geographical variations and
differences in demographic and social structure. In addition
to this, each of the occupying powers had influenced policy in
its zone in its own way, and there was the further differentiating
factor of the political complexion of the individual *Land*
governments. This complexity resulted inevitably in inequalities
of provision. The efforts of individual *Länder* to ease the
financial problems of school attendance varied. Access to a
Gymnasium could virtually be ruled out in some rural areas
where the local *Volksschule*, sometimes staffed by only one or
two teachers for all the age groups, was the only school within
reasonable distance. While this kind of problem failed to arouse
much public interest in the Federal Republic, there was a
strong impulse to tackle it in the *DDR* in accordance with the
view that uniform standards of provision should be guaranteed
throughout the country.

The dissatisfaction in the West resulted not so much from
the inadequacies of provision as from the difficulties that arose
through lack of liaison between *Länder*. Thus, in cases where
families were obliged to move across *Land* boundaries, the
continuity of their children's education could be disrupted. The
sequence of modern languages taught in the *Gymnasium* was a
particular source of irritation. Though these were the problems
of a small minority within a minority group, namely the
clientele of the *Gymnasium*, it comprised a highly articulate and

Administrative Districts of the DDR after 1952

politically effective body of opinion. Another example was the
reluctance of *Land* authorities to recognize qualifications
acquired outside their own boundaries, which could give rise
to serious grievances in questions of career opportunities, such
as entry to various forms of higher and further education. It
became increasingly clear in the course of the early 1950s that
this debit side of cultural federalism required urgent attention
in the form of some standardization of the educational programmes of the *Länder*. So while the view prevailed that *Land*
autonomy in education was beneficial, there was increasing
agreement on the need to impose a reasonable degree of unity
on this diversity.[3] Despite the growing call for standardization,
however, the variegation in the Federal Republic contrasts very
obviously with the uniform pattern of provision that characterized the system in the *DDR*.

The two approaches derive from different ideological
assumptions and this was already implicit in the wording of the
respective constitutions. In the case of the *DDR* it was stated
that 'each child must be given the possibility of all-round
development of his physical, intellectual and moral powers'.
The use of the term 'all-round development' is an echo of the
Marxian assertion that in capitalist society the masses are
educated only sufficiently to enable them to fulfil single functions in the production process thereby making them little
more than extensions of the machines they operate. From
1949 the importance of 'many-sided' education was continually
stressed and it became an essential element in the resolution of
the Party leadership in 1952 to educate young people as
rounded personalities (*allseitig entwickelte Persönlichkeiten*), 'able
and prepared to build up socialism and to defend the achievement of the workers to the utmost'.[4] This statement, which is
generally considered to have given the final impulse to the
'systematic building up of socialism', serves to reiterate the

[3] See for example *Jahrbuch der SPD*, 1950/51, p. 23; 1952/53, p. 37.
[4] *Dokumente zur Geschichte des Schulwesens* . . . Monumenta Paedagogica VI,
Berlin, 1970, p. 419.

fundamental importance of the social class issue. The educational system was seen as an instrument for the redressing of the grievances of generations of underprivilege by ensuring that the mass of the people would no longer be educated merely to the minimum level required to enable capitalist industry to operate profitably, but rather to a point where they would themselves be capable of becoming the controlling force in society.

The educational situation of the working class was regarded as the product of a scale of values according to which the highest prestige attached to a concept of general education of which the ultimate purpose and justification was the self-fulfilment of the individual regardless of vocational considerations. This view of the supreme aim of education constitutes the essence of the *Gymnasium* tradition, and, in the Federal Republic, its retention as the preserve of a minority was the mainspring of the formulation of policy. There was an assumption, at least implicit, that the ideals of disinterested scholarship held no attraction for the great majority, and that for them it was more appropriate that narrowly defined vocational considerations should remain uppermost. The preservation of the traditional values which stress the individualistic aspects of education was not, however, regarded as undemocratic in the Federal Republic. Though the *Gymnasium* was frankly admitted to exist for the purpose of educating the leaders in society it was freely open to children from all classes to compete for entry to it and for those reluctant to do so it was considered to be the responsibility of the parents to provide the necessary encouragement. In order to promote fair competition in this respect there was a series of initiatives in the individual *Länder* during the early 1950s to provide financial assistance where necessary and eventually to abolish fee-paying.[5] However, this view of how democratic principles were to be realized in education contrasted sharply with the approach to the question in the East.

[5] *Bericht des Vorsitzenden des Schulausschusses der Ständigen Konferenz*, 1951/52, p. 4; 1952/53, p. 3; 1954/55, p. 1.

In the *DDR* the historical development of the system which had resulted in the pre-eminence of the *Gymnasium* was regarded as inseparable from the class issue and the denial of democracy that was considered to be associated with it. *Gymnasium* education had for generations been the virtual monopoly of the middle classes so that the working class was regarded as having been conditioned to accept the second-class education of the *Volksschule* as their normal lot, thereby accustoming themselves to subservience. Already in the constitution it was made clear that 'the education of young people must not be dependent on the social and economic character of the home', and that the entire range of educational provision should be available to all classes on an equal basis. Furthermore the same article indicated that 'special consideration is to be given to children who are at a disadvantage through social circumstances'. Consequently it was natural that the available resources in the *DDR* should be channelled towards the *Volksschule* in order to raise the educational standards of the majority rather than towards the *Gymnasium* for the benefit of the personal cultivation of a minority. The fundamental difference between the ideologies of the two States lies in the fact that in the Federal Republic the individualism of the traditional system was reinstated along with the entire scale of humanistic values associated with it, whereas in the *DDR* the aim was to find a policy that would collectively benefit the working-class majority.

Such a policy was already launched by the time the *DDR* was created. The 1946 Law had brought about the organizational precondition for the abolition of the segregation which was considered to promote the educational monopoly of the middle class. The eight-year *Grundschule* which it introduced, however, was not totally undifferentiated, and it soon became clear that it was once again the middle-class children who most readily chose the courses which were more academically oriented in the traditional sense, and hence more likely to lead to entrance to the *Oberschule*, the truncated remnant of the *Gymnasium*. Furthermore the *Oberschule* by and large held

stubbornly to its humanistic traditions.[6] As it became clear
that the purpose of the reorganization of the educational
system was not merely to provide greater social justice, but to
create the necessary educational conditions for the dominance
of the working class in society, it was equally obvious that this
aim was jeopardized by the continued success of the middle
class within the new system. Consequently the 1946 Law was
followed by the gradual elimination of all differentiation within
the *Grundschule* unless it was of a remedial nature or was closely
linked to the ideologically oriented activities of the youth
movement. The statement in the constitution regarding those
'who are at a disadvantage through social circumstances' is
therefore the confirmation of a trend towards conscious promotion of the educational opportunities of the working class
by means of positive discrimination in its favour and corresponding curtailment of the opportunities for the middle class.

   Thus, despite the superficially anodyne wording of the two
constitutions, both of which were perhaps envisaged as applying
ultimately to a reunited Germany, there is a marked difference
in emphasis. Whereas in the Federal Republic the concern was
to guarantee basic rights within an existing social framework
and to eschew any *dirigisme* in educational policy, it was a considered aim in the *DDR* to change the existing social framework, using the educational system as an instrument towards
this end. This contrast in basic aims provides the starting-point
for a number of interesting comparisons, above all the question
of which approach was more apposite in the context of the problems of post-war economic recovery which faced both States.

Structural and Curricular Developments in the West

The call for standardization in the Federal Republic exerted
pressure to conform on those *Länder* which had deviated from

   [6] K.-H. Günther/G. Uhlig, *Zur Entwicklung des Volksbildungswesens . . .,*
Berlin, 1968, p. 34.

the general, orthodox pattern—Schleswig-Holstein, Hamburg and Bremen. The key point of divergence was over the extension of common primary schooling from four to six years and the consequent postponement by two years of selection for the *Gymnasium* and *Mittelschule* or their equivalents. Those opposed to the innovations in the *Länder* concerned made the urge to conform with the remainder of the Federal Republic a leading element in their campaign for a reversion to the traditional system. They argued furthermore that the changes introduced had been motivated by party politics, had largely gone against the wishes of parents and had been purely organizational measures, unaccompanied by the necessary revision of the curriculum and by care to ensure that sufficient teachers of the appropriate kind were available.[7] Inevitably some of the latter criticism was justified in schools which were still inadequately housed and overcrowded as a result of the flood of refugees. Schleswig-Holstein bore a particularly heavy burden in this respect. In all the *Länder* involved the decreasing support for a radical educational policy was reflected in the growing strength of the right-wing parties among which the *CDU* were particularly active opponents of the changes that had been introduced. The relevant laws were rescinded in Schleswig-Holstein in 1951, in Hamburg in 1954 and in Bremen in 1957 so that transfer to the *Gymnasium* once again became possible after four years of primary school.

This gradual falling into line of the more innovative *Länder* illustrates the conspicuous lack of enthusiasm for any modifications of the established highly selective system. Even in the professional association in which elementary teachers were strongly represented, the *Gewerkschaft Erziehung und Wissenschaft*, a proposal for a two-year comprehensive stage that could effectively postpone the age of selection from ten to twelve was not adopted.[8] And in the remaining sectors of the profession

---

[7] *Material- und Nachrichten-Dienst*, 8/1951, pp. 3–11.

[8] C. Kuhlmann, *Schulreform und Gesellschaft in der BRD 1946–66*. In S. B. Robinsohn, *Schulreform im gesellschaftlichen Prozess I*, Stuttgart, 1970, p. 1/36.

—the *Gymnasium*, the *Mittelschule* and the *Berufsschule*—there was general hostility to any such notion.[9] The opposition of the *Philologenverband*, the professional association representing the *Gymnasium* teachers, was particularly implacable and any suggestion of structural change was roundly denounced as undermining the consolidation of the traditional system which was now regarded as well advanced after the harm done to it by the attemps to introduce comprehensive education in the immediate post-war period.[10] Since the *CDU/CSU*, the German Party and the *FDP* all advocated restorative policies there was little prospect of the *SPD* achieving any real political influence. An indication of the general mood as regards educational policy at this time is given by the popular catch-phrase 'No experiments' (*Keine Experimente*) which was as effective as it was simple.

The course taken by educational policy during this period was therefore primarily one of coordination within the general restorative pattern, a task which naturally fell to the *Kultus-ministerkonferenz*. The climax to this work came with the Düsseldorf Agreement of February 1955 in which a considerable degree of rationalization was achieved. The practical benefits were above all in the easing of problems of migration from *Land* to *Land*. Administrative arrangements regarding the duration and timing of the school year were standardized, as was the system of assessment. Uniform nomenclature was introduced although terms traditionally used locally could be retained as an additional designation. Most important of all, mutual recognition of qualifications was agreed, and special procedures were established for cases of hardship in transferring from school to school. Thus for example where a pupil was faced with a change in the modern languages offered in the curriculum it was possible to waive the examination in one subject in the leaving certificate.

[9] For the attitude of teachers in *Mittelschulen* and *Berufsschulen* see E. Lippert, *Berufserziehung von Morgen. Material- und Nachrichten-Dienst*, 49/1953, pp. 9, 10. Also G. Ried, *Dokumente zur Schulpolitik*, Frankfurt/M., 1956, p. 128.   [10] Ried, op. cit., pp. 21–7.

The standardization achieved in the Düsseldorf Agreement makes it convenient to give a general description of the school system in the Federal Republic as a whole. Primary school (*Grundschule*) was an integral part of the *Volksschule* which in its senior stage provided the full-time education of most children up to the school-leaving age. Depending on the *Land* it was possible to transfer to a selective school after either four or six years in the *Grundschule*. There were two main kinds of selective school: firstly, the *Mittelschule* which offered a four- or six-year course leading to the intermediate qualification, the '*mittlere Reife*', after a total of ten years of education; secondly, the *Gymnasium* in which the course lasted either seven or nine years and led to the *Abitur* and university entrance. The three types of *Gymnasium* were standardized as the *altsprachliches Gymnasium* biased towards classical languages, the *neusprachliches Gymnasium* biased towards modern languages and the *mathematisch-naturwissenschaftliches Gymnasium* biased towards mathematics and natural sciences. For all three types the nine-year course was designated normal; the seven-year alternative was accepted only in the case of the latter two. Though the curricula were not fully standardized, a fairly uniform pattern was established for the sequence of foreign languages studied. A ten-year period was agreed upon for the validity of the Düsseldorf Agreement to which Bavaria alone refused to be a signatory, being unwilling to adapt to its provisions.

Certain elements stand out in a review of the general movement towards standardization of practice and the creation of a pattern for the educational system which was recognizable and coherent at a national level. The first is the extent to which it was marked by the concern to preserve traditions. Perhaps the foremost illustration is the restoration of the ninth year of the *Gymnasium* course, underlining as it does the importance attached to this minority sector and its need to make up the ground lost through the meddlings of the National Socialists. By comparison the raising of the minimum school-leaving age to 15 was a lesser priority. The preservation of the *Gymnasium* ethos was further safeguarded by ensuring that the main expansion in the selective schools took place in the *Mittelschule*. The second element is a concern that, however selective the system, its criteria should be based purely on scholastic ability and not on financial circumstances—in this respect the steady move towards the abolition of school fees reflects the earlier pressure exerted by the Allies and the agitation of the Social Democrats in this period. Finally there is a marked tendency to concentrate mainly on administrative matters. The Düsseldorf Agreement was a valuable contribution in this way, removing various anomalies created by the different ways of structuring the school year and the different curricula and leaving certificates. But it did not reflect any profound consideration of the implications of restoring the tripartite system unaltered.

For such consideration the *Kultusministerkonferenz* was however not the appropriate body, a fact which had been recognized in 1953 when a special committee, the *Deutscher Ausschuß für das Erziehungs- und Bildungswesen*, was set up on the joint initiative of the Federal Ministry of the Interior and the *Kultusminister-konferenz*. The task of this committee was to produce recommendations for the educational system which, it was emphasized, were to be independent of any particular political or religious line. At the inauguration of the *Deutscher Ausschuss* it was made clear that its ultimate task was to devise a plan for the reshaping of the *entire* educational system. It was however not until the latter half of the decade that its activities began to bear fruit.

Structural and Curricular Developments in the East

In the *DDR* on the other hand the *SED* was committed to active policies and was constantly preoccupied with the possibility of a further restructuring. The changes introduced by the 1946 Law were merely the first stage of the total transformation of the school system that was envisaged. The eight-year *Grundschule* was already established and the new developments

F

were concerned with provision beyond this stage. In this respect the early and mid-1950s were a turbulent period characterized by political and bureaucratic excesses and dissension in the teaching profession and among the public at large.

The major innovation was the introduction of intermediate or 'ten-class' schools (*Zehnklassenschulen*) announced by Ulbricht in 1950 (Diagram in Appendix VIII). The reason given was the need to bring more young people up to the standard of entrance to the schools which trained technicians (*Fachschulen*) in order to make possible the fulfilment of the Five-Year Plan. To meet the demand for qualified manpower it was considered essential to encourage as many pupils as possible to continue their full-time education beyond the school-leaving age. But in this respect the *Oberschule* had been unsatisfactory largely because of its middle-class ethos. The intermediate school on the other hand appeared more suited to the task of guaranteeing a flow of pupils to the higher levels of vocational and technical training.

The coexistence of the *Oberschule* and the *Zehnklassenschule* was somewhat uneasy. The former remained primarily devoted to preparation for university. Its curriculum was heavily loaded and its inevitably demanding nature tended to convey an impression of academic exclusiveness similar to that which had characterized the traditional *Gymnasium* (see Appendix II). Many of the teachers had set about making their pupils acquire in a shorter time the same kind of general culture for which a much longer period had previously been at their disposal. Since the curriculum of the *Zehnklassenschule* was less demanding, it did not enjoy the same prestige and eventually a certain flavour of competition, if not of mutual hostility, developed between the two kinds of school. The *Oberschule* was accused of having bourgeois tendencies and there were various calls to find one comprehensive form of upper school which would provide similar opportunities for all. The pressure to fuse the *Oberschule* with the *Zehnklassenschule* in one comprehensive institution reached its peak in 1953. At this time the influence of Soviet education was also at a peak and it was argued that the Soviet Union was planning a transition to a ten-year school as the standard type of institution for the education of all children. Accordingly it was advocated that the *Zehnklassenschulen* should be extended by one year to become eleven-class schools leading to the *Abitur*, and that the *Oberschulen* should be phased out.[11]

Reorganization along these lines was promulgated in May 1953 and the new three-year upper school course was to have a comprehensive character with the traditional division into three main branches (modern languages, classics and mathematics/natural sciences) abolished. In all schools Russian was to be compulsory as the first foreign language. New programmes were to be introduced to achieve 'a high general level of culture and to develop polytechnical education', to bridge the gap, that is, between general and vocational education.[12] The two reasons given for the reorganization were that the growing need for qualified manpower demanded a quicker and better preparation for university study and that the measure would enhance the educational prospects of working-class children. At the root of the issue lay a problem of curriculum. There was a feeling that the values embodied in the existing curriculum of the *Oberschule* were appropriate neither for the country's economic nor its social needs. It is in this context that the discussion of 'polytechnical education' must be understood, exploring somewhat hesitantly ways in which education could be more directly related to life and the means of production. But the conference on the subject, which was held shortly after the announcement of the reorganization, was not notably successful and during the next few years bore fruit only in isolated initiatives.[13]

Equally, the creation of *Elfklassenschulen*, as the proposed

---

[11] *Die neue Schule*, 16/1953, p. 16; 17/1953, p. 7.

[12] S. Baske/M. Engelbert, *Zwei Jahrzehnte Bildungspolitik . . . Dokumente*, Vol. I, Berlin, 1966, pp. 230, 231.

[13] K.-H. Günther/ G. Uhlig, *Geschichte der Schule in der DDR 1945 bis 1968*, Berlin, 1969, pp. 82, 83.

new institutions were sometimes called, proved premature and the order was withdrawn before it could come into force. The explanation of the withdrawal given by Otto Grotewohl was that a radical measure of this kind might prove an obstacle to the future reunification of Germany, but the Education Minister, Frau Professor Zaisser, admitted also that the authorities had lost touch with the general public and failed to take account of its wishes. It became clear from subsequent criticism that a peak of bureaucratic control had been reached at this time.[14]

After this brief episode—little more than a month elapsed between the announcement of the measures and their withdrawal—a good deal of energy went into building up the *Zehnklassenschulen*, so that by 1955 they were as numerous as the *Oberschulen*. But though it was made clear that they were the favoured model for the education of the entire school population in the future, there was after 1953 a general loss of momentum in the drive to transform the system in this way, evidenced above all in the spread of 'revisionist' thinking. By the mid-1950s, therefore, the school system in the *DDR* had not developed as far in accordance with comprehensive principles as many politicians and administrators had wished. The existence of an intermediate school appeared to many to create a hierarchy that was uncomfortably reminiscent of the one which marked the system in the West, even though selection in the East took place much later. Indeed the term *Mittelschule* was used in both States. Several more years were to elapse before it was possible to take a further step towards the elimination of this kind of differentiation.

Educational Implications of Policies

The policy of restoration adopted in the Federal Republic in the early 1950s was an expression of the belief that the

---

[14] *Die neue Schule*, 26/1953, pp. 7, 8; 27/1953, p. 4; 36/1953, pp. 6, 7; 41/1953, pp. 4–6.

source of regeneration after National Socialism lay in a reversion to pre-1933 practice. The efforts of the British, American and French authorities to stimulate a desire for change had if anything confirmed the Germans in this conviction. There were two main strands in the educational tradition. The first was the *Gymnasium* ideal of disinterested scholarship as a preparation for university and the learned professions, the second the minimum rudimentary general education of the *Volksschule* as a preparation for apprenticeship and the exercise of a trade. Concurrent with the period of apprenticeship was compulsory part-time attendance at a vocational school (*Berufsschule*). This dualism between the academic and the vocational was to some extent modified by the existence of the small intermediate sector represented by the *Mittelschule*. In this hierarchy the status of the *Gymnasium*, in its classical or 'humanistic' form in particular, was supreme. In the post-war period this status was reinforced by its teachers' claim of resistance to National Socialism so that the humanism that it stood for could be represented as a source of inspiration for the reconstruction of German society.[15] A second source of inspiration was the Church on the strength of the resistance shown by some groups of Christians, and the role of Christianity in the rebuilding of the school system was repeatedly stressed in the post-war period.[16] The significance of these two pillars of educational reconstruction, humanism and Christianity, was that both conveyed a sense of the resumption of the best in German educational traditions and virtually guaranteed the failure of the majority of the attempts to reorganize the school system along comprehensive lines. They were reinforced by a strong disinclination to bring in any measures that might appear to follow the trend of development in the Democratic Republic.

[15] R. Eilers, *Die nationalsozialistische Schulpolitik*, Köln und Opladen, 1963, pp. 80–2.

[16] Cf. M. Knappen, *And Call it Peace*, Chicago, 1947, pp. 48–50. Also L. Kerstiens, *Die höhere Schule in den Reformplänen der Nachkriegszeit. Zeitschrift für Pädagogik*, 11 (1965), pp. 551–5.

The status of the *Gymnasium* is inseparably bound up with the concept of *Allgemeinbildung* which as noted in the opening chapter had acquired its dominance in the time of Humboldt. Essential to it was the view that in the acquisition of knowledge and the refinement of aesthetic appreciation vocational considerations were irrelevant. Education was seen not as resting ultimately with the assimilation of something imposed from outside, a particular accumulation of knowledge and skills necessary in order to earn one's livelihood in society but as characterized by something generated from within, the urge to cultivate the intellect and the aesthetic sense to the highest degree possible. For Humboldt the striving for this ideal had required immersion in the literature of ancient Greece and this had been the *raison d'être* of the classical *Gymnasium*. Subsequently, it will be recalled, circumstances had modified the nature of *Allgemeinbildung* to the extent that two additional major types of *Gymnasium* had taken their place alongside the original classical one. And furthermore, it was often alleged that the inspiration of the Humboldt era had been betrayed by the subordination of the individual pursuit of culture to the need to bring all *Gymnasium* pupils up to a preconceived standard, the norm represented by the *Abitur*. But whatever the truth of the accusations that the *Gymnasium* was a '*Lernschule*', there was no gainsaying the immense prestige it enjoyed by virtue of its tradition of scholarship.

The new ideological departure in the *DDR* clearly implied the rejection of this favoured position. The process had begun in 1946 and the viability of the changes introduced at that time had been due in no small measure to the support of teachers versed in the theories of the *Reform* movement of Weimar and earlier. Many had felt that the new system being introduced provided an opportunity to break with the *Lernschule* tradition that was denied in the West as a result of the restoration of the *Gymnasium* in its pre-1933 form. In particular they regarded the *Reformpädagogik* tradition, with its emphasis on independent activity and thought, as a highly acceptable antidote to the authoritarian legacy of the Third Reich. Following this argument there was in the Soviet Zone renewed enthusiasm for the child-centred approach exemplified by the creative activity of Kerschensteiner's *Arbeitsschule*: the true worth of education was to be seen in the individuality of the child's achievement.

From 1949 onwards, however, not only was the main *Gymnasium* tradition of general culture rejected in the *DDR* but the theories of the minority tradition of *Reformpädagogik* also fell into disrepute. At the Fourth Educational Congress the *Arbeitsschule* ideal was labelled the product of the 'epoch of bourgeois imperialistic decline' and it became clear that its adherents were either to be won over to the new official line or censured:

... we must adopt a critical attitude to pre-1933 *Reformpädagogik* and prevail over it, not from the standpoint of the past but from the standpoint of the future of our new democratic school. In this we must always strive to distinguish very clearly between those progressive colleagues who on the basis of an uncritical attitude and a lack of understanding of the basic truth that every new social order must create anew the corresponding educational theory, are still prejudiced in favour of the errors of the various conceptions of the *Arbeitsschule*—these we wish to convince and win over—and those who are under the Anglo-American influence of pseudo-democratic Western theorists of the *Arbeitsschule* who see their main business in the falsification of formerly progressive educational theories and the exploitation of the fundamentally reactionary ideas of Kerschensteiner for the purposes of neo-fascist educational theories—these are the ones we wish to combat.[17]

The particular quarrel with Kerschensteiner's theories was that implicit in them was acceptance of the existing social order, and that, however valuable his conception of the complementary nature of intellectual and practical activity, it still assumed a school system which assigned the overwhelming majority of children to an education which fitted them for little other than skilled and semi-skilled trades, and thereby buttressed the educational privileges of the middle class.

[17] Baske/Engelbert, op. cit., Vol. I, pp. 129-30.

The quarrel was thus at root political and ideological. The school system was seen first and foremost as the instrument of social revolution and its fundamental task was therefore the inculcation of socialist ideology. The general tenet of *Reformpädagogik* that education should be child-centred was merely an obstacle to the achievement of this objective. In so far as the individualistic theories implied that the teacher should withdraw into the background in order to allow children to form their own attitudes spontaneously and independently, they represented for the *SED* activists an abdication of the crucial role of the teacher in the building of socialism.[18] To fill the gap left after the discrediting of the *Reform* movement the speakers at the Fourth Educational Congress turned to two sources, firstly to those educationists in German history, such as Friedrich Diesterweg, who could be shown to have struggled for the betterment of the lot of the working class, and secondly to the socialist educational theory of the Soviet Union.

As a result of the reversal of policy a new authoritarianism restored something of the *Lernschule* character to the schools, but in the service of different ends. The school was seen as having a vital role to play in the political re-education of the population as a whole and three major agencies were enlisted to carry it out, the teaching profession itself, educational theory in respect of teaching method and curriculum, and the youth movement. Marxism-Leninism became a standard constituent of teacher training. As an incentive to professional achievement the new title of *Verdienter Lehrer des Volkes* was created and strong political conviction was an important criterion in its award. At the same time there was a much tighter grip on teaching method. Exhaustive instructions were given as to how lessons were to be prepared and structured, which methods were to be used, and how work was to be evaluated. In contrast to the freedom advocated in the *Reform* movement teachers

---

[18] G. Uhlig, *Die Entwicklung des Schulwesens . . . Wissenschaftliche Zeitschrift der Karl Marx Universität Leipzig*, 3/1961, p. 377. Also Günther/Uhlig, *Zur Entwicklung . . .*, op. cit., p. 206.

now had a rigid model which they were obliged to follow. Finally there was the role of the youth movement in reinforcing the work of the teacher. The formation of the *Verband der Jungen Pioniere* is significant in this respect. The rigid organization of the Pioneers was closely modelled on the Soviet organization from which they drew their name. But whereas the *Freie Deutsche Jugend*, which had already been in existence for some time, had been an extra-curricular activity, the Pioneer organization, designed for a younger age group, was now consciously used to create an atmosphere of disciplined learning in the classroom and to promote ideological commitment. Its objectives thus overlapped with those of the school curricula.[19] From 1949 on the *FDJ* also ceased to be purely extra-curricular and its activities were correspondingly intensified with the number of school branches of the organization showing an increase of 60 per cent within a year.[20]

Thus all possible forces were mobilized to realize in practice the implications of the transition from an educational theory founded largely on the principles of the *Reform* movement tradition to one which drew its primary inspiration from Soviet theory and which was designed to serve the cause of political and ideological re-education. It was the ideological content that constituted the major changes in the curriculum. But the attempt to bring about a radical reorganization of the balance of studies at the *Oberschule* level proved premature. Consequently the traditional acceptance that *Gymnasium* general culture was essential as a preliminary to university study was not by any means disposed of. Moreover, with the loss of ideological momentum after 1953, it was not till later in the decade that a new educational theory was developed to the point where a curriculum of a different kind could begin to be devised as a replacement for the legacy of *Gymnasium* general culture.

Although this legacy had been taken over in the Federal

[19] M. Feist, *Der Pionierauftrag. die neue schule*, 34/1950, p. 7.
[20] Günther/Uhlig, *Zur Entwicklung . . .*, op. cit., p. 202.

Republic it did not go unquestioned. The structure whereby the *Gymnasium* remained segregated from the rest of the system was not seriously challenged but there was a good deal of concern over its overloaded curriculum. This encyclopaedism was denounced in the report of a working party of school and university teachers in 1951 with the memorable maxim *Arbeiten Können ist mehr als Vielwisserei* (The ability to work is more important than the accumulation of factual knowledge). The report known as the Tübingen Resolutions (*Tübinger Beschlüsse*) reflected the criticism of the *Gymnasium* as a *Lernschule*, concerned more with the quantity than the quality of its work, and pointed out that true intellectual understanding was hampered by a surfeit of purely factual knowledge and that general phenomena could be better learnt if illustrated by one specific and well-chosen example. This argument contained the essence of what subsequently developed into a theory of paradigmatic learning (*exemplarisches Lernen*) according to which those topics are taught which best exemplify the theory and method of the discipline as a whole. The removal of the emphasis from how much is studied to the way in which it is studied was designed to foster the ability to apply what is learnt to new situations. The early explorations of the theory were mainly in the field of natural science, where its application could be more clearly illustrated, than in the humanities, where the debate was less fruitful.[21]

The emergence of the theory of *exemplarisches Lernen* is a measure of the reluctance to abandon any of the traditional components of the *Gymnasium* curriculum. The broad range of studies, with its marked linguistic and literary bias, was regarded as essential to the general culture transmitted in all three kinds of *Gymnasium* (see Appendix I). Any reduction by way of specialization in the upper forms, as practised for example in England, was regarded as an erosion of the cultural heritage. If it could be made operational, *exemplarisches Lernen*

[21] Cf. M. Wagenschein, *Zur Selbstkritik der höheren Schule. Die Sammlung*, 7/1952, pp. 142–52.

offered a way of reducing the burden on pupils and at the same time retaining the constellation of humanistic values intact.

Ultimately the educational implications of the policies adopted in the Federal Republic and the *DDR* were related above all to curricular problems. It is significant that the idea of *exemplarisches Lernen*, the most notable development in German educational theory in the early 1950s, was concerned specifically with the *Gymnasium* while comparatively little attention was paid to other sectors of the system. The main preoccupation was with finding a way of preserving traditional values in the context of the 'internal reform' that was considered necessary. In the *DDR* the task was only beginning of finding the appropriate curricular content to bring about the eradication of the traditional values which at this stage were still in evidence, particularly in the *Oberschulen*.

The Social Dimension

The lack of criticism of the very obvious social stratification in the school system of the Federal Republic is surprising, at least in retrospect. The *Gymnasium* was demonstrably dominated by the middle class and was concerned with producing a cultivated élite. The numbers entering this privileged group from the working class were extremely low. For example, in a survey carried out in Schleswig-Holstein in 1951 the percentage of children who, in their seventh year of schooling, were in selective schools, i.e. *Gymnasien* or *Mittelschulen*, was calculated for five occupational categories as follows: upper class (high managerial and professional), boys 79·7, girls 70·8; upper 'white collar', boys 39·6, girls 31·5; lower 'white collar', boys 11·9, girls 8·7; upper working class, boys 4·5, girls 2·4; lower working class, boys 0·7, girls 0·4; total school population, boys 12·8, girls 9·4.[22] Though the pattern may not have been

[22] K. Valentin Müller, *Begabung und Soziale Schichtung in der Hochindustrialisierten Gesellschaft*, Köln und Opladen, 1956, p. 27.

quite so marked in the more populous and highly urbanized *Länder*, there is little doubt that it was broadly similar. The prevailing interpretation of the sociological data was that the higher socio-economic groups had been constituted as a result of a sifting process in which intelligence was a fundamental criterion and that since heredity was the major determinant of intelligence it was in the nature of things that children from these groups would perform in a superior manner. Thus the distribution of intelligence was regarded as corresponding very closely with the social structure. In this way psychological and sociological theories served to justify the vertical structuring of the system and the early selection of an élite.[23]

A factor that appeared to corroborate this finding was the working-class attitude to the exclusiveness of the *Gymnasium*. Its aura was intimidating and for those parents who were keen on advancement for their children the *Mittelschule* offered a more acceptable route. The most noteworthy feature of this so-called *Bildungsabstinenz* of the working class is the fact that its essential ingredient was indifference rather than resentment. For the parents, attendance at the *Berufsschule* and the acquisition of a trade qualification at the end of the period of apprenticeship represented a tangible achievement with a guarantee of security, in comparison with which the somewhat nebulous pursuit of general culture appeared far less attractive.[24] And among young people the value attached to vocational as opposed to general education was very marked—in the *Berufsschulen* the teacher of vocational subjects enjoyed much greater prestige than the teacher of general subjects. There was moreover a strong element of social prestige in the acquisition of skilled worker status.[25] Thus the general pattern of social attitudes tended to support the tripartite structure of *Gymnasium, Mittelschule* and *Volksschule*.

[23] Ibid., pp. 115-21.

[24] J. Leimig, *Wirtschaft und Berufsausbildung. Material- und Nachrichten-Dienst*, 48/1953, p. 2.

[25] H. Steglich, *Aufstieg über die praktische Lehre. Die deutsche Berufs- und Fachschule*, 12/1955, p. 909.

The consensus rested on the belief that these three major educational levels corresponded to three main types of ability:

The *Volksschule* provides the basic education for the large sector of the population which is predominantly manually employed, the *Realschule* (*Mittelschule*) for those people whose jobs involve a combination of initiatory and executive, practical and theoretical activity, that is to say who, as thinking responsible practitioners in industry and commerce, in artisan trades, agriculture and administration, and in the social, welfare, technical and artistic professions are in a position to grasp dominant ideas rapidly and with certainty and have them carried out sensibly and accurately. The *Gymnasium* forms the appropriate preparatory institution for the intellectual leadership which is responsible for activity of a directional, planning and scholarly nature.[26]

This view of the differentiation of ability clearly complemented the prevailing theory regarding its social distribution and contributed to the justification for segregation in the system.

It was vigorously attacked in the *DDR* as a specious form of reasoning designed to bolster up the educational privilege of the middle class. This privilege, so ran the counter-argument, could be eliminated by removing the conditions which created it and which were essentially environmental rather than hereditary, a function of the lack of opportunity and the systematic inculcation of erroneous conceptions of potential. A major task of the drive towards a socialist interpretation of the function of education was to convince the children of industrial and agricultural workers of the importance of knowledge and of their duty both to themselves and to the workers' cause in general to strive to educate themselves beyond the traditional minimum which had for generations constituted their horizon. This explains the preoccupation with the additional dimension given to education through the uniting of the concept of *Bildung* with that of *Erziehung*.[27] Whereas *Bildung* involved the

[26] *Gesamtband Deutscher Mittel- und Realschullehrer, Leitsätze* . . ., Ried, *Dokumente* . . ., op. cit., p. 128.

[27] C. Lost, *Zur Entwicklung der Lehrpläne für die allgemeinbildende Pflichtschule in der DDR im Zeitraum 1951 bis 1959.* Unpublished thesis. Berlin, 1970, p. 419.

traditional elements of acquisition of knowledge and skills, *Erziehung* was concerned with affective qualities directly related to motivation and commitment. A conscious effort was to be made to invest the thoughts and actions of children with qualities of character such as 'strength of will, stamina, determination, courage, purposefulness and steadfastness'.[28]

The logical practical outcome of this rejection of what was termed the bourgeois theory of ability and of the limitations traditionally assumed to apply to the working class, was the urge to reach a situation in which the representation of this class at all levels of the educational system would correspond directly to its representation in the population at large. In the *SED*'s Guidelines for Educational Policy of 1949 this objective was clearly stated—'the selection of *Oberschule* pupils from working-class backgrounds is to be increased along with the special encouragement of children of activists and the progressive intelligentsia corresponding to the proportion of these classes in the population. . . .'[29] In a later *SED* statement Ministry officials were instructed to introduce measures, in collaboration with the *FDJ* and the Pioneers, to bring about the required increase.[30]

To achieve the objective there was a range of strategies. The core and course system was abolished when it became clear that the superior opportunities that it created for the more able were concentrated in certain urban areas and not accessible to between 70 and 80 per cent of the school population.[31] This situation was, at least in part, due to the existence of a large number of rural schools staffed by only one or two teachers, so that there were immense practical difficulties in introducing a standard curriculum which would offer all children equal prospects of access to the *Oberschule*. Whereas for example in the largely industrialized *Land* of Saxony it

[28] Monumenta Paedagogica VI, op. cit., p. 419.

[29] Baske/Engelbert, I, op. cit., p. 144.   [30] Ibid., pp. 167-8.

[31] K. Ellrich, *Die Entwicklung des Grundschulwesens in der Sowjetischen Besatzungszone seit 1945. Pädagogik*, 6/1950, p. 284.

proved possible to provide instruction in a foreign language in some 90 per cent of schools, for the largely rural *Land* of Brandenburg the corresponding figure was 37 per cent.[32] The rationalization of this situation was pursued with vigour so that by the school year 1955–56 a total of 1745 centralized schools (*Zentralschulen*) had been created and only 55 one-class schools were still in existence.[33] The most thoroughgoing measure was, however, the issue of regulations to the effect that 60 per cent of the candidates accepted for *Oberschulen* were to be from the working class, a policy which was reinforced by financial support. For the *Zehnklassenschulen* the working-class intake was to be even higher, namely 80 per cent.[34] These high percentages were clearly somewhat unrealistic but none the less an increase was achieved in the working-class intake which, for the *Oberschulen* and *Zehnklassenschulen* combined, rose from 40·8 per cent in 1950 to 49·4 per cent in 1955.[35] There seems little doubt that this achievement was assisted by the high level of migration to the West, particularly of middle-class families, which accompanied the sharpening of the class struggle.

The new virulence of social policy is most clearly illustrated by a further dimension whereby its objective was not merely to achieve proportional representation of the working class in the educational system but to ensure that the leading positions in society would in the future be filled from its ranks:

The first priority is to prepare the children of working people better and more quickly for university. Through the new education thoroughgoing consideration is given especially to children of industrial and agricultural workers and of the creative intelligentsia. A position must be reached whereby in our State which is a State of industrial and agricultural workers and in which the working class has the leadership, the children of industrial and agricultural workers take over to an increasing degree the most important

[32] Ibid., p. 285.   [33] Monumenta Paedagogica VI, op. cit., p. 73.
[34] *Anweisung Nr. 83. Richtlinien für die Aufnahme von Oberschülern und Zehnklassenschülern. die neue schule*, 7/1951, p. 21.
[35] *Wissenschaftliche Zeitschrift der Karl Marx Universität*, Leipzig, 4/1967, p. 417.

positions in the economy and the administration and become qualified for this by the acquisition of the highest level of general education and by university study.[36]

Hence the struggle on behalf of the working class was not merely
a question of compensation for previous deprivement but of the
conscious assumption of the leadership and control of the State.
This underlines the importance attached to the ensuring of a
high working-class representation at the universities and explains later attempts to change drastically the normal route to
the *Abitur* so that the universities would recruit from the
vocational rather than the more formally academic route
within the educational system. It is here that as regards social
policy there is perhaps the sharpest contrast with the Federal
Republic. In the *DDR* it was claimed that by the middle of the
decade 53 per cent of university students were drawn from a
working class which accounted for roughly 69 per cent of the
population. In the West the working class has been calculated
as embracing 57 per cent of fathers of young people of university
age; the proportion of students actually drawn from this social
group was 4 per cent in 1950 and rose to 7·5 per cent in 1970.
Throughout the period in question approximately two-thirds
of all university students were financed entirely out of parental
income.[37] With such a small proportion of the student population drawn from the working class it was inevitable that the
leading positions in society in the Federal Republic were filled
almost entirely from the ranks of the middle class.

From the vituperative quality of mutual assessments of
social and educational development in the two States there
seems little doubt that the determination to bring about a total
reversal of the traditional social order in the *DDR* owed much
of its momentum to distaste for the stratification that had
reappeared in post-war society in the Federal Republic.
Conversely the determination in the West to resist democratiza-

[36] W. Groth, interview. *Die neue Schule*, 22/1953, p. 4.
[37] K. Hochgesand, *Soziale Herkunft der Studierenden an wissenschaftlichen
Hochschulen. Wirtschaft und Statistik*, 5/1971, p. 293.

tion was strengthened by extreme disapproval of the imposition from the centre of measures to change society in the East. After the high point in this polarity, which was reached in 1953, the extreme ideological line was for a time pursued with less vigour in the *DDR*, and in the Federal Republic the beginnings of an inclination to devote to educational problems not merely administrative expertise but serious consideration within a wider social context were in evidence. Any sense of rapprochement between the two systems was, however, extremely limited and ultimately illusory. By the end of the decade the lost momentum in the build-up of socialism had been regained in the East and the overwhelming conservatism of educational policy in the West had once again been demonstrated.

Economic Influences

If the ultimate aim of Marxist-Leninist policy was to create a new social order which would eliminate the kind of hierarchy that had re-established itself in the Federal Republic, the means of achieving this aim were closely bound up with the problems of economic recovery. Only a high rate of production could create the wealth necessary to meet the needs of the new society envisaged for the *DDR*. With the economy crippled by the dismantling of industrial plant carried out by the Soviets after the war, and with its resources further drained by the reparations demanded, it was inevitably necessary to place immense emphasis on the needs of productivity. The Federal Republic was equally concerned to rebuild its economy but in contrast to the *DDR* its revival was boosted by the aid received through the Marshall Plan. For both States it was a matter of foremost importance that the educational system should fulfil its obligations in furnishing industry with the labour force it required.

In the West the traditional system did so without any great

G

problem arising, and this success was one of the foremost factors working against change. Throughout society there was a strong motivation to work hard to recover the losses of the war years and to leave behind the austerity of the immediate post-war period. Among the working class this was accompanied by an understandable impatience with lengthy schooling and unnecessary postponement of the age at which earning could begin. This dynamic factor coupled with the serious approach to industrial training provided the Federal Republic with an enviable skilled labour force and could not but have made a strong contribution to the now somewhat legendary resurgence of the economy which was already under way by 1951. The spectacular economic success of the period suggested that the country was getting what it required from the schools. Consequently in economic terms there seemed to be no valid reason for disturbing the existing state of affairs. This was confirmed by the general endorsement of the policies of the Christian Democrat/Liberal coalition in the 1953 *Bundestag* election.

In view of the significance of vocational and technical education in the Federal Republic and of its contribution to the economic revival of the 1950s, it is appropriate to examine the system in some detail. Although the great majority of children left school at fourteen, compulsory part-time education continued for at least two further years at a *Berufsschule*, usually in conjunction with an apprenticeship; only a small minority began their working life as unskilled labourers without training of some kind. The system had grown out of the medieval tradition of apprenticeship, through the developments of the late nineteenth and early twentieth centuries when the larger industrial firms organized the training of skilled workers on a large scale, to the point where in the Weimar period it became legally binding on employers to release apprentices to attend the *Berufsschule* for one, in some cases two whole days a week. The interest of the trade unions had contributed to the establishment of this legal position which ensured the cooperation of recalcitrant employers.

The urge towards quality of workmanship that characterized vocational training was expressed in detailed surveillance of the progress made by apprentices at their place of work. Employers were under an obligation to keep a work book, which was periodically inspected to ensure that adequate time was being spent in acquiring all the skills laid down in the trade profile (*Berufsbild*). Throughout the system national standards were laid down by the various trade councils, the examinations were conducted by the chambers of commerce, industry and handicrafts and the entire operation of the network was supervised at federal level by the Ministry of Economic Affairs. Its efficient working was guaranteed not only by the eagerness on the part of the apprentices to acquire skilled status but also by pressure on the employers to ensure that an acceptable proportion of their candidates in fact did so, failing which their entitlement to take on apprentices could be removed. Thus a positive sense of achievement attached to the acquisition of a skilled qualification (*Facharbeiterbrief*), which greatly affected prospects of pay and promotion.

From an educational point of view the system was in some respects unsatisfactory. One day in the *Berufsschule* and four or five days in the factory amounted to a very demanding week for fifteen-year-old apprentices. Moreover despite the surveillance of their training there was always the risk that they were being used as cheap labour in the firm's interests rather than in their own. Their payment was small, technically regarded as a grant towards their education (*Erziehungsbeihilfen*). In the *Berufsschule*, too, lack of facilities and staff often caused the statutory eight periods of instruction to be reduced to four. Yet in the early 1950s there was little dissatisfaction on these scores. A significant factor was the tradition of acceptance of low earnings as an investment for the future when possession of the *Facharbeiterbrief* would ensure considerable financial rewards. From the employers' point of view and from the point of view of the economy as a whole, there is no doubt that the traditional educational system was serving the country well in providing an appropriate labour force. It is hardly surprising that in this respect there was little incentive to embark on any changes in the tripartite structure.

In the *DDR* on the other hand the challenge was much greater and the need for qualified manpower was rendered more acute by the extensive migration to the West. Consequently it was vital from the point of view of the economy to raise overall standards and encourage the system to yield a swiftly increasing proportion of trained manpower. In very general terms this economic requirement was in harmony with the social objective of fostering the educational ambitions of the working class. In terms of specific policies, however, this was not wholly the case. The reorganization of 1946, in creating an eight-year *Grundschule* followed by a four-year *Oberschule*, had removed the intermediate sector, the *Mittelschule*, completely. This was consistent with long-term social aims since the notion of such a sector seemed irrevocably identified with a hierarchical tripartite structure. In the Federal Republic, where the *Mittelschule* was becoming an increasingly important sector of the system, it carried precisely the petty bourgeois label which confirmed the revulsion felt in the *DDR* for the kind of class-consciousness which it was considered to stand for.[38] But, whatever the social overtones of the *Mittelschulen* of the Federal Republic, they had the quite explicit economic function of providing the 'appropriate school preparation for the new generation in higher-level practical employment in agriculture, trade, crafts, industry and administration, as well as nursing, social, technical, artistic and domestic employment for women'.[39] This clear role was attested by the intermediate leaving certificate, the *mittlere Reife*, which was a substantial concept occupying a conspicuous place on the educational ladder.

[38] H. Löbner, *Bedeutung und Aufbau der Zehnklassenschulen. Pädagogik*, 7/1952, p. 512.
[39] *Vereinbarung der Ständigen Konferenz der Kultusminister der Länder vom 17.12.1953.*

The disappearance of the *Mittelschulen* in the 1946 reorganization in the Soviet Zone was detrimental to the prestige of the *mittlere Reife* which became a kind of consolation prize for those who failed to stay the *Oberschule* course. Moreover the demand for an independent *mittlere Reife* on the old model persisted:

The curricula of the *Oberschulen* are designed as a four-year course. The training in these schools leads to university study. Despite this clear and necessary objective, up to now many *Oberschule* pupils have been leaving after the tenth class while the departures from the other classes were markedly less numerous. A study of these departures showed that many pupils were accepted who from the beginning did not intend to pursue their studies to *Abitur* level. The idea of the so-called *mittlere Reife* still haunted the minds of the parents, so that they only wanted two years of education beyond the minimum for their children in order to avoid the greater financial burden. For even the guarantee of exemption from fees and the provision of maintenance allowances cannot completely meet the costs arising from school attendance.[40]

This constituted a serious dysfunctionality from the economic standpoint, particularly in view of the acute need for qualified manpower experienced in the *DDR* at this time. An output of premature leavers who had not been able to come to terms with the academically oriented curriculum of the *Oberschule* compared unfavourably with an output of school leavers who had followed a shorter and less demanding curriculum with a clearly defined terminal qualification, corresponding more accurately to their needs and wishes.

The gap between the *Grundschule* and the *Oberschule* was one which the *DDR* could therefore not afford not to fill. In introducing the *Zehnklassenschulen* Ulbricht stressed the economic argument: that to make possible the expansion of production that was envisaged, it was necessary to meet a shortage of trained manpower to fill the middle cadres in industry, administration and teaching. They were also to provide a supply

[40] Löbner, op. cit., pp. 504-5.

of entrants to the higher vocational schools, especially the engineering schools, a function which their counterparts also fulfilled in the Federal Republic.[41] A further similarity with the Federal Republic was that in sparsely populated areas where access to an *Oberschule* was difficult it was in practice easier to provide the facilities of an intermediate school.

In the *DDR* however any suggestion of similarity between the *Zehnklassenschule* and the *Mittelschule* of the West was firmly repudiated on two counts. The first was the already familiar social one that whereas the *Mittelschule* had been primarily a middle-class school, the *Zehnklassenschule* was primarily an institution for the working class. The second was an economic one expressed in the nature of the curriculum. The *Mittelschule* education of the past was alleged to have been one-sided and narrowly vocational, as befitted an institution designed to prop up the economic structure of the capitalist ordering of society. The *Zehnklassenschule* was meant to educate for flexibility and versatility and this was considered to contrast with capitalist unscrupulousness in training young people in a one-sided way to fulfil specific functions and thereby denying them the full flowering of their individuality.[42]

In practice it is difficult to see much substance in this argument in the early 1950s. The curriculum of the *Zehnklassenschule* was not very different from that of the *Mittelschule* as far as the relative balance of the various components was concerned (see Appendices III and IV). As regards the actual content within the individual subjects, it is certainly true that a good deal more effort went into the revision of syllabuses in the *DDR*, particularly on the basis of Soviet models. As a result of this the emphasis on the practical application of mathematics and science was increased by the introduction of a vocational element related to future employment in agriculture or constructional, mechanical, electrical or chemical engineering. But the process of working out systematically the implications for the school curriculum of the Marxian notion of

[41] Baske/Engelbert, I, op. cit., p. 162.   [42] Löbner, op. cit., p. 512.

versatility and flexibility, of finding the appropriate method of applying the ideas of *poly*technical education which had already been formulated by early Marxist writers did not reach a decisive stage till the latter half of the decade. In practice during the middle 1950s the *Zehnklassenschule* bore considerable similarity to its counterpart in the Federal Republic in that both were concerned with providing sufficient education for those at the middle levels of responsibility in the economy. Hence it is scarcely surprising that the Western term *Mittel-schule* was not infrequently used in the East also.

In the vocational sector the traditional 'dual system' of part-time attendance at a *Berufsschule* during the period of apprenticeship had been carried on in the *DDR* in much the same way as in the Federal Republic. The main new departure in policy was the creation of a new type of *Berufsschule*, housed and administered by the large nationalized industrial concerns and known as the *Betriebsberufsschule*. The first of these were in fact set up late in 1948 in conjunction with the Two-Year Plan. With the Five-Year Plan which followed, their number was steadily increased. The concentration of training within large concerns in this way offered numerous advantages in terms of facilities for the study of modern machinery and techniques, rationalization of instruction to relate theory to practice and increased output of trained apprentices.

In these respects the *Betriebsberufsschulen* paralleled the train-ing schemes operated by large combines in the Federal Re-public, but any suggestion of similarity was repudiated on the grounds that the latter lay outside the State system, and were therefore designed to produce highly trained specialists, and thereby to neglect their obligation to provide a general educa-tion that aimed beyond the fulfilment of a single, highly specialized function. This danger, that the responsibility for general education would be sacrificed to narrowly conceived interests of production, existed, however, in the *DDR* as much as in the West. At the Second Vocational Educational Congress in October 1948 misgivings had been expressed as to whether it would be avoided in the *Betriebsberufsschulen*.[43] In practice each side could well have claimed that the other was exploiting apprenticeship training for the benefit of productivity, without risk of well-founded contradiction, since the same system of qualifications had been inherited in both States, one which was fragmented into hundreds of individually demarcated trades, each codified in its own *Berufsbild*. Any claim on either side to have advanced beyond the training of workers for something more than the practice of a comparatively narrowly defined specialism really depended on a rationalization of this situation. While the need for such a development was an integral element of Marxist theory and was consequently more clearly recognized in the *DDR* than in the Federal Republic, it was some years yet before any practical progress could be recorded. There were in fact fewer trades in the West at this time—718 in 1950 and 649 in 1955—than in the *DDR* where there were still 972 in 1957.[44]

The vocational education sector therefore, as well as the *Zehnklassenschulen*, failed to break free of the traditional mould that was characteristic of their counterparts in the West at this stage. The development of both was intimately connected with the problems of polytechnical education, which was as yet no more than a controversial issue in discussion. In this respect it provided a gauge of the desire to embrace wholeheartedly a new dimension that would finally confirm in practice the divergence of paths in educational policy. For however much had been said regarding the inculcation of Marxist-Leninist principles and the building of socialism, any really fundamental change depended in practice on the corresponding step in the reorganization of the curriculum and the qualifications system. The debate on polytechnical education revealed the lukewarm nature of the desire to move on from the system which had developed in the immediate post-war 'anti-fascist democratic' phase and which, as has just been seen, incorporated much that had been inherited jointly with the Federal Republic.

[43] Günther/Uhlig, *Zur Entwicklung* . . ., op. cit., p. 171.
[44] A. Hegelheimer, *Berufsbildung im Wandel*, Berlin, 1971 (manuscript), p. 3.

Policies and Constraints

The initial assumptions on which educational policy was based in the two States in the period under review stood in marked contrast to one another. In the Federal Republic the educational system developed in response to the free play of social and economic forces. The economic factor was the dominant one, and the dynamism it created through the rapid growth of prosperity was instrumental in forestalling any serious discontent. As a result the most marked feature of the period is the absence of a coherent policy at national level. In the *Länder* education did acquire political significance in cases where controversial legislation had been introduced in 1948 and 1949. But in by far the greater part of the country the development of policy was primarily in the hands of administrators seeking to improve the particular sectors for which they were responsible.

Educational development in the *DDR* was founded on the belief in the integration of political, social and economic objectives, not left to the free play of independent forces and pressure groups within individual *Länder*, but centrally planned and directed. In the early 1950s these various objectives did not obviously coincide at all points. The acute shortage of manpower necessitated developments in the system that made it uncomfortably similar to that of the Federal Republic in terms of structure and objectives. In turn the attempt to push ahead with a more acceptable social policy through the fusion of the *Zehnklassenschule* with the *Oberschule* was a political failure, and it proved necessary to tolerate a substantial body of opinion which was opposed to the thoroughgoing implementation of socialist educational principles. Whereas the Federal Republic at this time enjoyed a stability that derived from consolidation of longstanding practices, the *DDR* experienced the uncertainty of a major transition for which the political will was not yet strongly in evidence.

From one standpoint the introduction of the *Zehnklassenschule* appears as a concession to short-term economic pressures in view of the failure to harness the *Oberschule* to the needs of the economy. The similarities which the new school bore to the *Mittelschule* suggest a partial reversion to a tripartite pattern. However much this is true for the short term, it should however be made clear that the *Zehnklassenschule* subsequently developed into the prototype for an institution providing compulsory education for the entire school population. It was in the course of the early 1950s that this transition began, and in 1956 the plans for a gradual progression to universal ten-year education were announced.

This function of the *Zehnklassenschule* is illustrative of the dominant leitmotiv of policy in the *DDR*, namely the raising of the educational standard throughout the entire population. A clearer illustration of this impulse is provided by the strenuous efforts to reduce the inequalities of provision as between urban and rural areas. The growth of a network of *Zentralschulen*, and the corresponding reduction in the number of schools staffed by only one or two teachers, was in marked contrast to the inertia regarding the problem in the Federal Republic. It is perhaps this organizational achievement above all others that suggests that policy was motivated by a concern for the collective good of society as a whole. In the Federal Republic the most consistent objection to structural reorganization was that such changes in themselves were no guarantee of progress and that individual local initiatives taken on a pragmatic basis offered prospects of more genuine improvements. However tenable this view, the indictment of policy as regards rural schools, which reached something of a crescendo in the 1960s, suggests that in fact the impulse to deal with the problem was very weak.

The urge to raise the general standard of education throughout the *DDR* was further characterized by the tenet of faith that this rise was directly related to an increase in potential productivity. Thus in theory the long-term economic view was in harmony with social objectives and provided a further incentive for a policy that concentrated on the improvement of the basic education of the entire community. The experience of the Federal Republic in the early 1950s, however, suggested that the existing level of general education was quite sufficient to serve the needs of productivity. The industrial success provided ample evidence to justify the *status quo* on economic grounds. But while in the *DDR* concessions had to be made in recognition of the truth of the Western case in the short term, by the middle of the decade the prospects of achieving comparable growth were very largely considered to depend on the long-term policies for the educational system which formed an integral part of the Second Five-Year Plan introduced in 1956.

However, the extent to which it would be possible to implement policies geared to the collective advantage of the entire community rather than to the sectional interests remained doubtful. A marked reluctance to follow a thoroughgoing socialist programme had become evident in the teaching profession, in administration and among educationists. The outcome of the struggle with this 'revisionist' element was to be of crucial importance later in the decade.

CHAPTER 4

Growing Divergence: 1955–60

Central Direction and Federalism

One of the interesting features of the early 1950s was the fact that despite the contrast in the initial assumptions on which policies were based, the school systems of the two States retained a good deal in common in respect of the educational values to which many teachers and administrators subscribed. Furthermore, the degree to which policies could diverge in practice was limited by economic necessities and social realities. The latter half of the decade saw the first major initiative to work out a coherent alternative to traditional humanism in the *DDR*. The prolonged debate which ended with the demise of 'revisionism' ushered in an era of consciously socialist educational policy in which the traditional educational values were not only rejected in theory, but supplanted in practice by a set of aims which envisaged gearing the entire school system to productivity and the reordering of society. In terms of practical policies this meant attaching foremost importance to ensuring that the content of educational programmes was relevant to the future employment of those who followed them and hence guaranteeing a supply of the appropriate kind of trained manpower.

In order to ensure that the educational system would serve the interests of the economy in this way, it was regarded as vital that the *Mittelschule*, as the intermediate *Zehnklassenschule* had come to be called, should be built up to a position where it could compete in attractiveness with the *Oberschule*. The significance of the *Mittelschule* was above all that it aimed to educate its pupils to 'have at their disposal secure, *applicable* scientific and technical knowledge'.[1] The later 1950s saw increasing efforts to reduce the theoretical bias of the *Oberschule* so that the first years of education would lead just as logically to the *Mittelschule* as to the *Oberschule*. Moreover, the former with its emphasis on technical instruction was in any case ultimately to be the model for universal ten-year education. Thus the change in emphasis was from a preoccupation with turning out more and better educated young people within the framework of existing curricula to a reanalysis of curricular objectives in general and a corresponding revision of their content. The new panacea to emerge was polytechnical education, a concept which has since been, in its various interpretations, an integral part of the educational policy of the *DDR*.

The polytechnical principle had in fact been implied in the decision of a Party conference in May 1952 to begin the 'systematic building of socialism' and in the *Politbüro* statement which followed soon after regarding the need to raise standards in the schools. Among the points made in the latter was the need to emphasize the close relationship between education and life, especially industrial and agricultural production. A good deal of discussion about polytechnical education followed, notably at a conference at the *Deutsches Pädagogisches Zentralinstitut* in 1953. It was a controversial issue. On the one hand there were those who deplored the gulf between theory and practice in schools and demanded some kind of reorganization which would enable it to be bridged to the general benefit of industry and agriculture. On the other there was the resistance to such demands largely on the grounds that a major reorganization was premature, that while it might be appropriate for the stage in the development of socialism reached in the Soviet

[1] *Dokumente zur Geschichte des Schulwesens* . . ., Monumenta Paedagogica VII/1, Berlin, 1969, p. 23.

Union, this was not so in the case of the *DDR*.[2] The issue over-lapped to a considerable extent with the equally controversial introduction of the *Elfklassenschule* in the same year. The failure of this measure had been simultaneously a setback for the cause of polytechnical education and while individual initiatives continued to be pursued the debate did not regain real promi-nence until the boost given to it by Ulbricht's speech introdu-cing the Second Five-Year Plan. The transition to a new Plan was an appropriate time to take stock of progress and to reaffirm the government's determination to ensure that the school system would effectively serve the needs of the economy.

No such centrally directed initiative was possible in the West on account of the division of responsibility within the federal system. The need for standardization of policy which had steadily become more obvious in the early 1950s, and had resulted in the Düsseldorf Agreement, had certainly focused attention on this problem. In the course of the deliberations of a parliamentary committee on cultural affairs there was a certain amount of support for a proposal to extend federal responsibility in education, which up till then had been con-fined to the promotion of scientific research, to include stan-dardization of the school system. Any such proposal implied the setting up of a federal ministry of education and this, too was suggested. After some two years of discussions, however, the final recommendation, made in 1956, was that there should be no attempt to change the constitution in this way. The *status quo* was to be retained. This outcome reflected the over-whelming opposition of the *Land* governments to any diminu-tion of their responsibilities.

Thus even after the Düsseldorf Agreement it remained impossible to speak of a national policy. The *Kultusminister-konferenz* continued to act as a forum for discussion of problems common to the various *Länder* and the exchange of information no doubt hastened the progress of such measures as the aboli-

[2] K.-H. Günther/G. Uhlig, *Geschichte der Schule in der DDR 1945 bis 1968*, Berlin, 1969, p. 82.

tion of school fees. But the only initiatives that can be regarded as really transcending the interests of the individual *Länder* came from the *Deutscher Ausschuss*, the work of which gradually drew limited attention to the shortcomings and omissions of the existing system in the preceding years. The support of this body for the Düsseldorf Agreement was guarded, since it took the view that the German school system 'has not adapted to the changes which in the last fifty years have altered the situation and the consciousness of society and the State, and has largely held to the characteristics which originate from past intellectual, economic and political viewpoints'.[3] These reservations were largely on two specific counts. The first was that the Agreement, while somewhat grudgingly permitting experiments within the framework which it set up, insisted that these must preserve the essential individual character of the established types of school. This excluded innovation of the radical kind associated with comprehensive reorganization. Secondly, the *Deutscher Ausschuss* considered that ten years was too long a period to bind the *Länder* to the provisions of the Agreement and that long before it elapsed there would be a need for a more extensive restructuring and standardization of the school system. In the course of the later 1950s the publications of the *Deutscher Ausschuss* became steadily more detailed and analytical, culminating in the Outline Plan for future development (*Rahmenplan zur Umgestaltung und Vereinheitlichung des allgemein-bildenden öffentlichen Schulwesens*) in 1959. It was this publication which brought the *Deutscher Ausschuß* into real prominence with the general public.

The events of 1959 in fact provide an apt illustration of the contrasting views of the nature of policymaking in East and West. In the *DDR* the 'Law regarding the Socialist Development of the School System in the *DDR*' (*Gesetz über die sozialistische Entwicklung des Schulwesens in der DDR*) gave statutory form to the outcome of the controversies over differentiation and the

---

[3] *Empfehlungen und Gutachten des Deutschen Ausschusses, Folge 1*, Stuttgart, 1955, p. 51.

introduction of polytechnical education. The sharp differences of opinion had come to a head, the 'revisionist' line had been officially rejected and a clear basis had been laid down for future policy which conceived of the educational system as an integrated whole whose function was to further the development of socialist society. On the other hand, the *Rahmenplan* proposals, put forward by the *Deutscher Ausschuß* in the Federal Republic in the same year, were of a purely advisory nature, the result of the deliberations of a group of leading figures in society more or less directly concerned with education. The plan was in the nature of a forecast of the kind of compromise which the group thought might be acceptable but in the event there proved to be no question of it leading directly to political action. Its achievement was to arouse sufficient interest for education to become for the first time a matter for sustained discussion in a national context. But the responsibility to act remained with the individual autonomous *Länder*, within which the varying strengths of individual pressure groups were the main determinants of policy.

Structural and Curricular Developments in the West

Such criticisms as there were of the existing system in the Federal Republic were diffuse and carried little weight with the general public. The demands for change gathered momentum very slowly, for education proved to be no more of a political issue than it had been in the first half of the decade. The question of social justice in a highly selective system had faded into the background in the context of the general decline of interest in the class struggle on the part of the *SPD*. The markedly moderate programme adopted by the Party at Bad Godesberg in November 1959 contained no proposals for a comprehensive system, though it did urge that the minimum period of full-time education should be raised to ten years. The economic problem of the supply of manpower aroused greater political interest, but it was regarded not so much as a problem of the school system but rather a matter of increasing provision of *Fachschulen*, specialist technical colleges for the training of technicians. In 1957 an agreement was concluded providing federal financial assistance for this kind of training but it was stressed that this was in no way a curtailment of the autonomy of the *Länder*.[4]

In the *Länder* the main guideline was the Düsseldorf Agreement which had consolidated the system that had emerged as a result of the policy of restoration. Policy initiatives remained within the framework which this provided and therefore could bring about no fundamental structural changes. Nevertheless there can be discerned in *Land* policies some interest in a greater spread of selective opportunities over the whole community. By the school year 1958–59 school fees had either been abolished or were being phased out in almost all *Länder*.[5] Thus one of the achievements of the later 1950s was the removal of the more obvious financial barriers to school attendance beyond the minimum. Selection procedures however remained severe, based on examinations at the age of ten. In 1959 Rhineland-Palatinate was the first *Land* to dispense with these and select on the basis of the primary school recommendation.[6] Such efforts as were made to offset the irrevocability of the selection procedures were largely in the domain of vocational and further education. By 1957 almost all *Länder* had provided facilities for the acquisition of the *Abitur* in special evening *Gymnasien*. According to an agreement of the *Kultusministerkonferenz* these institutions were to provide a three-year course of twenty periods per week following a curriculum of which the demands were to be comparable with those of a normal *Gymnasium*. This constituted such an exacting way of qualifying for university entrance, however, that the numbers taking advantage of it were minimal.[7]

[4] *Bericht des Vorsitzenden des Schulausschusses der Ständigen Konferenz 1957/58*, p. 3.   [5] *Bericht* . . ., 1958/59, p. 2.   [6] *Bericht* . . ., 1959/60, p. 527.
[7] Between 3 and 4 per cent of all *Abiturienten* qualified in this way. S. B. Robinsohn/H. Thomas, *Differenzierung im Sekundarschulwesen*, Stuttgart, 1969, p. 38.

H

The numbers admitted to the *Gymnasium* showed no very great increase over the period in question[8] and it remained the case that prospects for university entrance were largely decided at the age of ten. Only the *Gymnasium* offered the kind of curriculum that led logically to the *Abitur* and it was not till the end of the decade that it became relatively common for the *Länder* to explore ways of facilitating transfer to its senior classes at the end of the *Mittelschule* course. This irrevocability was further aggravated by the slow pace of development of the *Volksschulen*. Some of these did have special promotion streams (*Aufbauzüge*) particularly in Hesse, Schleswig-Holstein and Baden-Württemberg but they constituted a very small proportion of the age group, under 2 per cent, in the Federal Republic as a whole.[9] One of the earliest recommendations of the *Deutscher Ausschuß* had been to develop the *Volksschulen* by raising the school-leaving age to provide for a ninth compulsory year of full-time education. There was however no widespread implementation of this largely on account of lack of buildings and teachers. By 1959 it had been introduced in the city states and Schleswig-Holstein; elsewhere it was beginning to be tried out on an experimental basis in a few selected districts in Hesse, Rhineland-Palatinate and North Rhine Westphalia.[10] Consequently the demand that it should be implemented forthwith throughout the Federal Republic was reiterated in the *Rahmenplan*.

In practice therefore throughout the 1950s the great majority of children left school to take up an apprenticeship at fourteen. It was however becoming steadily clear that this was too early for genuine vocational choice to be possible. As verification of this it was being calculated at the end of the decade that only some 50 per cent of apprentices were continuing to work in

[8] Cf. F. J. Weiss, *Statistik des Bildungswesens, Teil* I: *Die allgemeinbildenden Schulen. Jahrbuch für Wissenschaft, Ausbildung und Schule, WAS 71.* Frankfurt/M., 1971, p. 164.
[9] F. J. Weiss, *Entwicklungstendenzen des Besuchs allgemeinbildender Schulen in den Ländern der BRD. Deutsches Institut für Internationale Pädagogische Forschung,* Frankfurt/M., 1964, p. 10.   [10] *Bericht . . .,* 1958/59, pp. 6, 7.

the trade for which they had qualified.[11] Hence the nature of the ninth school year was very relevant, and the *Kultusminister-konferenz* had in its discussions come to the conclusion that its curriculum should comprise a synthesis of general and pre-vocational education with the object of making the choice of apprenticeship more easy. This in turn created a degree of apprehension in the *Berufsschule* sector which saw suggestions regarding the increasing importance of the *Volksschule* as a partial threat to its existence.

The uncertainty about vocational education, particularly the apprenticeship system, was evident in other respects. The trade union movement was in favour of greater State control and advocated the passing of an all-embracing law, in order that greater pressure could be exerted on employers to ensure high standards in instruction. The resistance to such a proposal on the part of the *CDU* and the *FDP* was, however, such that there was no possibility of it being acted upon.[12] The lack of action was in fact markedly characteristic of the administration of the apprenticeship system at this time. It lay outside the compe-tence of the *Kultusministerkonferenz*, and in a period of virtually unprecedented economic success employers were not generally disposed to treat the matter with any urgency.

Thus the general impression over the system as a whole was of failure to get to grips with fundamental problems. It was in this context that the *Rahmenplan* appeared, setting out pro-posals to break the rigidity of the existing structure which were accompanied by suggestions regarding the rationalization of the curriculum (Diagram in Appendix VII). The plan was that after the four years of a common *Grundschule*, which was more or less undisputed as the basis of the system, the great majority of the children were to enter a two-year stage known as a *Förderstufe* designed for observation of developing talents so that the subsequent choice of type of school could be based

[11] *Bericht über das sechste Gespräch des Ettlinger Kreises*, Weinheim, 1960, p. 8.
[12] *Öffentliches Berufspädagogisches Gespräch. Material- und Nachrichten-Dienst*, 81/1957, pp. 22, 23.

on evidence of some substance. This stage was to resemble the *Volksschule* rather than the *Gymnasium* in avoiding premature contact with intellectual abstractions and for this reason it was considered preferable that it should be regarded as an extension of primary education rather than attached to a *Gymnasium* or *Realschule*. After the *Förderstufe* the choice would lie between the *Gymnasium*, either the modern languages or the mathematical variety, the *Realschule*, or the '*Hauptschule*', the new type of school which was to replace the senior forms of the old *Volksschule*. In this tripartite division the committee continued to subscribe to the notion of the major vocational strata arrived at after three different lengths of full-time schooling. The process of selection or, the preferred term, choice was postponed, however, by two years with the one exception of the '*Studienschule*', simply another name for the classical *Gymnasium* which was to continue to recruit those of outstanding ability at the age of ten and offer them the traditional nine-year course, strongly language-based with Latin and English in the curriculum from the outset, followed three years later by the addition of either French or Greek. This was 'the school of the European educational tradition'.[13] The entire system was intended to be characterized by an abundance of opportunities for lateral transfer based on examinations.

The *Rahmenplan* stimulated a certain amount of action in the *Kultusministerkonferenz*. While the ministers considered that many of the suggestions required further discussion and information, there were three areas in which action was to be taken without delay. The first was the expansion of the *Oberstufe* of the *Volksschule* and the introduction of the ninth school year throughout the Federal Republic. The second was a reorganization of the *Oberstufe* of the *Gymnasium* to reduce the pressure on pupils and allow greater scope for individual work. The third was the refinement of the selection processes for entry to the *Mittelschule* and the *Gymnasium* to ensure that

---

[13] *Empfehlungen und Gutachten des Deutschen Ausschusses Folge 3*, Stuttgart, 1959, pp. 16-19.

they were open to all children on the basis of ability and irrespective of family means or background. Furthermore, the ministers requested the *Deutscher Ausschuß* to produce further recommendations for the vocational sector as soon as practical.[14] The proposals regarding the ninth school year and the selection processes were left to the individual *Länder* to implement in their own ways.

In the question of the reorganization of the upper reaches of the *Gymnasium*, however, further concerted action was to follow in the form of the Saarbrücken Outline Agreement of September 1960. Here the influence of the *Rahmenplan* on policy is very obvious. The recommendations had been very specific as regards the reduction of the curriculum: four main subjects were advocated for the *Oberstufe*, together with an optional one which could be given up two years before the *Abitur* was taken.[15] The Saarbrücken Agreement followed this formula, spelling out the details. The four basic subjects were to be: in the classical *Gymnasium* German, Latin, Greek (or French), mathematics: in the modern languages *Gymnasium* German, two modern languages, mathematics: in the mathematical *Gymnasium* German, mathematics, physics, one modern language. Furthermore civic education, physical education and art or music were also to be compulsory. The additional optional subject was to be chosen from among modern languages, physics, chemistry, biology and geography. Religious instruction remained a matter for the individual *Länder* to regulate. For the *Abitur* examination the *Rahmenplan* recommendations were also followed and the *Land* authorities were left free to hold the examination in one of the four basic subjects at the end of the eleventh or twelfth grade, thereby completing the course and allowing for increased specialization in the last one or two years. In addition to the four written examinations there were to be oral tests in the four major

[14] *Kultusministerkonferenz, Pressemitteilung aus Anlass der 73. Plenarsitzung am 24/25.9.1959 in Berlin*, p. 2.
[15] *Empfehlungen und Gutachten ... Folge 3*, op. cit., p. 42.

subjects, and in civic education and an optional subject. Furthermore, there was to be an examination in physical education and in religious instruction under *Land* arrangements. The Agreement was to be implemented forthwith, beginning with the school year 1961 and the *Abitur* regulations were to come into force at the latest by 1965.[16] Thus the one question on which the *Kultusministerkonferenz* acted with collective vigour was that of the *Oberstufe* curriculum. Indeed in the context of the longstanding curriculum of the 'fourteen-subject school' as the *Gymnasium* had been called, the proposals in the Saarbrücken Agreement appeared quite radical and were the subject of substantial controversy in the years that followed.

What is significant above all however is that the most radical proposal in the *Rahmenplan*, the introduction of the *Förderstufe*, was not included among the items to which priority was given. The consensus was that the system could stay basically as it was in terms of structure and that the problems should be tackled by way of 'internal reform'. By concentrating on internal reform it was possible to display concern that the system should be improved while at the same time remaining faithful to the general aversion to new departures conveyed by the popular slogan '*Keine Experimente*'.

Structural and Curricular Developments in the East

A slogan such as *Keine Experimente* would have been highly inappropriate in the context of policy in the *DDR* at this time. After a period of uncertainty the impetus towards radical change gathered momentum and reached a climax at the end of the decade. The years 1956 and 1957 saw sporadic developments designed to improve productivity. The transformation of *Berufsschulen* into *Betriebsberufsschulen* was speeded up so that vocational education became more directly linked with pro-

---

[16] *Kultusministerkonferenz, Rahmenvereinbarung zur Ordnung des Unterrichts auf der Oberstufe der Gymnasien. 29.9.60, Beschluss Nr. 175.*

duction. In view of the higher standard of those leaving the *Mittelschulen*, as compared with the normal post-*Grundschule* apprentices, it was stipulated that special classes should be provided to train them for those trades which required a higher general education.[17] The entire rationalisation was aimed at raising the standard of technical education, encouraging as many apprentices as possible to work for higher qualifications, and guaranteeing a steady supply of labour for the nationalized industries. A further effort to strengthen the relationship between education and industry followed when a measure was introduced to recruit production workers into the teaching profession at all levels, but particularly with the *Mittelschulen* in mind on account of the desire to promote the study of technical subjects.[18]

Another concern was to increase the labour force by raising the proportion of women employed. A drive had begun in 1950 to increase the number of women obtaining educational qualifications.[19] A logical sequel to this policy was the effort to build up a network of pre-school education in order to facilitate the employment of married women. The kindergartens were generally attached to industrial and agricultural enterprises. Apart from the practical advantages of the arrangement it was considered to have social and ideological ones.

In our State, in which the industrial working class and the agricultural workers create the preconditions for a happy future for children, the direct exercise of the influence of the workers in socialist enterprises on the education of children is necessary. The organisational form of this help is the sponsorship system which represents a kind of binding mutual agreement and sets out the mutual obligations of the sponsoring enterprise and the kindergarten. These obligations must have as their objective to give employees' children of kindergarten age a happy childhood and to educate them to respect for working people.[20]

[17] Monumenta Paedagogica VII/1, op. cit., p. 43.
[18] S. Baske/M. Engelbert, *Zwei Jahrzehnte Bildungspolitik . . . Dokumente*, Vol. I, Berlin, 1966, pp. 319–21.   [19] Ibid., p. 162.
[20] Monumenta Paedagogica VII/1, op. cit., p. 57.

Thus it was intended that children should regard a situation in which both parents were employed in productive work as natural, conducive to a happy life and good.

At this time too, various structural proposals were developing out of the arguments of the 'revisionists'. One suggestion was the restoration of the thirteenth school year as in the West, a proposal that would have extended the *Oberschule* course to five years. Another idea was that the transition to the *Oberschule* should take place after six years for the more gifted with the remainder completing their time in the *Mittelschule* which was eventually due to comprise ten years of compulsory education for all.[21] Such a plan would have made the age of selection for the *Oberschule* the same as for the *Gymnasium* as envisaged in the *Rahmenplan,* although the latter retained selection after four years of primary school for the proposed classical *Studienschule.* These similarities of structure reflected similarities of outlook in so far as foremost consideration was given to the propaedeutic functions of the school system as they related to the needs of the academic professions. The views expressed by the revisionists were the subject of bitter controversy in 1957, and the denunciations rose to a crescendo in the early months of 1958. In April of that year at the *SED* Education Conference the demise of the group was finally confirmed.

Thereafter there was a surge of activity. After blaming the slow development of previous years on the infiltration of reactionary theories the Conference statement spoke of 'widespread demands for the formation of a school system closely related to the development of socialism'. The unity of theory and practice, of learning and life was then declared to be the most important educational principle of dialectical materialism and for its realization specific measures were called for. The first was the raising of the level of instruction in the system as a

---

[21] H. H. Becker, *Über das Wesen der Allgemeinbildung. Pädagogik,* 9/1957, p. 663 and 10/1957, p. 727; A. Tebbe, *Zur Diskussion über Probleme der Allgemeinbildung. Pädagogik,* 3/1957, p. 184; O. Mader, *Bemerkungen zu Fragen der Allgemeinbildung. Pädagogik,* 5/1957, p. 361.

whole which required extensive revision of curricula, textbooks and educational equipment. The second was the introduction of polytechnical education 'with the aim of developing
in all pupils the socialist consciousness and high regard for
work and the working class'. This required that pupils learn
the processes of production, and the solution arrived at was to
set aside one whole day in the week which pupils and teachers
would spend working in a factory or on the land. The third
measure called for was the full realization of the *Mittelschule*
programme, and the fourth the completion of the development
of schools in rural areas.[22] These demands were further
elaborated in the course of the Fifth *Parteitag* of the *SED* in the
following year at which the introduction of polytechnical
education was declared to be the central question.

The major innovation was the idea of devoting a whole day
per week to production in industry or agriculture. This had
been the subject of a certain amount of experimental work over
the previous few years and was now becoming increasingly
familiar to teachers through reports in the press.

As long ago as 1956 the *Comenius-Mittelschule* decided in favour of a
weekly *Produktionstag*. The intention was to ensure for the pupils a
certain continuity in the observation of technological processes and
productive work. The staff also saw in this the only opportunity for
the real merging of instruction with productive work throughout the
year. Finally they also wished to achieve palpable educational
effects on the pupils through weekly contact with the workers.[23]

This experiment is characteristic of a series of similar initiatives
generally regarded as significant advances in the search for
ways to reduce the rigidity of teaching and create a realistic
relationship to life.

The experimental work was largely the preserve of the
Mittelschulen which were thereby enabled to find a progressive
role for themselves. The accounts suggest that it was carried

[22] Monumenta Paedagogica VII/1, op. cit., pp. 103–4.
[23] F. Busch, *Wöchentlich Einmal in der Produktion. Deutsche Lehrerzeitung*
17/1958, p. 6.

out by teachers who were highly dedicated to the cause of socialism. There are distinct moralizing overtones about the value of work and the worthiness of the working class and a hint of preciosity creeps into some of the descriptions:

Oily hands were what the pupils got who worked in the vehicle section. Under the direction of apprentice-trainer Esche and motor mechanic Siepert they helped in the repair of a potato-harvesting machine. Screws were undone and done up again, driving chains were cleaned, checked and assembled—important jobs with a deadline. Here too a good combination of work and instruction.[24]

The main problem was the difficulty of reconciling the *Unterrichtstag in der Produktion* with the existing curriculum which still had to be followed. The report on the *Comenius-Mittelschule* experiment pointed out that an innovation of this kind necessarily entailed a revision of the curriculum.

The new timetables for 1958–59 took this into account. They were designed to guarantee the introduction of the polytechnical principle throughout the system and provided for a considerable amount of time to be spent in productive work. In order to obviate organizational problems the time was computed as a block period for the year but it was indicated that schools were expected by September 1959 to be in a position to have one *Unterrichtstag in der Produktion* per week. Elements of polytechnical education were included in the programme of all classes. The amount of time gradually increased from 35 periods in the year for classes 1 and 2 to 130 for class 6: this was devoted to manual skills, needlework and 'socially useful work'. In the last two classes of the *Grundschule* (7 and 8) 120 periods were provided in the year for factory or farm work together with 80 periods for manual skills. In classes 9 and 10 of the *Mittelschule* the time devoted to outside work reached 160 periods in the year of which 70 were intended for a consecutive 14-day practical. A further 90 periods were for a new subject in the curriculum, providing an 'introduction to socialist pro-

---

[24] '*Tag der Produktion*' *bewährt sich. Deutsche Lehrerzeitung*, 16/1958, p. 1.

duction' which included technical drawing. In the *Oberschule* the pattern was similar. All classes had 160 periods of factory or farm work of which 70 were reserved for a consecutive 14-day practical and in classes 9 and 12 a further 60 and 90 periods respectively were designated for the introduction to socialist production.[25]

This latter new subject contained a strong ideological element as the following extract indicates:

The pupils are made acquainted in theory and practice with the basic questions of State direction and the cooperation of working people in the control of a socialist economy and of production; and also with the powerful economic and political achievements of the working class and of all employed people in the struggle for the victory of socialism. That means that in this new subject the ideological-political side of a socialist economy and of production is given priority of treatment. The instruction in this subject thereby has great *educational* significance.[26]

Following this objective it was intended that the new subject should be closely coordinated with the teaching of civics which included a basic course in political economy, Marxist-Leninist philosophy and the theory of the socialist state. The subject matter was differentiated to ensure that pupils in predominantly industrial areas were given some understanding of production in agricultural areas and vice versa. This was considered especially desirable since the skills and processes taught in the context of production were of necessity determined by the nature of the employment available locally.

Despite the long debate and the experimental work that had preceded it the wholesale introduction of polytechnical education was a drastic step. It was a far cry from attempting the complex organization involved in selected schools, where a strongly committed staff enthusiastically embraced the idea, to doing so in *Oberschulen* with a long tradition of purely theoretical instruction. Even if the value of the exercise for those wanting a career in industry or agriculture was conceded, it seemed

[25] Monumenta Paedagogica VII/1, pp. 113–16.   [26] Ibid.,p . 162.

pointless for those with other prospects for the future. It created difficulties for some teachers who were ill at ease in the surroundings of the factories or farms whose managers, too, were caused considerable problems by the weekly invasion of large numbers of young people. To ensure that they were not mere observers, but were actually employed in some capacity which contributed to the manufacturing process, was an immense task. There is little doubt that the preparations had not been sufficiently thorough. A commission which reported on the problem in October 1958 declared it to be essential to work out a system for the *Unterrichtstag in der Produktion*, and to provide facilities to give teachers the additional training necessary to enable them to do what was asked of them.[27]

To dispel the uncertainty among the general public the agencies which had in the past been enlisted to support official policy were again mobilized for this purpose, the *FDJ* and the Pioneers, the workers' organization (*Freier Deutscher Gewerkschaftsbund*) and the parents' committees for which a national conference was staged at Fürstenwalde at the beginning of the school year 1958–59. In the report of a State commission in January 1959 the entire administrative machinery of the *DDR* was instructed to give every possible help and support in the realization of the plans for polytechnical education and to ensure the coordination of the work of the various agencies. In order to ensure that the appropriate atmosphere prevailed, the instruction in the processes of production was to be entrusted to those workers who 'educate the children in a class-conscious way, influence them in respect of socialist morality and pass on sound knowledge'.[28]

What was in fact being attempted in 1958–59 was to incorporate in the normal school curriculum some of the basic components of an industrial or agricultural apprenticeship. The relevance of this is only fully apparent when it is seen in combination with the other main preoccupation of this period, the introduction of universal ten-year education. Though it was

[27] Ibid., p. 170.   [28] Ibid., p. 176.

several years since this had first been envisaged it had been somewhat overshadowed by the polytechnical education question. The situation became favourable for its introduction once the dispute over the advocated reduction of the common *Grundschule* to six years was over and the comprehensive principle vehemently reaffirmed, and the *Schulkonferenz* of the *SED* of 24/25 April 1958 called for obligatory *Mittelschule* education for all children. But polytechnical education nevertheless remained the chief preoccupation during the remainder of 1958. In January 1959 a lengthy statement of the Central Committee in the form of 'Theses on the Socialist Development of the School System in the *DDR*' set out a new programme. In order to achieve the higher general standard of education it was proposed that the eight-year *Grundschule* should be replaced as the normal compulsory school by a ten-year school, the *allgemeinbildende polytechnische zehnklassige Oberschule*, a new type resembling the *Mittelschule* (Diagram in Appendix VIII). It was to have one curriculum for the entire ten years which were to be obligatory for all children by 1964. The amalgamation of general and polytechnical education over this longer period was to ensure that subsequent vocational training began at a higher educational level and that consequently the entire labour force would be better qualified than before.[29]

The new school was to be referred to as the *Oberschule*, a term which by its longstanding connotations indicated that universal secondary education leading to the possibility of some sort of higher education was being introduced. This step was considered a major landmark in the progress towards the final realization of socialist objectives. The polytechnical element guaranteed close links between education and life so that the school could be said to be in step with developments in the society for which it prepared its pupils. The comprehensive structure guaranteed a framework within which special efforts could be made to encourage working-class children to pursue their education over a longer period. The old four-year *Oberschule*

[29] Ibid., p. 180.

was to remain in being under the new name of '*erweiterte Oberschule*' and take its pupils in at the end of their eighth year in the new *Oberschule* but was no longer to be accepted as the main route to higher education. This was now to be via vocational training so that all those leaving the new *Oberschule* were to have the opportunity to work for the *Abitur* during their apprenticeship. Those leaving the new *erweiterte Oberschule* already equipped with the *Abitur* were to complete a year's apprenticeship leading to a trade qualification before becoming eligible for university. Thus the definition of *Hochschulreife*, general fitness for university study, had changed in accordance with the new conception of general education to include direct experience of employment in a practical capacity.

The implications of the new policy for the entire field of vocational education were far-reaching. The changes in the schools meant that those entering on apprenticeships would be better educated. There was at the same time a feeling that the instructional programmes for these apprenticeships had not kept pace with the developments in industry and agriculture. The creation of *Betriebsberufsschulen* had resulted in an appropriate overall organizational structure within which the cooperation of vocational education with industry and agriculture could be achieved. But the detailed structure comprising upwards of some 900 different trade qualifications was regarded as outdated in an age when flexibility and adaptability in the labour force were considered to be of paramount importance. Just as the 'Theses' had set out the lines of development for the school system, a document of similar significance was issued by the Central Committee of the *SED* in July 1959 calling for a thorough rethinking of policy in order to give a broader base to vocational education.[30] A debate of some magnitude was thereby initiated ensuring that in the next period of development the structure of trade and professional qualifications would be given urgent consideration.

The policy developments of the 1950s culminated in the

[30] Ibid., pp. 275–93.

passing of the 1959 Law which subsumed all the measures contained in the various isolated directives that had gone before. The preamble laid emphasis on the aim to build a new social order in which power would be in the hands of the workers and the urgent need to raise the standard of education in the labour force as a whole and to encourage as many people as possible to acquire higher technical qualifications. The new *zehnklassige allgemeinbildende polytechnische Oberschule* was proclaimed as the vehicle for this and its systematic introduction was to be completed by 1964.

Educational Aims

A prominent feature of development in the *DDR* in the early 1950s had been the survival to a substantial degree in the *Oberschule* of the traditional attitudes to general culture and its attendant hierarchy of academic prestige which had dominated German education since the early nineteenth century. In the latter half of the decade this tradition was seriously challenged in both East and West so that the deliberations over the relevance of this culture were of central significance for the future of the two systems.

There was a certain similarity as regards the economic origins of the challenge. In the *DDR* the familiar theme of the importance of meeting manpower requirements was reiterated with the launching of the Second Five-Year Plan. In the Federal Republic a similar preoccupation became increasingly evident during the later 1950s. In a major debate in the *Bundestag* in 1956 the starting-point was the proposition 'that the training of technical manpower in sufficient numbers and of sufficient quality is for the present and the foreseeable future not an internal problem for individual elements in the economy but a task which affects the vital interests and the economic future of the entire population'.[31] Representatives of

[31] *Deutscher Bundestag. 2. Wahlperiode. Drucksache 2374.*

all parties joined in deploring the manpower shortage and recommending vigorous action. The atmosphere of general agreement did not indicate any great dissatisfaction or controversy over structural matters, but rather a feeling that a greater effort was needed to dynamize the existing system, and there were echoes of the feeling that it was the decentralization brought about by the federal structure that was the main obstacle to the formulation of enterprising policies. The same debate further revealed the growing awareness of competition between the capitalist and socialist States in terms of output of manpower. Much was made of the contrast between, on the one hand, the progress of the Soviet Union and the *DDR* in the training of scientists, engineers and technicians, and on the other, the relatively poor performance of the United States and West Germany in this respect.[32] The crucial issue for the comparison of policies in the Federal and Democratic Republics is the reaction to these pressures in the ideological, social and economic contexts and in this the 'revisionism' that developed in the *DDR* in the later 1950s is of central significance.

Much of the revisionist writing was concerned with reinterpreting the concept of general culture which had dominated German education since the early nineteenth century. This reinterpretation was claimed to be wholly consistent with socialist development—to embody equal rights for all and the nullification of former class privilege, to bridge the gap between general and vocational education and to imply an all-round education that took due account of intellectual, aesthetic, social and moral, polytechnical and physical dimensions. It was an attempt to give a different connotation to the term *Allgemeinbildung*, suggesting primarily its accessibility to all and in this respect its protagonists declared it to be quite different from the Western élitist concept.

In a number of respects however the assumptions that underlay the revisionist arguments bore a marked similarity to

[32] *Deutscher Bundestag. 2. Wahlperiode. 148 Sitzung Stenographische Berichte 1956*, p. 7847.

those of Western educationists. One of these was that the
traditional academic standards of the universities were in
jeopardy as a result of the drop in the standard of the *Abitur*
which had accompanied the reduction of the *Oberschule* to a
four-year establishment and that it was of the utmost importance to preserve them.

. . . Finally the point at issue is the preservation of the academic level
of our higher education. The present *Oberschule* education has
failings—that has been emphasised often enough before—and it does
not achieve in many respects what society must demand of it. . . .
With the building up of socialism the demands on our universities
have also grown and they can only fulfil their greater tasks if their
students have at their disposal that higher basic general education
which is indispensable for successful university study. For this reason
we must not thrust aside the character of the *Oberschule* as a school
providing general education but secure and increase it.[33]

In the Federal Republic the concern for the preservation of the
academic level of the *Gymnasium* was in some respects comparable to the preoccupation illustrated above.

The failure to maintain the traditional standards in the *DDR*
was to some degree put down to a lack of stimulation of
individual effort and a failure to adjust the educational demands in accordance with individual capabilities. This had
been illustrated by the problems of the undifferentiated eight-
year *Gundschule*. The attempt to bring as many children as
possible up to the standard of the leaving certificate had over-
extended many pupils, as the high proportion of grade repeaters
showed. While too much was obviously demanded of these
pupils there was also a smaller group for whom the standardized
course was not demanding enough. The revisionists wished to
see more concern to arouse individual interests in pupils in
order ultimately to develop the urge to continue their education throughout their lives on their own initiative. This approach was contrasted with the exaggerated encyclopaedism
which had characterized the *Grundschule* and the *Oberschule*—

[33] Becker, *Über das Wesen* . . ., op. cit., p. 740.

'what is decisive for the assessment of our schools . . . is there-fore not how comprehensive is the treasury of knowledge which their pupils can display in a leaving examination (which is then forgotten a few weeks thereafter) but the decisive thing is what powers and abilities, what desire for education the schools have developed in the young people'.[34] In this line of argument very similar ideas were being expressed to those of the more progressive theorists in the Federal Republic who were trying to free the *Gymnasium* from its '*Lernschule*' tradition.

The urge to reduce encyclopaedism in the *Oberschule* of the *DDR* can be compared in particular with the *Rahmenplan* proposals in the Federal Republic for more flexible subject grouping in the upper forms of the *Gymnasium*, the Saarbrücken Agreement to put them into effect, and the Stuttgart Recom-mendations which indicated how an alternative approach to the customary accumulation of extensive factual knowledge was to be encouraged. The objective was to steer *Oberstufe* teaching away from its alleged emphasis on memorization of purely factual knowledge in order 'to make possible a deepen-ing of instruction and to foster the education of the pupil towards intellectual independence and responsibility'.[35] The Agreement picked up the threads of the *Tübinger Beschlüsse* of 1951 emphasizing limitation of content through paradigmatic choice. But it also went very much further by reducing the number of compulsory subjects studied in the last three years of the *Gymnasium*. In relation to the development of academic education since 1900 this was a quite radical measure which went against the views of the various professional associations of *Gymnasium* teachers which considered any reduction in the traditional curriculum as undermining the value of general culture. The universities too were opposed to a reduction but it would appear that the *Kultusministerkonferenz* regarded this as one of the less controversial issues raised in the *Rahmenplan* which could be acted upon fairly quickly. Seen in retrospect

[34] Ibid., p. 729.
[35] *Kultusministerkonferenz, Rahmenvereinbarung . . .*, op. cit., p. 1.

the Agreement was an untimely initiative. The conception on which it depended for its successful implementation involved a new approach to teaching in the *Oberstufe* for which *Gymnasium* teachers were by and large unprepared. Consequently the more radical opportunities for specialization which it offered, such as for example the dropping of a major subject like mathematics two years before the end of the *Gymnasium* course, were soon shown to be unacceptable.[36]

The debate on the subject of the *Gymnasium* curriculum was related to the problem of the rigid structuring of the school system. The defenders of the traditional *Gymnasium* held firmly to the view that in order to fulfil the demanding requirements of an undiluted *Allgemeinbildung*, selection at the age of ten for a nine-year course was essential. The alternative seven-year course which was provided in some *Aufbaugymnasien* was only grudgingly accepted. The opponents on the other hand were beginning to argue with increasing clarity for a more horizontally structured comprehensive system. If the recommendations were to have any prospect of being acted upon, the *Deutscher Ausschuß* had to steer a course between these two extremes. In the *Rahmenplan* the committee expressed its view on the crucial question of selection at the age of ten as follows:

With the majority of ten-year-old children . . . the nature and the extent of their ability cannot, by means of a single examination however careful and extensive, be recognised with the degree of probability that would be necessary to make possible a responsible decision. Admittedly the result of the examination can be supported by a professional opinion from the primary school; but the demands and methods of the primary school must, if it is not to lose its individual character, be different from those of the secondary schools. The judgment on the achievements and efforts of a child, arrived at by the primary school, therefore needs to be complemented. The unusual situation of an examination, taken in a strange school in front of strange teachers, in conjunction with the under-

[36] H. Scheuerl, *Vom Sinn der Hochschulreife* (1965). In H. G. Herrlitz (ed.), *Hochschulreife in Deutschland*, Göttingen, 1968, p. 55.

standable anxiety of the parents, gives rise to a mental pressure which in many children falsifies the picture of achievement. Since in addition some parents attempt to improve their children's prospects of success through private coaching, something which can neither be prevented nor controlled, since in certain cases special primary school classes are even set up to prepare for the examination, it is often not possible to establish to what extent good examination results derive from ability or astute preparation. The introduction of psychological tests has admittedly an undeniable value in complementing the examination; but judging from experience with them so far, they, too, do not permit a sufficiently reliable prediction of performance at secondary school.[37]

Alongside this virtual carbon copy of the arguments against selection at eleven in England the committee however maintained that in the case of very highly gifted children the need for early selection had to be faced.

Civilisation confronts us today, intellectually, politically and economically with demands which cannot be met if we do not succeed in trading an intellectual élite of high standard; for this purpose the most impressionable years of children of specially high ability must be made full use of.[38]

It was on the basis of this reasoning that the compromise embodied in the plan as described earlier was arrived at.

Thus the common ground that some Western educationists had shared with the revisionists in the East was abandoned because there was a general consensus in the academic world that any danger of diluting the traditional culture must be avoided. As for the *DDR* any reasoning which recognized the importance of the *Oberschule* in any way ran counter to the general trend of official policy established in 1958. This was progressively to dismantle the existing *Oberschule* and to make the *Mittelschule* the model for the education of the entire school community over the proposed compulsory ten-year period.

[37] *Empfehlungen und Gutachten . . . Folge 3,* op. cit., p. 10.
[38] Ibid., p. 11.

The Polytechnical Principle and Economic Objectives

The central aim in building up the *Mittelschule* in the *DDR* was to eliminate the former dualism between academic and vocational education. But if these two traditions were to be merged successfully there had to be some common denominator to give a meaning to what would otherwise have been an artificial collocation of quite disparate elements. As indicated earlier, this common denominator eventually emerged as the principle of polytechnical education, one which had its roots in early communist writings and which by 1959 had become the new leitmotiv of policy.

The origins of the polytechnical principle are to be found in the writings of Marx and Engels on education though they owe a certain debt to earlier theorists of socialism such as Thomas More and Robert Owen. The ideas were subsequently developed by Soviet thinkers, notably Lenin and his wife Krupskaya, and given specific form in the Bolshevik programme of 1919, which stated as one of its objectives 'the complete realisation of the principles of the *Einheitsarbeitsschule* with instruction in the mother tongue, with common instruction for the children of both sexes, a school which is entirely secular, that is, free from all religious influence, in which there is a close relationship between instruction and socially productive work and which produces versatile members of communist society'.[39] Krupskaya subsequently wrote at length about this relationship between education and production, ascribing immense significance to polytechnical education which 'is not any special subject of instruction, it must penetrate all subjects, must reveal its influence in the choice of material, in physics, in chemistry, natural and social science'. These subjects were to be coordinated and linked with practical activity, especially with manual skills. In this way manual skills would cease to

[39] *Quellen zur Geschichte der Erziehung*, Berlin, 1968, p. 371.

be isolated from the remainder of education but would acquire a genuine polytechnical character.[40]

The reasoning behind the idea of polytechnical education is based on the Marxist view of the role of education in bringing about a new social order. This entails the control of the means of production by the workers in order to bring about the unprecedented expansion of productivity, which would be the natural consequence of the freedom from the constrictions of private gain. This expansion would create sufficient wealth of material goods to meet the needs of the whole of society, so that ultimately class differences and the division of labour would become obsolete concepts.

The division of society into different classes which are in opposition to one another . . . becomes superfluous. But it becomes not only superfluous, it is positively incompatible with the new social order. The existence of classes is the product of the division of labour and the division of labour in the form it has taken hitherto disappears completely. For in order to bring industrial and agricultural production to the level that has been described, mechanical and chemical means are not enough; the abilities of the people who set these means in motion must also be developed to a corresponding degree. Just as the peasants and craftsmen of the last century changed their whole way of life and even became quite different people when they were drawn into large scale industry, so the common operation of production by the whole of society and the new development of production that will follow from this will require and also produce quite different people. The common operation of production cannot be carried on by people like those of the present day, each of whom is subordinated to one single branch of production, chained to it, exploited by it, each of whom has developed only *one* of his abilities at the expense of all others and knows only one branch or a branch of one branch of the total production process. Present-day industry has already less and less use for such people. Industry operated communally and in a planned manner by the whole of society requires exclusively people whose abilities are developed in all directions, who are in a position to survey the total system of

[40] Ibid., p. 373.

production. The division of labour which makes one man an agricultural worker, another a cobbler, a third a factory worker, a fourth a financial speculator has already been undermined by the advent of machines and will completely disappear. Education will enable young people to work quickly through the entire system of production, enable them to go from one branch of production to the other in turn, according to how the needs of society or their own inclinations dictate. It will thus remove from them the one-sided character which the present division of labour imposes on every individual. In this way the communistically organised society will give its members the opportunity to make use of all the varied abilities that have been developed in them.[41]

The ideas expressed in this passage are fundamental to the aims of educational policy as they developed in the later 1950s. They provide the theoretical justification for a comprehensive educational system which was intended to ensure that no children were channelled into an activity from which they were subsequently unable to escape, but that all would acquire an all-round *poly*technical education which guaranteed them choice and mobility. Polytechnical education must further be seen in the context of the practical revolutionary Leninist development of Marxist thought which declared education to be an instrument for the overthrow of capitalist society, a society that had created the kind of schools which were most appropriate for the exploitation of the working class, providing general education for a privileged minority and vocational training for the majority in order to produce operatives capable only of attending to one detail of the process of production.

The growing preoccupation with polytechnical education in the *DDR* was influenced by developments in the Soviet Union. There the experiments with polytechnical education which had taken place in the 1920s had not been conspicuously successful and had been followed by a formalized, more easily manageable interpretation of the curriculum. At the Nineteenth Congress

---

[41] Ibid., p. 286.

of the Communist Party in 1952 the possibility of reviving the polytechnical principle was aired and in the years that followed was the subject of increasing discussion. In a major pronounce-ment in 1956 Krushchev declared that the schools had lost touch with society as a whole, and that their pupils were not adequately prepared for employment. From then on the move towards the general introduction of polytechnical education gathered momentum, culminating in the reforms of 1958 which brought an increase in the time devoted to manual skills during the eight years of compulsory education and allowed for one-third of the curriculum of the upper secondary schools to be spent in some form of theoretical and practical study of the workings of industry or agriculture.[42] Various explanations have been offered for this development, principally the eco-nomic factor of meeting manpower requirements and the social issue raised by Krushchev, who deplored the growing tendency to look down on manual labour. The reasoning behind the introduction of polytechnical education in the *DDR* was similar, and the debt to the Soviet Union in the matter of methods of putting the principle into practice is generally acknowledged.

The economic emphasis of polytechnical education as introduced in the *DDR* is clear from an analysis of the objec-tives, which began from the Marxist assumption that the production of material goods is the most urgent task and that consequently technology is of foremost importance. The first function of polytechnical education was therefore to convey the fundamental technical and economic knowledge necessary for an understanding of the principles of all aspects of production and hence of the entire manufacturing process from raw mater-ial to finished product. Beyond this it was to foster a creative attitude to the process by encouraging pupils or workers to think out the implications of the process and, accordingly, to use their initiative to improve it and to innovate: the creative activity here was particularly directed at the schools where

[42] N. Grant, *Soviet Education*, London, 1964, pp. 87, 98–9.

interests and abilities with a technical bias were to be specially fostered. A third aspect was the development of the appropriate skills, both the traditional manual ones, and those associated with the operation and servicing of modern machinery. Fourthly, polytechnical education was to be seen as a preparation for work. Work was to be recognized as important, indeed revered as the source of social wealth, which was only possible through production. Finally, it was to provide an education for responsibility, in particular collective responsibility. Children and workers were to learn that all stages in production are interdependent and that they shared common responsibility in a common enterprise of which they shared the ownership.[43]

The general tenor of curriculum development in the *DDR* stood in marked contrast to the situation in the Federal Republic where the challenge to the traditional values of the *Gymnasium* was vigorously resisted. Most of the criticism of the early 1950s had been directed at the encyclopaedic nature of the curriculum but only in isolated cases had the basic assumption been questioned that the task of the *Gymnasium* was to provide an essentially humanistic, non-vocational education for future leaders of society. In the later 1950s however, as a result of the awareness of the shortage of trained manpower in essential sectors of the economy, the curriculum was called into question in a more fundamental way. It was no longer taken for granted that the traditional concept of general culture embraced those fields of knowledge which were most relevant to modern needs. The fact that the socialist countries had reshaped their educational systems, largely in accordance with the demands of science and technology, aroused misgivings that the Federal Republic was in danger of falling behind in economic competitiveness.

The resistance to the basic assumptions that underlay the predominantly humanistic *Gymnasium* curriculum is illustrated by the defensive position taken up by the *Arbeitsgemeinschaft Deutsche Höhere Schule* which maintained that 'there would not

[43] H. Klein, *Polytechnische Erziehung in der DDR*, Hamburg, 1963, pp. 57-8.

be [public] support for a move to make German *Gymnasium* education dependent on vocational considerations'[44] and that it was important to preserve the tradition of *Allgemeinbildung*. The federation did not deny the need for an increased supply of manpower, especially in the realm of science and technology, but maintained that this was not the responsibility of the *Gymnasium*. It welcomed any increase in the *Mittelschule*, or *Realschule* sector as it was now more commonly called, and in the capacity of the higher technical schools to which it gave access. The *Realschule* sector, being proud of its own identity, in turn welcomed expansion. This separate development is illustrative of the way in which the various sectors of the school system in the Federal Republic were conceived of as fulfilling functions which were quite different in kind. As a result the formulation of policy was always a composite affair meeting the demands of each sector separately. There was little opportunity to relate them to one another on account of the strength of the individual interest groups.

In the Saarbrücken Agreement the *Kultusministerkonferenz* did create a more flexible pattern for the upper forms of the *Gymnasium* but without changing its basic traditionally academic character (cf. Appendix V). The need for a more vocationally oriented secondary education was dealt with through the continuing expansion of the *Realschulen* and the higher technical schools. The *Volksschule* was different again, being closely related to the apprenticeship system. Yet the dangers of rigid categorization were recognized and individual initiatives to ease transfer from one sector to another became increasingly common in the later 1950s. But if there was any common element which determined the degree of mobility within the hierarchy it was a humanistic one, since it was believed that the qualities developed by a humanistic education were ultimately those that provided the best credentials for the exercise of responsibility. On this issue the *Arbeitsgemeinschaft*

[44] *Arbeitsgemeinschaft Deutsche Höhere Schule, Bildungsauftrag und Bildungspläne der Gymnasien*, Berlin, 1958, pp. 15-16.

Deutsche Höhere Schule framed the characteristic apology for the *Gymnasium*:

. . . life in the national community is not the same as activity in a factory in which skilled workmen and foremen control the quality of the products through their special skill, but in which all including the leaders of the enterprise are active in pursuit of the same goal. Rather it is continually multi-form in the material and still more in the intellectual and emotional needs of men who want to have the possibility guaranteed them of leading a life which appears to them individually to have a purpose. In the degree to which the life of the community becomes more complex and embraces the whole human being, there will be demanded of those in leading positions greater insight and deeper understanding of human activities and desires, as well as greater ability to secure our material existence.[45]

The survival of the *Gymnasium* unscathed from the controversy over the relevance of education to the demands of a modern industrial economy is sufficient evidence that educational policy was based on a widespread acceptance of this scale of values.

Social Considerations

While the economic emphasis was the dominant one in the introduction of polytechnical education in the *DDR* there was also a strong social element in the more general field of policy-making. The revisionists had maintained that their proposals for differentiation need have no adverse effect on social policy but that it would be just as easy, if not easier, to further the prospects of working-class children by beginning the more intensive academic *Oberschule* education two years earlier. The main emphasis in their argument was on the need to halt the decline in educational standards among those taking the *Abitur* and entering university. This decline in the standard of the *Abitur* was inevitable as compared with the corresponding situation in the West where the whole of the restored nine-year

[45] Ibid., p. 18.

course in the *Gymnasium* was directed towards guaranteeing a high academic level. At the time of the dispute over revisionist proposals a high proportion of *Oberschule* leavers, estimated at one-quarter of those obtaining the *Abitur*, were migrating to the Federal Republic where six-month preparatory courses were arranged to enable them to reach the standard required for university entrance.[46] Those who argued the revisionist case were clearly concerned at the discrepancy. Whereas in terms of scholarship the Federal Republic had been able to restore the traditional norms, in the *DDR* these had been to some extent eroded.

The desire to restore academic standards was interpreted among the opponents of revisionism as a thinly disguised revival of the 'bourgeois theory of ability' which would lead to a differentiation on a social basis. The entire argument for the lengthening of the *Oberschule* in order to guarantee the kind of general education regarded as an indispensable precondition for admission to university implied acceptance of a category of theoretically gifted children who could be identified quite young—in this case after six years of primary school—and given the necessary preparation to enable them to fill the leading positions in society. This had in the past led to the dominance of the middle class, and it was feared that it would continue to do so until the conditions that were conducive to the survival of educational privilege had been removed. It may have been that the revisionists were assuming with genuine optimism that this latter stage had been reached and that the social aspects of policy had therefore lost much of their relevance. It seems more likely however from the tenor of their arguments that social policy did not actively concern them and that they did not regard it as inseparable from educational policy. Ulbricht himself attacked them for maintaining that there was such a thing as the 'neutrality of instruction'.[47]

The tendency to separate education from ideological and social considerations had in fact permeated the system during

---

[46] *Bericht . . .*, 1957/58, p. 14.   [47] *Deutsche Lehrerzeitung*, 9/1958, p. 4.

the mid-1950s and now came under severe attack in the
educational press:

Although from 1952 on the socialist educational aim was laid down
for school work, in the years that followed there was no purposeful
realisation of it. This has ideological causes. In opportunistic interpretation of the New Course nothing was said for years about
socialist education by Party members, administrators and teachers.
The politico-ideological education of teachers was greatly neglected
and in its place a one-sided subject-oriented teacher education was
practised. . . . There are even whole school staffs where not a single
teacher subscribes to *Neues Deutschland* or where only 50 per cent
subscribe to *Deutsche Lehrerzeitung*. (Sometimes even fewer, especially
in the *Oberschulen!*—editor.) No socialist consciousness can develop
in this way. This situation led to tendencies to separate politics from
education and encouraged various manifestations of revisionism in
the sphere of education.[48]

Those who, as in the passage just quoted, denounced this
outlook were at the same time denouncing the prevailing
attitude in the Federal Republic where there was a general
reluctance to view educational policy as an instrument of social
change. There during the later 1950s the school system continued to correspond very closely with a hierarchical social
structure. It remained the prevailing view in the social sciences
that this situation reflected the distribution of ability, according
to which it was to be expected that the great majority of the
category of 'theoretically gifted' would be drawn from the
middle class, and almost all the category of 'practically gifted'
would be from the working class. This stratification, further
consolidated by the qualifications system, was a generally
accepted feature of society in the Federal Republic and for a
number of reasons already explored did not generate a great
deal of discontent. Certainly the *Deutscher Ausschuß* expressed
misgivings in a very general way, maintaining that the educational system had not come to terms with the changes in

[48] W. Neugebauer, Director of Central Committee Education Department. *Deutsche Lehrerzeitung*, 13/1958, p. 2.

society. But even the *Rahmenplan* proposals of 1959, which marked such a significant advance in the discussion of future policy, were still based on the premise of three main types of ability, theoretical, theoretical/practical and practical for which three different types of curriculum were considered appropriate.

In so far as the revisionists in the *DDR* appeared, by virtue of their disinterest in an active policy to promote social change, to be approaching the acceptance of social stratification as inevitable, if not desirable, they incurred the odium of those who took an uncompromising line on social policy. The 'bourgeois theory of ability' came under vigorous attack, particularly as interpreted in the West by the leading sociologist Karl Valentin Müller who was accused of formulating specious propositions of innate ability and social sifting in order to justify the class structure within the school system, purporting to prove that democratization was impracticable:

Following this artificially concocted premise of 'innate ability' and 'social sifting' it is no longer difficult for Müller to justify the class bias of the West German school system and to oppose school reform. According to him 'it is neither accidental nor to be wondered at that the *Gymnasien*, which today even more than in years past make their selection according to the principle of ability, are to a dominant degree attended by the sons (significantly no account is taken of daughters throughout Müller's work) of the upper and middle classes. Even the most radical school reform would not be able decisively to alter this "fact". The actual class bias of the *Gymnasium* is explained "predominantly by the extensive natural coincidence of school sifting and social sifting. It would be an illusion" ', thinks Müller, "to achieve any essential 'democratisation' (Müller himself puts this word in inverted commas) by a system of incentives and scholarships." '[49]

This abhorrence of the hierarchical nature of the school system of the Federal Republic, which enabled the middle class to

---

[49] W. Reischock, *Das Bildungsmonopol und die 'Begabung'. Deutsche Lehrerzeitung*, 23/1958, p. 5.

monopolize academic education, was strongly characteristic of educational thinking in the *DDR* at the end of the 1950s.

In fact the policies pursued in the *DDR* had already resulted in a very different social composition in the schools from that which obtained in the Federal Republic, and the revisionist view was that this was a sufficient degree of democratization and that priorities now needed to be altered. The uncompromising line of their opponents remained that variations in intelligence did not relate to social differences and that therefore it was necessary to continue to pursue active policies of conscious promotion of the working class until complete proportional representation had been achieved. This reaffirmation that the class struggle was still the *raison d'être* of educational policy conveys accurately the tone of discussion after the denunciation of revisionism at the *SED* Education Conference. It had now been stated unequivocally that the leadership of the working class was a foremost priority and that education was an instrument to be used to achieve this. It was consistent with this view that the interests of the majority should be put before those of any minority and that the emphasis should be placed on the raising of the general level of education throughout the entire school population by reaffirming the inviolability of the undifferentiated eight-year *Grundschule*. Moreover, the rejection of any dualism was seen as extending eventually to the ten-year *Mittelschule* which was to become the standard institution for all.

The nature of policy in the Federal Republic at this time differs sharply in two obvious ways. Even the *Rahmenplan*, which was if anything regarded as radical rather than conservative, still fundamentally accepted the traditional vertical structuring which had been denounced in the *DDR*. Secondly, while in the *DDR* it was planned to increase the duration of compulsory education to ten years, the addition of a ninth compulsory school year was, as regards the Federal Republic as a whole, still only a proposal. This distinction was however at this stage more one in theory than in practice. The original plan in the *DDR* only envisaged by 1960 an entry of 40 per cent of the relevant age group to the *Mittelschule* after eight years of *Grundschule*,[50] and even this figure was not necessarily achieved. Though precise statistics are not available, it is unlikely that by 1960 the number continuing beyond eight years in full-time education in the *DDR* greatly exceeded the corresponding figure in the West. The full implications of the divergence of policy as regards the raising of the school-leaving age were not readily visible till the following decade.

Political Contrasts

By the end of the 1950s in the *DDR* a new phase of determined socialism had been ushered in which represented a major step towards achieving the unity of the political, social and economic aims of the educational system. Differentiation along the lines practised in the Federal Republic had been rejected and the *Zehnklassenschule* or *Mittelschule* had not merely held its own but was officially designated the standard school for the entire population and renamed the *zehnklassige allgemeinbildende poly-technische Oberschule*. The use of the term *Oberschule* was particularly significant in that it proclaimed that secondary education was now the prerogative of all children. The old *Oberschule*, renamed *erweiterte Oberschule*, had been divested of much of its exclusiveness in terms of academic curriculum by combining with the preparation for the *Abitur* an element of vocational training leading to a trade qualification. Though it was going to require a number of years for the provisions of the 1959 Act to become operative, it was already clear how marked the contrast would be over the next five years with the Federal Republic where the limited modifications of the traditional structure suggested in the *Rahmenplan* caused so much controversy that very little change could be anticipated.

This controversy revealed the strongly conservative stand-

[50] Monumenta Paedagogica VII/1, op. cit., p. 25.

point of secondary teachers who firmly rejected the proposals, defending vigorously the existing forms of the *Gymnasium* and *Realschule*. The *Volksschule* was defended no less energetically by religious groups which maintained that the reform proposals jeopardized the right to educate children in accordance with the dictates of conscience. The interest of the Churches lay above all in retaining control of the confessional schools. Since these were mainly *Volksschulen* they feared that a new State system aiming to reduce in size and reorganize this sector would erode their influence. Towards the end of the decade the Protestant Church had become less committed than before to exclusively confessional schools, and more prepared to endorse the '*Simultanschule*' in which the religious element in the curriculum was confined to the lessons in religious education given separately by representatives of the various denominations.[5] Spokesmen for the Catholic Church maintained however that the *Simultanschule* was no substitute for the confessional school since for Catholics religion was 'not one subject among others but the fundamental principle of all instruction'.[52] The *Rahmenplan* and the *Bremer Plan* clearly constituted a major challenge to the authority of the Churches and protests against the advocacy of secularization that these documents were considered to imply were voiced with particular force by parents' organizations.[53] Conservative stances of this kind still reflected the consensus view with regard to educational policy more accurately than the more radical reactions to the *Rahmenplan*. It consequently remained true that foremost importance was attached to fostering separately the achievement of

[51] For the change of attitude in the Protestant Church see *Wort der Synode der Evangelischen Kirche in Deutschland zur Schulfrage. Vom 30.4.1958*. In H.-M. Schreiber, *Interaktion Kirche-Schule*, Hamburg, 1971, pp. 146–8.

[52] J. Pohlschneider, Bishop of Aachen, *Erklärung der deutschen Bischöfe zu Bestrebungen hinsichtlich der Umgestaltung des deutschen Schulwesens anläßlich der Fuldaer Bischofskonferenz in September 1960. Schul-Korrespondenz Nr. 19*, 11.10.1960.

[53] See K. Bungardt, *Der 'Bremer Plan' im Streit der Meinungen. Eine Dokumentation*. Frankfurt/M., 1962, pp. 59–61, 87–8.

K

specific groups. Moreover this approach accorded with the general social climate in which resentment at the middle-class dominance of the selective schools was not particularly strongly expressed.

By contrast the new *DDR* policy was consistent with Marxist-Leninist principles in placing its emphasis on the collective aspects of education. The main uncertainty was whether such an approach was wholly desirable from an economic point of view. It was important to make the best use of the most highly gifted young people in the spheres of languages, science and technology. This the *Gymnasium* in the Federal Republic was equipped to do, but it was less easy to achieve in a system where all teaching was totally undifferentiated for the first eight years. It was in this context that the idea of specialist schools was mooted by Ulbricht in 1958.[54] But while it was an obviously sensible idea from an economic point of view, it was politically difficult to reconcile with the collective principle which pervaded the post-revisionist enthusiasm for undiluted socialism. The momentum created by this ideological enthusiasm was the strongest motive behind policy at the time while the economic consideration of the optimal exploitation of above average ability, which objective analysis would have shown to be important, remained in the background.

[54] Baske/Engelbert, I, op. cit., p. 412.

CHAPTER 5

Years of Inquiry: 1960–65

Research and the Growth of Political Interest

After a decade of vicissitudes in educational policy in the *DDR* it had in 1959 proved possible to shape a law which could be presented as a response to ideological, social and economic requirements at one and the same time. On all these counts the new ten-class comprehensive school—the *zehnklassige allgemein-bildende polytechnische Oberschule*—appeared irreproachable. It offered lasting evidence of the repudiation of any desire to restore the kind of differentiation that had existed in the early years of the Occupation period and hence of any suggestion of rapprochement with the system of the Federal Republic. It was seen as an agency for the promotion of a united society in which no group was allowed the opportunity to remain academically aloof. Economically, from the standpoint of the Seven-Year Plan it was expected to be instrumental in raising the standard of education throughout the labour force, a development which it was assumed would have a direct bearing on productivity. These objectives had been voiced many times before, but were now given a new practical meaning through the introduction of polytechnical education which injected into the curriculum an element designed to guarantee an output of young people committed to socialism and trained to take an active part in industrial or agricultural production.

The early 1960s were characterized by the energetic efforts to realize the objectives of the 1959 Law. To begin with, the

overriding preoccupation was to ensure the success of polytechnical education in the context of a rise of two years in the
school-leaving age. The practical problems which were thrown
up by the implementation of the policy however showed that
the total conception of the 1959 Law, with its abhorrence of
differentiation and obsession with practical experience in
industry or agriculture, did not combine the various objectives
as harmoniously as had been envisaged. It was during this
period that the vagueness about a general rise in educational
standards, which would have the effect of turning out a versatile
labour force, gave way to increasing precision about what the
manpower requirements really were. As a result it could no
longer be taken for granted that the uncompromising collecti-
vism that had inspired the 1959 Law offered at the same time
the most effective solution to economic problems of manpower
supply. Thus a transition took place. The policy that had been
formulated in the wave of thoroughgoing socialism that had
followed the demise of revisionism was modified in accordance
with objective assessment of the needs of the economy. Planning grew in sophistication as a result of the increase in research
activity, which ceased to be individualistic but became increasingly interdisciplinary in character, carried out in new
research centres specially set up for the purpose. A new centre
for the coordination of research plans was created at the
Deutsches Pädagogisches Zentralinstitut and when in 1962 the
first major programme of educational research was officially
approved, one of the foremost priorities was the study of long-term
planning issues affecting the development of educational policy.[1]

In the Federal Republic too there was a marked growth in
research activity, but it did not have the same function as that
which took place in the *DDR*. In the latter case research work
was integrated into the central planning process, and it was
not readily obvious to what extent its findings conflicted with
existing policies. In the West, on the other hand, it played an

[1] K.-H. Günther/G. Uhlig, *Geschichte der Schule in der DDR 1945 bis 1968*,
Berlin, 1969, p. 137.

independent role. The main developments in the system in the 1950s had been the result of economic pressures exerted piecemeal but without any great thought being given to long-term implications. The advocates of change had made re-markably little impression as the reception to the *Rahmenplan* showed. One of the most striking features of this debate was the lack of statistical evidence available so that arguments on either side were seldom supported by objectively compiled informa-tion. On the radical side very little empirical research had been carried out to test the assumptions about social injustice. Its extent could therefore be the subject of interminable unin-formed argument. The traditionalist view that, for example, a good measure of transfer—*Durchlässigkeit*—took place within the existing system was equally unsupported by factual data. What was now becoming apparent was that without the kind of evidence that empirical investigation could yield the debate would remain in a position of stalemate.

This was perhaps most clearly recognized by the *Ettlinger Kreis*. Having first pointed out the lack of precise statistical material, it went on to make two suggestions. The first was for a sizeable increase in the collection and publication of statistics both at federal and at *Land* level. The second was that, since statistics of population development were only of limited use, research should be put in hand to obtain the more complex additional data required: 'since the educational system is in the closest interaction with the other sectors of society, re-searchers of several disciplines must work together . . . to create the necessary bases for decision in matters of educational policy'.[2] It was this line of thought which ushered in a quali-tatively new phase in the development of policy-making in the early 1960s. When the volume of research activity increased accordingly, it served to reveal the omissions of existing policy and to stimulate pressure for change.

[2] Ettlinger Kreis, *Entschließung zum Rahmenplan und zur Kulturstatistik (Fünftes Ettlinger Gespräch)*, 1959. In A. O. Schorb, *Für und Wider den Rahmen-plan. Eine Dokumentation*, Stuttgart, 1960, p. 25.

The fact that much of this research work challenged the prevailing political attitude which was opposed to change emphasizes the contrast to the situation in the *DDR* where research activity was closely related to political decision-making and findings had to be in accordance with Marxist principles. At the time of the revisionist controversy there had been an outcry in Party circles over the acceptance by the Education Faculty of the Humboldt University in Berlin of research which had no affinities with Marxism, and university teachers who declined to underpin their work with socialist ideology were denounced.[3] The climate for research in the early 1960s was quite clearly defined:

It was a precondition for [the] new methodology of educational science that traditional conceptions which were inhibiting at this phase of the development of science should be overcome in practical activity, above all the traditional individualistic method in research, but also theoretical opinions which had their origin in bourgeois science, such as for example the 'separation of politics and education', the 'search for a timeless psychology and methodology unrelated to class issues' or shallow empiricism in research.[4]

Thus individual research divorced from ideological commitment became impossible. By contrast, in the Federal Republic the impact of research findings had the effect of calling into question the ideology according to which the educational system was organized. By the middle of the decade the inadequacies of provision had been mapped out in some detail and there appeared to be sufficient evidence to suggest serious discrepancies between supply in terms of the qualified manpower turned out and demand as represented by national needs. Thus the social and economic arguments were seen as complementary. To put right social injustices by giving educational opportunities to those who had been previously denied them was at the same time to identify the unused reserves of ability on which the future health of the economy depended. During

[3] *SED III Hochschulkonferenz. Deutsche Lehrerzeitung*, 10/1958, p. 7.
[4] Günther/Uhlig, op. cit., p. 137.

the early 1960s these ideas became more and more influential and were reflected in isolated measures taken in individual *Länder*. A survey of the needs of the school system for the period 1961–70 carried out for the *Kultusministerkonferenz* showed that an immense expansion of demand was imminent.[5] As a result of this a number of *Land* ministries began to show a new concern with planning for the future.

In sheer statistical terms the achievements of the early 1960s were unimpressive, largely because of the lack of concerted action in the previous decade. This situation was suddenly projected before the general public by a series of articles by Georg Picht, which appeared in 1964 under the ominous title of the 'German Educational Catastrophe' (*Die Deutsche Bildungskatastrophe*), and which had a quite extraordinary impact.[6] A succession of carefully chosen data portrayed the Federal Republic as educationally one of the most backward countries in Europe. The figures came principally from an OECD survey which had shown a projected increase of at least 100 per cent in the number of school leavers obtaining the equivalent of the *Abitur* in eight European countries,[7] while on the basis of the current trends the expected increase in West Germany was put at 4 per cent. On such data Picht based his forecast that without a dynamic political initiative the system would become unworkable.

This comparative perspective focused interest once again on the machinery for policy-making, and it became important to evaluate the achievements and role of the *Deutscher Ausschuß*. This body had continued to produce recommendations, the main purpose of which was to elaborate on the *Rahmenplan*

---

[5] *Kultusministerkonferenz, Bedarfsfeststellung 1961 bis 1970 für Schulwesen, Lehrerbildung, Wissenschaft und Forschung, Kunst und Kulturpflege*, Stuttgart, 1963.

[6] First published in *Luthersche Monatshefte*, then in *Christ und Welt*. Reprinted in book form: G. Picht, *Die Deutsche Bildungskatastrophe*, Olten/ Freiburg im Breisgau, 1964.

[7] Yugoslavia 148, Norway 165, France 154, Belgium 100, Sweden 138, Italy 110, Denmark 124, Holland 100 per cent. Ibid., p. 27.

proposals, above all as regards the content of the curriculum and the teaching methods appropriate for the various stages of the school system. It examined too the system of vocational education and came out basically in favour of the existing way of organizing apprenticeship training, though recommending developments at the higher levels. But its importance was dwindling with the realization that it was able to exert very little practical influence on the course of policy. The *Rahmen-plan* proposals, for all the adroitness they showed in compromising between two extremes, proved impossible to implement. By the middle of the decade it was clear that there was no longer a significant role for an advisory committee totally divorced from the political and executive power to carry out its recommendations. With its dissolution and replacement in 1965 by the German Education Council (*Deutscher Bildungsrat*), a body constituted on different lines, a new phase began in the relationship between the work of federal advisory bodies and the educational policy of *Land* governments.

It would however be unjust to describe the work of the *Deutscher Ausschuss* as fruitless. Its impact was considerable in stimulating ideas and in creating an atmosphere in which the *Kultusministerkonferenz* showed itself much more open to them. When the Düsseldorf Agreement expired in 1964 it was succeeded by the Hamburg Agreement (*Hamburger Abkommen*) which was less restrictive on the signatories as far as experimental innovations were concerned. It recognized the concept of a *Förderstufe*, while still leaving the decision to the individual *Länder* as to how extensively and in what precise form it should be introduced. It also allowed for the possibility of experiments outside the existing framework, though the *Kultusministerkonferenz* retained nominal control over these by stipulating that its approval had to be obtained in advance. In general the relations between the federal and the *Land* authorities improved at this time, and a number of agreements to increase cooperation were concluded.[8] These were largely in

---

[8] *Kultusministerkonferenz, Kulturpolitik der Länder 1963–64*, p. 4.

the sphere of higher education since the *Länder* still jealously guarded their autonomy as far as school policy was concerned. Nonetheless the improved atmosphere was at least to some extent auspicious for school affairs and appeared to bring a standardized national educational policy based on detailed planning a step nearer.

Structural and Curricular Developments in the West

In the Federal Republic the detailed course of educational policy in the early 1960s appears unspectacular in view of the ferment of discussion which followed the *Rahmenplan*, and which was further stimulated by the growing volume of educational research and of publications to popularize it. But as already noted, only towards the end of the period did the issue really catch the public imagination. Nevertheless, in individual *Länder* there was a steady increase in measures designed to mitigate inequalities and hardships. Increasing attention was now devoted to the *Volksschule*, reflecting the repeated warnings of the *Deutscher Ausschuß* about neglect of this sector. A number of *Länder* pushed ahead with the conversion of its upper classes into a genuine *Hauptschule* by providing the staff and facilities necessary to operate the kind of curriculum that would make transfer to the *Realschule* a viable proposition, and by introducing a compulsory or at least a voluntary ninth school year. However, though the extent of the *Durchlässigkeit* achieved was statistically unexplored, it seems clear that beyond the age of thirteen prospects of transfer were slender.[9]

One of the major difficulties was the task of developing the *Volksschule* sector in largely rural areas. All the *Länder* faced with this problem initiated measures to amalgamate small village schools staffed by only one or two teachers into central schools known as *Mittelpunktschulen*. But the overall picture of

[9] See the section on West Germany in S. B. Robinsohn/H. Thomas, *Differenzierung im Sekundarschulwesen*, Stuttgart, 1968.

rural school provision remained a bleak one as sociological research subsequently revealed. The greatest expansion took place in the *Realschulen*. In 1961 they contained 386,640 pupils, an increase of nearly 11 per cent over the previous year. Throughout the early 1960s the increase continued at a rate of between 5 and 7 per cent so that by 1965 the number had reached 531,602. At the same time growing importance was attached to transfer to the *Gymnasium* at the end of the course in the *Realschule*. In a number of *Länder* special 'transition classes' were set up at the *Gymnasium* to ease this process. In Hesse, for example, as a result of these classes it was possible for nearly 9 per cent of all those who completed the *Realschule* programme to transfer to the *Gymnasium*.[10] Outside the orthodox school system there were signs of steady expansion in the *zweiter Bildungsweg* with the development of various types of institution providing full-time courses leading to entrance to the higher vocational colleges and in some cases to university. The reports on policy of all the *Länder* reflect the impact made by the *Kultusministerkonferenz* manpower survey, in that they displayed a concern to draw on the untapped resources of the 'pool of ability'. *Bildungsreserven* had become a ubiquitous catch phrase.

The developments at federal level can best be traced through the proceedings of the *Kultusministerkonferenz*, which remained the only body that could be said to formulate anything approaching a national policy. At the beginning of the period in question the main concern was with the *Gymnasium* curriculum. In 1961 the 'Stuttgart Recommendations' interpreted the Saarbrücken Agreement on the pattern of the curriculum and teaching methods.[11] In 1962 the specific area of civic education (*Gemeinschaftskunde*) was dealt with in guidelines for the top two classes of the *Gymnasium*. This was to be a composite

[10] *Bericht des Vorsitzenden des Schulausschusses der Ständigen Konferenz*, 1961/62, p. 21; 1962/63, p. 23; 1963/64, pp. 19, 22; 1964/65, pp. 19, 24.

[11] *Kultusministerkonferenz, Empfehlungen an die Unterrichtsverwaltungen der Länder zur didaktischen und methodischen Gestaltung der Oberstufe der Gymnasien im Sinne der Saarbrücker Rahmenvereinbarung. Beschluss Nr. 175.1.*

subject comprising elements of history, geography and social science and was recommended as a particularly fruitful field for the way of working that the Saarbrücken Agreement had declared to be peculiar to the upper forms of the *Gymnasium*. This document was the culmination of protracted action on the question of political education which had originated with a recommendation published by the *Deutscher Ausschuß* in 1955. Individual *Land* programmes in this domain were now gathered together as part of one nationally recognized syllabus.

In 1964 the Hamburg Agreement generally consolidated the attempts made at standardization by its Düsseldorf predecessor (Diagram in Appendix VII). It made the raising of the school-leaving age to give nine years of compulsory school attendance binding on all *Länder*. For the *Gymnasium* sector it stated that curricula were to diverge significantly only after the tenth year. The only differentiation up till this point was to be on the basis of languages studied and this was very slight as the first foreign language was to be either Latin or English. If Latin was chosen as the first, English had to be the second. This confirmed the provisions of the Düsseldorf Agreement on this score. As regards the *Realschule*, the normal compulsory foreign language was to be English and a second foreign language was to be offered as an optional extra subject. In this way the possibility of transfer from the *Realschule* to the *Gymnasium* became genuine provided that the appropriate courses could be offered. The new Agreement, as indicated earlier, was receptive to a number of ideas put forward in the *Rahmenplan*. It gave official recognition to the concept of a *Förderstufe* and showed the willingness of the *Kultusministerkonferenz* to countenance more radical experimental programmes, provided that they were first submitted for its approval. The most controversial issue was that of the restricted rights of entry to university conveyed by the term *fachgebundene Hochschulreife*. It had always been an exclusive feature of the *Gymnasium* that its leaving qualification conferred an unrestricted right to enter any faculty (*allgemeine Hochschulreife*). The use of the term *fachgebundene Hochschulreife* in the Agreement, apropos of further education, implied approval on the Conference's part of the notion that university entry, restricted to certain faculties, could be secured outside the *Gymnasium* on the basis of leaving certificates which did not conform to the *Tutzinger Maturitätskatalog*. The exact scope of the controversial term remained undefined but the debate, stirred up by its very use, foreshadowed the problems that surrounded university admissions in the later 1960s.

By 1965 the educational policy agreed at federal level had begun to display some pattern. There was an obvious awareness of the social and economic arguments for change and a readiness to bring in expansionist measures that would create a greater demand for upper secondary education. At the basis of the policies actually initiated lay a general aversion to any radical restructuring of the entire system along comprehensive lines. The *Gymnasium* retained its immense prestige as the pride and inspiration of the entire school system and hence remained to all intents and purposes inviolable. But all other means that could be devised for developing the system were beginning to be mobilized. Ultimately the success of the vertical structure depended on the ease of lateral movement from one branch to another. In this connection there was one overriding problem, the differences in the curricula of the types of school. Since there was immense reluctance to dilute the *Gymnasium* curriculum the only viable course was to develop the curriculum of the other branches. Here the key question was the provision of foreign-language teaching since it was necessary to have studied two foreign languages to obtain the *Abitur*. In addition to the arrangements for language teaching in the *Realschule* referred to above, it was laid down that one foreign language should be available for all pupils in the *Hauptschule*. This was not sufficient to meet the demands of unrestricted lateral transfer at the end of the tenth school year, the *mittlere Reife* stage, but it was a step in that direction. In the later 1960s the problem of curriculum was to be recognized with still more clarity as perhaps the most vital one of all school policy.

Structural and Curricular Developments in the East

In the *DDR*, measures to ensure the successful implementation of the 1959 Law began to be taken soon after its promulgation. A decree reorganizing the parents' committees stressed the need for cooperation with teachers and with the youth movement if polytechnical education was to be successful and the objectives of the Seven-Year Plan accomplished. It became obligatory to form a committee at every school.[12] Other links between the schools, the youth movement and sectors of society at large were actively fostered. The Ministry of Education reported early in 1960 on the sponsorship of school classes and youth groups by trade union 'brigades' and made various recommendations as to how such liaisons could be improved. The social purpose was a particularly strong feature of this aspect of policy and it was pointed out that 'the most important precondition for the further development of sponsorship arrangements between brigades and school classes and Pioneer or *FDJ* groups lies in making clear to all teachers the necessity and significance of the increase in influence of the working class on education'.[13] Finally, the bonds between all these various agencies were to be strengthened by a revision of teacher training.

A *Politbüro* decision regarding the development of polytechnical instruction in the *Oberschule* reflects the same emphasis on the cooperation of all sectors of society, in particular the industrial and agricultural concerns and the trade unions. Courses in electrical and mechanical engineering were to be improved since these two areas were regarded as of foremost importance and had a shortage of qualified labour. The teaching of manual skills in schools was likewise to be improved. The shortcomings that had so far been evident in this respect were blamed on the inadequate training of primary stage teachers;

[12] *Dokumente zur Geschichte des Schulwesens*, Monumenta Paedagogica VII/1, Berlin, 1969, p. 323.   [13] Ibid., p. 331.

provision was made for an increase in the time devoted to methods of teaching manual skills. The more general implications of polytechnical education were also considered important so that the significance of the new subject 'Introduction to socialist production' was emphasized. A further measure to channel the general interest of pupils in the approved direction was the introduction of the *polytechnisches Kabinett*, a kind of recreation room stocked with display material, models which could be dismantled and assembled, and charts to illustrate technical processes. It was made the responsibility of management to provide the necessary facilities and equipment and there was the familiar insistence on the supporting role of the youth movement.[14]

The last remaining item in the *Politbüro* decision concerned the *erweiterte Oberschule*. From September 1960 the *Unterrichtstag in der Produktion* was to be used to furnish pupils with the basis of an apprenticeship training simultaneously with the *Abitur*. This would enable all pupils to acquire a trade qualification after one year of employment, before going on to higher education. This idea of combining the highest level of academic work in schools, symbolized by the *Abitur*, with acquisition of a trade qualification was further extended by a directive providing for special *Abitur* classes within the domain of vocational education, as stipulated by the 1959 Law. These classes were regarded as carrying 'a high degree of political responsibility in the education of a new socialist intelligentsia', and were ultimately to constitute the main route to university. Of all *Oberschule* leavers 10 per cent were expected to enter them in 1961 and 1962, 15 per cent in 1963 and 1964 and 20 per cent in 1965. The curriculum was to be an amalgam of the normal work of the relevant trade training, the *Oberschule* and the *erweiterte Oberschule* and there was to be no fall below the standards of the latter.[15]

These measures form part of a more general preoccupation

<hr>

[14] S. Baske/M. Engelbert, *Zwei Jahrzehnte Bildungspolitik . . . Dokumente*, Vol. II, Berlin, 1966, pp. 74–80.   [15] Ibid., p. 100.

with the structure of vocational education as a whole, revealed in a major document of 1960 establishing the 'basic principles for the further development of the vocational education system' (*Grundsätze zur weiteren Entwicklung des Systems der Berufsbildung in der DDR*). There were two main tendencies in this. The first was the intention to link vocational training as closely as possible with life, especially socialist production.

The young people should be trained as early as possible in the departments of the concern and not predominantly in the instructional workshops. The instructors should therefore work in close cooperation with the workers, especially the socialist brigades, study their experiences and evaluate their relevance to education. Thereby the working class gains the opportunity more than hitherto to have a direct effect on the education of the coming generation. The links already created with the socialist concern in the *Oberschule* through the *Unterrichtstag in der Produktion* are further developed and strengthened.[16]

The social significance of this and its direct economic relevance are equally clear. The second tendency was influenced by more far-sighted economic considerations and is expressed in the concern to extend the theoretical knowledge of young people, above all in mathematics and science. From September 1960 the structure of an apprenticeship was to be on a two-tier basis. The first stage, lasting one year, consisted of a broad general training applicable to several trades. This was followed by a specialist training also lasting one year or in exceptional cases up to two years. The content of the apprenticeship courses was to be revised in accordance with the advocated reduction in their number. Each trade was to acquire a new profile of knowledge and skills (*Berufsbild*) and all the relevant authorities were to cooperate in the reorganization involved. The overriding aim was flexibility and in support of this a new wage structure was introduced, replacing the former rigid categories and scales by incentives, payable in accordance with productivity.[17]

[16] Ibid., p. 87.   [17] Ibid., p. 89.

The conflict between the policies, firstly of linking vocational education very closely to practical production work in a
specific capacity, and secondly of raising the theoretical content
of the courses, came into prominence in the context of the
introduction of compulsory ten-year schooling. The two additional years would obviously provide the opportunity to
extend theoretical knowledge as was constantly being demanded. Yet at the same time there was a good deal of pressure
to retain a strongly vocational element at this stage. In polytechnical instruction which was intended to relate theory to
practice, surveys showed that it was the practical aspects which
made the most impact on young people:

In these constantly repeated expressions of opinion the need of
young people for genuine productive work is expressed. In this
context the pupils estimated that they had not conceived of their
polytechnical instruction in the slightest as serious activity but more
as a game and a way of being kept occupied. From this they deduced
that the teacher-pupil relationship had not the same clear demanding
character as their present relationship of foreman-apprentice.[18]

The strong urge to acquire a specific qualification as soon as
possible was clearly the overriding consideration for the
majority of young people from the age of fifteen onwards and
it would be surprising indeed if this view had not been largely
echoed by the production workers with whom they came into
contact in the course of their induction into industrial or
agricultural life. Thus as the introduction of the ninth and
tenth compulsory school years began to take effect there were
strong forces pushing the polytechnical education of the period
in the direction of very specific vocational training.

The uncertainty can be described as the tension between the
'tendency towards the general' and the 'tendency towards the
specialized, the concrete and towards productive work'. It
illustrates the continuing problems of interpreting polytechnical education. At this point, however, it was becoming

[18] Ibid., p. 171.

clear that the intention was to solve the problem by a more directly vocational interpretation of the task:

However useful and significant on the one hand the tendency towards the general and instructional in polytechnical education, it would on the other be questionable to the same degree to orient oneself purely to this side. A general polytechnical education does not yet enable the school leaver to take part directly in the production process. Also the work in *modern* production demands alongside general polytechnical education a specialised training, directed towards a specific job. In the framework of general polytechnical education it is also difficult to organise genuine obligatory productive work for pupils. And polytechnical education oriented towards the general will also not be sufficient to direct the inclinations and interests of our pupils towards specific economically important professions and jobs in production. In this respect one only needs to look at how slight the influence of our school is in general on the vocational wishes of children in rural districts. For these reasons the demand is raised by various practising teachers to relate polytechnical education more strongly and more decisively to the concrete and specific conditions of production that obtain on the spot, to make polytechnical education more specific. We regard this demand as worthy of consideration and the tendency towards the concrete and specialised as just as right and necessary as the tendency towards the general. The task will be to realise both sides.[19]

This thinking strongly affected the interpretation of the *Unterrichtstag in der Produktion*. It had been established that the conduct of this hitherto had caused the actual time devoted to work by the pupils to be reduced to a minimum. This had a deleterious effect on recruitment to apprenticeships, especially in rural areas. It was for example discovered that in one district 101 apprentices were required in a particular year for agricultural production but only 40 were forthcoming. Of the 114 children of the local farming families who were of the appropriate age only 19 took up agricultural apprenticeships, so that of the total number, which was itself far from adequate, there was a majority from urban areas.[20] This was regarded as

[19] Ibid., pp. 192–3.   [20] Ibid., p. 193.

a characteristic outcome of the flexible all-embracing nature of polytechnical education, which had not been solely related to local industrial and agricultural patterns, but had sought to give urban children an understanding of agriculture and rural children an understanding of industry. Since it resulted in discrepancies of supply and demand in the labour market, it was unacceptable on economic grounds and indicated a need for tighter organization and increased emphasis on specialization.

The culmination of the move away from the flexible interpretation of polytechnical education came in a joint decision of the *Politbüro* and the Ministerial Council in July 1963. Following this the polytechnical programme was reorganized so that in classes 7 to 10 of the *Oberschule* pupils were to follow a basic apprenticeship course in either industry or agriculture (*Grundlehrgang Industrie* or *Grundlehrgang Landwirtschaft*). In classes 9 and 10 the amount of time spent in production was doubled to two days a week, and for this work pupils were to receive monthly remuneration. The recently introduced 'Introduction to socialist production', which had been intended to provide the general theoretical framework for polytechnical instruction, ceased to exist as a separate entity but became incorporated in a revised form in the *Grundlehrgang*. The courses in industry and agriculture were more closely related to local employment patterns and labour requirements. Consequently vocational guidance began as early as the sixth class and by the time the pupils reached the ninth and tenth classes they were engaged on a specific vocational training.[21]

It was this same document which made provision for the setting up of specialist classes and schools designed to prepare pupils for careers in 'those specialist professions of the leading branches of the economy and of agriculture which are of fundamental significance for the achievement of scientific and

---

[21] Cf. I. Szaniawski, *Organisatorische und didaktische Probleme der allgemeinbildenden Schule in der DDR im Zeitraum 1963–1966. Bildung und Erziehung*, 6/1966, p. 403.

technical progress . . . and demand a specially high degree of mathematical and scientific knowledge'.[22] The specialist schools and classes though attached to *Oberschulen* and *erweiterte Oberschulen* were to be organized separately, where possible on an all-day basis and in some cases with boarding facilities. In accordance with their *raison d'être* they were to have close links with the relevant enterprises. They were to recruit pupils who had shown outstanding ability on the basis of an aptitude test during their sixth school year. The intensified instruction began therefore in the seventh year with a course of 'general technical instruction', which was concerned with imparting an understanding of the foundations of technology and the economy. In the ninth and tenth years the syllabus was expanded to deal specifically with mechanical and electrical engineering and with automation. The vocational orientation of the specialist schools and classes was thus as marked as in the *Oberschulen* or the *erweiterte Oberschulen*.[23]

The danger of the strong vocational emphasis was that it would serve too narrow an interpretation of the needs of production and there were signs that this was being recognized in the period that followed. Major policy statements at this time conveyed a desire to correct the balance and see the fusion of instruction and productive work, as Margot Honecker, Minister of Education, put it, 'not only as a method for the increase of social production but as the only method for the turning out of fully developed people.'[24] The problem was seen as above all one of curriculum and this was to become the major preoccupation in the latter half of the decade.

The framework for further development was established in the new law introduced in 1965 (*Gesetz über das einheitliche sozialistische Bildungssystem*). This confirmed the provision for specialist schools and classes leading to a university entrance qualification, the *Hochschulreife*. The numbers involved were to be limited. In 1964 the idea had been developed to allow the

[22] Baske/Engelbert, op. cit., p. 284.   [23] Ibid., pp. 284–5.
[24] Monumenta Paedagogica, op. cit., Vol. II, p. 516.

direct attachment of the top classes to particular university departments so that instruction could be given by lecturers. Special syllabuses were to be worked out with a declared propaedeutic function in relation to the university. The average class size was to be 15 pupils and in the case of modern languages teaching was to be in groups of 5 to 8. The course was to include a vocational training but the nature of this was not specified.[25] The specialist classes became centres of enthusiastic experiment in methods of giving continuity of school and university education to the highly gifted. The small groups made it possible to include directed private study and seminar work.[26]

Leaving out of account the specialist schools and classes, the educational system acquired in 1965 a structure which can be regarded as the logical conclusion of the process of comprehensive reorganization[27] (Diagram in Appendix VIII). The *erweiterte Oberschule* was reduced from four to two years, so that the *Oberschule* was now to provide a ten-year course for the entire school population apart from the highly gifted and the handicapped. It should also be pointed out, however, that the tidiness of an organization whereby all but a very few followed the same curriculum for ten years was somewhat impaired in practice. Provision had still to be made for some to leave full-time education after the eighth class and at this point there had also to be preparatory classes for those expected to go on to the *erweiterte Oberschule*. But it was confidently expected that these deviations from the general pattern would soon be overcome and that the objective as embodied in the Law would be achieved. The key to the problems, in particular the relationship of the *Oberschule* to the *erweiterte Oberschule* and to the special schools, lay in the matter of curriculum. The Law gave a general indication of how, pedagogically speaking, the

[25] Baske/Engelbert, op. cit., p. 359.

[26] See for example M. Helm, *Spezialklassen—ein Beitrag zur Begabtenförderung. Hochschulwesen*, 3/1965, pp. 173–8.

[27] Cf. O. Anweiler, *Strukturprobleme des allgemeinbildenden Schulwesens in der DDR. Bildung und Erziehung*, 4/1970, p. 265.

Oberschule was to be organized. But this was only a starting-point for a major attempt to tackle the problems of the curriculum. From the early 1950s the authorities had been talking about curriculum planning. Brave statements of aims were generally followed by recriminations when the planners went astray in the labyrinthine byways of polytechnical education. Only from the middle 1950s onwards was there an obvious systematic plan carried through without debilitating interruption.

Social Issues

The 1959 Law had embodied a reaffirmation of the social objectives of educational policy in the *DDR*, namely the removal of the educational privilege which it was alleged still existed in the Federal Republic. The total absence of differentiation in the new ten-year *Oberschule* was intended to ensure that equal opportunities were available to all. Though the former *Oberschule* now renamed *erweiterte Oberschule*, continued to recruit its pupils after their eighth year of school, the whole tone of the Law placed the emphasis on the ten-class institution beside which the *erweiterte Oberschule* was to decline in importance. The declaration that the main route to higher education was to be via the ten-class school and vocational education, made it plain that there was no longer to be any justification for the survival within the system of a sector geared exclusively to university entrance. This was emphasized by the requirement that all *erweiterte Oberschule* leavers must spend a year in productive work before entering university.

Even before 1960 it had been possible to claim that some 50 per cent or so of university students in the *DDR* originated from the industrial or agricultural working class as compared with between 5 and 7 per cent in the Federal Republic.[28] This was to a considerable extent the direct result of the policies

[28] Günther/Uhlig, op. cit., p. 141.

pursued in the East in the 1950s. Some of these, in particular the reform of the rural schools, had been constructive measures designed solely to spread educational opportunity to sectors of the community which had not previously enjoyed it. Others had involved active discrimination against the middle class in the matter of entry to the *Oberschule*. Also, the high proportion of university students drawn from the working class was in part a consequence of the exodus to the West of large numbers of the middle class, whether to escape this discrimination or on grounds of more general disaffection.[29] In turn this influx into the Federal Republic helped to increase the middle-class proportion of the university intake there.

Nonetheless the West fared badly in any comparison of provision of equal opportunity as the sociological research gradually revealed. The discrepancy, particularly in the matter of rural schools, illustrates once again the difference in ideological starting-points. In the *DDR* the Marxist objectives, both in their social and economic aspects, demanded a rationalization of the system of the kind that was largely effected during the early 1950s. The educational system was restructured with the aim of changing the social order. In the West, on the other hand, there was no consensus among the general public that education was an area of particularly severe underprivilege and no strong feeling that changes in the system were needed in order to facilitate the process of social reform. With no pressure forthcoming from the general public no overwhelming need was felt for political action.

In this apathetic atmosphere it became the role of those engaged in sociological research to indicate the precise extent of the underprivilege. At the beginning of the decade the prejudice against sociology had been particularly strong. Not only were there misgivings about the use of quantitative techniques in a field that was traditionally considered to

[29] Cf. K.-D. Mende, *Schulreform und Gesellschaft in der DDR 1945–1965*. In S. B. Robinsohn, *Schulreform im gesellschaftlichen Prozeß I*, Stuttgart, 1970, p. 2/70.

concern matters of value, but there was also a tendency to equate the discipline with Marxism and therefore to see in it a threat to the established order. By the mid-1960s, however, the effects of the sociological findings were beginning to make some impact on the general public and thereby to create the possibility that a demand for greater equality of opportunity would arise. But the forces working against a radical reorganization of the system on social grounds remained strong, not least because of the lack of incentive to compete with the *DDR* on this score. If comparisons were made they were more likely to confirm the aversion to democratization on ideological grounds.

One of the earliest starting-points for what could be called the sociological campaign was provided by an examination of the effects which the federal structure had on the provision of schooling. A comparative study of school attendance in the different *Länder* published in 1962 revealed large discrepancies between them. For example in the Saar only 19 per cent of 16-year-olds were in full-time education of any kind whereas the corresponding figure for Schleswig-Holstein was 39 per cent. In the same two *Länder* the proportions obtaining an intermediate leaving certificate were 4 and 24 per cent respectively. In Hesse proportionately twice as many boys obtained the *Abitur* as in Rhineland-Palatinate, in West Berlin twice as many girls did so as in Hamburg.[30] To establish the reasons further research was required since they were clearly many and complex. The authors were convinced that they were for the most part unrelated to innate ability. If this was so, then the principle of equal opportunity for all could not be said to be operating effectively. This proposition was the starting-point for widespread investigations into the precise extent of educational provision and for analysis of those factors as a result of which certain groups in society were at a particular disadvantage where education was concerned.

[30] R. von Carnap/F. Edding, *Der relative Schulbesuch in den Ländern der Bundesrepublik 1952–1960*. Frankfurt/M., 1962, p. 15.

An obvious indication of the pattern of opportunity was given by the numbers passing the *Abitur*, calculated as a percentage of the total age group. This technique had been used in establishing the differences between *Länder*. Another leading study went further, examining similar data at a more local level and finding striking differences between specific districts.[31] It was convenient to use *Abitur* results, since statistics were readily available, but they were a somewhat crude yardstick. The *Abitur* was particularly geared to the propaedeutic requirements of traditional university courses, while for careers outside the professions the upper forms of the *Gymnasium* did not necessarily provide the most appropriate preparation. In view of the large numbers of pupils that left prematurely, success in the *Abitur* could not strictly speaking be regarded as a measure of opportunity. The more sophisticated methods used by Hansgert Peisert provide a good illustration of the maturing of the techniques of measurement. His concept of 'concentration of educational provision' (*Bildungsdichte*) was based on the numbers of young people in the 15–19 age group in full-time education, that is to say from school leaving to *Abitur* age. These were analysed, taking in succession as the unit for comparison the various levels of local administration: *Land, Regierungsbezirk, Kreis* and *Gemeinde*. To work down to the level of *Gemeinde* was a laborious as well as a novel procedure since official figures, as for example in the 1961 census, were generally quoted only for the *Kreis*. This painstaking differentiation, however, produced the surprising result that in 33 per cent of all such units in the Federal Republic virtually no children stayed in full-time education beyond the school-leaving age and that less than 5 per cent did so in a further 15 per cent.[32]

Such research studies as had been done in the 1950s had explored inequality of opportunity mainly in terms of social

[31] R. Geipel, *Sozialräumliche Strukturen des Bildungswesens*, Frankfurt/M., 1965. See for example pp. 112–13.

[32] H. Peisert, *Soziale Lage und Bildungschancen in Deutschland*, München, 1967, p. 53.

class and by the end of the decade the prevailing interpretation of the data had begun to change. Where previously it had been argued that the social stratification was inevitable and virtually immutable, it now became more common to reject such an assumption and to advocate positive measures to equalize opportunity.[33] In the course of the more sophisticated investigations of the 1960s the disadvantaged groups became more finely differentiated. In addition to the industrial working class it became clear that Catholics, girls and those living in rural areas were particularly affected, and that different factors could be identified in each case. As far as purely physical amenities were concerned the problem was at its most acute in sparsely populated rural areas. A study of a number of these in Baden-Württemberg showed them to be remote from economic and cultural centres, lacking an adequate communications network and below average in resources and wealth. One such area was known locally as 'Siberia' (*Badisch-Sibirien*). The schools in these areas were correspondingly underdeveloped, the great majority of *Volksschulen* having only one or two teachers in all. Understandably this situation tended to be demoralizing for teachers, and appointment to schools of this kind was looked upon as something of a penance. These and other factors were subsumed within a general mentality according to which education beyond the minimum was so remote from everyday experience as to be a virtually meaningless concept.[34]

Many of these communities were predominantly Catholic, and it was sometimes suggested that membership of the Catholic Church was an additional disincentive to educational ambitions. Certainly from various studies of the relationship between confession and education the Catholics emerged as an underprivileged group, underrepresented to the extent of some 10 per cent at *Gymnasien*, and the thesis of a Catholic

---

[33] See for example H. Daheim, *Soziale Herkunft, Schule und Rekrutierung der Berufe. Kölner Zeitschrift für Soziologie und Sozialpsychologie. Sonderheft,* 5/1961, p. 214.   [34] Peisert, op. cit., pp. 137-8, 145-7.

'educational deficit' enjoyed widespread acceptance.[35] To some extent the Church had contributed to this situation. Reorganization of education in rural areas was against its interests since to centralize the *Volksschulen* meant reducing the control of the local clergy and the transfer of more pupils to secondary schools, which were usually non-denominational, would also lead to a reduction in Church influence. Moreover, many of the arguments for reform were of a socio-economic nature and did not enjoy the Church's approval. In the course of the 1960s the Churches increasingly came in for criticism on this score:

For this (the failure to reform the school system) the determined confessionalism which established itself after 1945 is not without blame. However much all the motives of Church and religious bodies for retracing steps and pausing for reflection after the period of National Socialist horror deserve recognition and respect, it must be said that very soon after the end of the war these motives acquired a flavour of worldly struggle for power, intolerance, political calculation and intellectual bondage. Georg Picht remarks in an essay in the *Luthersche Monatshefte*, rightly in my opinion, that the Churches used the post-war vacuum to secure the implementation of their formulae for educational policy, formulae which belong to the distant past. Hence all initiatives towards school reform consistently failed because of the political influence of the Catholic Church and for this reason the Churches could not be absolved of responsibility for the poor conditions existing at that time. For, since they had brought about the confessionalisation of the school system through political pressure, they now had to answer for its consequences.[36]

This attack was by Hildegard Hamm-Brücher, a leading spokesman on education for the *FDP*. At this time it was in particular by virtue of the efforts of this Party that the findings of educational research began to influence political thinking.

[35] Cf. K. Erlinghagen, *Katholisches Bildungsdefizit in Deutschland*, Freiburg, 1965, pp. 98–9.

[36] H. Hamm-Brücher, *Bildungspolitik—die Feuerprobe des modernen Liberalismus. XV Ordentlicher Bundesparteitag der Freien Demokraten*, Duisburg, 2.6.1964, p. 13.

An issue of statistically similar proportions to those revealed in the Catholic *Bildungsdefizit*, emerged in the case of girls, who as a category between 1950 and 1964 made up only 40 per cent of the total number of entrants to the *Gymnasium*, some 9 per cent below their representation in the relevant age group. As the cohorts proceeded through school the proportion of girls dropped to 36 per cent at *Abitur* level.[37] Within these global figures variations were revealed between the individual *Länder*. Exploration of the reasons again uncovered a complex of factors among which social origin appeared particularly significant. One survey of eight *Gymnasien* in medium-sized towns showed that out of a total of 1,723 pupils there were only 37 girls from working-class families. Elsewhere, where the initial entry was higher for such girls, this was offset by a high rate of early leaving, so that as the cohorts passed through the school the proportion of middle-class girls grew significantly, while it fell to a similar degree for those who came from the working class.[38]

The social class issue was in fact the one which continued to attract by far the greatest attention. This was particularly so in the urban areas where in contrast to the rural regions communications were adequate and *Volksschulen* were generally fully developed and staffed so that educational underprivilege could not so easily be attributed to lack of facilities. The working class in the Federal Republic was estimated as comprising 56·6 per cent of the population, but in the early 1960s the proportion of *Gymnasium* pupils who were of working-class origin was much smaller—16 per cent for classes 5-7, 10 per cent for class 10, 6·4 per cent for class 13.[39] In surveys of Berlin, Hamburg and Bremen, the areas of very low *Bildungsdichte* coincided for the most part with working-class districts.

---

[37] Peisert, op. cit., p. 101.
[38] H. Peisert/R. Dahrendorf, *Der vorzeitige Abgang vom Gymnasium. Schriftenreihe des Kultusministeriums Baden-Württemberg A1*, 1966, pp. 138-9.
[39] Assembled from composite sources by C. Kuhlmann, *Schulreform und Gesellschaft in der BRD 1946-1966*. In Robinsohn, op. cit., p. 1/74.

Furthermore in these districts there was a marked lack of *Gymnasien* since they tended to be concentrated in the middle-class residential areas. South of the 'Hamburg equator' for example, in the half of the city which is predominantly inhabited by the working class, there were only half as many *Gymnasien* per head of the population as in the more prosperous Northern half. A similar pattern was revealed in West Berlin and Bremen where again the majority of *Gymnasien* were sited in middle-class areas.[40] As in the case of other groups already discussed it seemed clear that the reasons for the *Bildungsabstinenz* were varied and that it could not simply be explained by lack of the required ability.

Though the research just alluded to took place largely in the early 1960s it was not till the middle of the decade that it began to be published in a form which brought it to the attention of the public at large and thereby provided fuel for a political campaign. In this respect a significant role was played by Ralf Dahrendorf, who founded the case for expansion of the educational system on the need for social justice. In particular his book, *Bildung ist Bürgerrecht*, coming a year after Picht's striking publication, consolidated the new topicality of education as a major preoccupation of national social and economic policy.[41]

Economic Issues

The empirical studies carried out in the West suggested not merely that opportunity was very unevenly distributed, but that this should be interpreted as a waste of human resources. It has already been noted how in the later 1950s there was a certain anxiety about the contribution of the educational system to the economy in terms of qualified manpower. To some extent the growth of this anxiety was held in check in the

[40] Peisert, op. cit., pp. 70–2.
[41] R. Dahrendorf, *Bildung ist Bürgerrecht*, Hamburg, 1965.

early 1960s. Where particular shortages appeared, as for example in the engineering industry, the result had been pressure to expand the sector concerned, in this case the *Realschulen* and *Ingerieurschulen*. But as piecemeal expansion of this nature increased without being subject to any overall regulation, it placed growing stress on the system as a whole, and it was in revealing the extent of this stress that the survey of needs for the period 1961–70, issued by the *Kultusministerkonferenz*, was significant.

The general public, it will be recalled, was given a vivid impression of the gravity of the situation by the publication of *Die Deutsche Bildungskatastrophe* in 1964. Though this was critical of educational policy on the social grounds of denial of opportunity to various sectors of the community already discussed, its fundamental theme was the threat to the economy. The key point of the entire argument was the relationship between economic development and the growth of the educational system. This was a proposition that had underlain educational policy in the *DDR* ever since its foundation. Ulbricht had repeatedly stressed the economic functions the schools were expected to fulfil in terms of output of manpower of the kind appropriate for industry and agriculture in an age of technology. It was the overriding motive behind the adoption of polytechnical education as the new element which was intended to revolutionize the nature of the qualifications of the labour force. In the Federal Republic, on the other hand, little had been made of the economic functions of the educational system on this kind of global scale. This had not been necessary. The pattern as it had been restored in the immediate post-war period had proved itself in practice by virtue of its contribution to the economic success of the 1950s, and the notion that an active policy of reorganization was required in order to extract more in the way of qualified manpower was not entertained to any substantial degree.

Picht's case was that satisfaction with the present had diverted attention from the need to plan for the future and that as a result a state of crisis was imminent. The shortage at the more highly qualified levels was in his view about to become acute. The partial vacuum created by the wartime losses had been filled, firstly by an older generation among whom active service had not taken such a great toll, secondly by a stream of refugees from the *DDR* and other Eastern territories. The first of these sources was drying up since most of the generation in question had reached the age of retirement, the second had been cut off by the erection of the Berlin Wall in 1961. Until the early 1960s therefore no very acute shortage of well-qualified manpower had been felt and in this situation the lack of any large-scale policy initiatives is hardly surprising. By the same token the *DDR* which was losing large numbers of its population, many of them well qualified or potentially so, was forced by circumstances to lay immense stress on increased output from the schools.

Though Picht himself did not draw comparisons with the *DDR*, his catalogue of omissions can be quoted to underline the contrasts in policy between the two States at this time. Yet again the neglect of rural areas was made clear in a forceful exposé which pointed out that, far from decreasing, the number of one-class schools in the Federal Republic had doubled in the post-war period. Moreover there appeared to be widespread acceptance of this situation and failure to recognize that it conveyed a conception of educational provision that was totally inappropriate for a modern economy:

Anyone who regards it as self-evident that this form of school, originating in the pre-industrial age, is no longer considered acceptable in the twentieth century has been misled. It finds passionate advocates who love to sketch a homely still-life of the fatherly figure of the village schoolmaster with children crowding round him like a family. In fact it requires little imagination to picture to oneself what a lesson must look like in which a teacher can no longer achieve the minimum of what every agricultural worker, industrial worker and craftsman needs in the way of education. The introduction of modern language instruction or preparation for transfer to higher stages of education is in these rural schools quite out of the question.[42]

By contrast the reform of rural education had been almost completed by the mid-1950s in the *DDR* and it was a constant element in policy to encourage rural children to pursue their education beyond the minimum.[43]

There were other contrasts. The period of compulsory education in the *DDR* was being raised to ten years while in the West it remained at eight or at most nine. There was also the structural question. Access to university in the Federal Republic was still almost exclusively via the *Gymnasium*, which had to all intents and purposes a monopoly of the *Abitur* which conferred the right of entry. While the *zweiter Bildungsweg* did exist it was intensely demanding and very rarely were alternative criteria to those of the traditional academic nature accepted. By contrast the 1959 Law in the *DDR* if anything overdid the attempt to correct any such imbalance through the insistence that the normal route to university was via vocational training and employment. Picht argued that the situation in the Federal Republic required urgent measures to raise the numbers of those obtaining the *Abitur*. His suggestion that in order to do so the best strategy would be to bypass the *Gymnasium* and develop the *zweiter Bildungsweg* is particularly interesting in view of the established policy for access to university in the *DDR*.

The picture that emerged from Picht's publication and the debate that followed it was of a critical situation that had resulted from fifteen years of relative passivity in educational policy. There seems little doubt that this lack of political will had largely resulted from the economic prosperity of the period and that a willingness on the part of the general public to alter priorities was a prerequisite for political action. In the *Bundestag* debate which was held in the wake of the controversy which Picht had stirred up, Franz-Josef Strauss, the *CSU* leader, gave an exposé of the demands on government finance and summed

---

[42] Picht, op. cit., p. 36.   [43] Günther/Uhlig, op. cit., p. 84.

up in striking terms the root cause of the disregard for educational planning and policy:

Finally I believe that federal government and *Land* governments and all responsible bodies . . . should enlighten the population on the relationship between restraint in consumption today and provision for one's existence tomorrow. Whoever desires and promises everything today must necessarily jeopardise the foundations of the life of the next generation. . . . We must at last have the courage . . . to acknowledge in political practice that restraint in consumer spending today is the necessary sacrifice for the achievement of the objectives of tomorrow.[44]

In the *DDR* where economic recovery had been a more difficult task than in the Federal Republic it had been considered necessary to place much greater emphasis on planning the educational system in accordance with the future requirements of industry and agriculture than to meet the demand for consumer goods. At the same time it would appear that the proportion of the national income devoted to education was higher than in the Federal Republic.[45]

The proposition that was widely put forward in the West as a result of the controversy sparked off by Picht, namely that there was a close relationship between the success of the economy in terms of productivity and the output of the educational system in terms of qualified manpower, was one that had always been a basic assumption of *DDR* policy, as the following statement by Margot Honecker makes clear:

Never before has our work, education, had such significance. When we study thoroughly the documents and decisions of our Party we perceive that they are all impregnated with the fundamental idea that there is a close link between the economy and education. A

[44] *Deutscher Bundestag. 4. Wahlperiode. 118 Sitzung. Stenographische Berichte 1964*, p. 5476.

[45] Expenditure as proportion of national income *DDR*—1954: 6·0 per cent; 1960: 6·0; 1961: 6·0; 1962: 6·0. Federal Republic—1957: 3·5 per cent; 1960: 3·5; 1961: 3·5; 1962: 3·7. UNESCO Statistical Yearbook 1964, p. 319.

high level of education is one of the determinants of the pace of our progress.[46]

Moreover at the time when this controversy was at its height in the Federal Republic it was being made clear in the *DDR* to what extent long-term planning was considered essential:

The requirement to apply to an increasing degree scientific criteria to our work, to the planning, direction and orientation of our social development corresponds to the objective lawfulness of socialism. Socialism cannot be built up other than through conscious systematic use and application of the economic laws of socialism and of the development of the economy and society corresponding to the highest level of science and technology. The demand for scientific leadership, planning and direction applies not only to the economy but also to the education of the younger generation.[47]

It was above all in the context of this commitment to scientific planning that the implications of the interdependence of education and economic development were explored.

Though the comparison between the two States seems in retrospect very striking, with a few exceptions[48] very little was made of it in the Federal Republic at the time, whether due to ignorance of developments in the East or reluctance to evaluate them positively. The yardstick for the measurement of achievement in the West was much more the other countries of Western Europe. Particularly telling was the comparison with France where educational planning had been adopted and where forecasts suggested that the number of those obtaining the *baccalauréat* would by 1970 treble the number of those obtaining the *Abitur* in the Federal Republic. It was on this basis that the fear arose that in comparison to France German living standards would drop through the failure to train sufficient people to a sufficient extent to guarantee the maintenance of a competitive position in Europe:

[46] Monumenta Paedagogica, op. cit., p. 514.
[47] Ibid., pp. 514–15.
[48] E.g. *Bildungsnotstand in Ost und West. Ein Interview mit Dr Ulrich Lohmar (MdB) SOPADE Rednerdienst*, 2.3.64.

M

The number of *Abiturienten* is a gauge of the intellectual potential of a nation and in the modern world the competitiveness of the economy, the level of the national product and the political position are dependent on the intellectual potential. For the remainder of the twentieth century the balance of influence in Europe will be determined by the fact that, despite a smaller population, France will for an indefinite period of years produce almost three times as many *Abiturienten* as the Federal Republic; at the same time no one can maintain that the standard in French schools is lower than in German ones. The French sociologist Alfred Sauvy bases on this the convincing forecast that France will be the centre of Europe in 1970. On the other hand the Federal Republic will in the near future on account of the backwardness of its educational system only be able to play a subordinate role both economically and politically.[49]

The outcome of the controversy was fairly general agreement as to the seriousness and urgency of the problems. Though it proved possible to find flaws in Picht's calculations regarding the future shortage of teachers, and though some of his assumptions about French education were somewhat dubious, he had indicated accurately a series of omissions in previous policy that could not easily be denied.

Expansion therefore became a dominant theme of policy declarations, presented less as a reparation for past shortcomings than as an expression of the desire to fall into line with developments in the rest of Western Europe at a time when 'increasing European integration and the needs of modern industrial society common to all States give with fresh vigour renewed impulse to the further development of school and university policy' as the statement issued after the 100th session of the *Kultusministerkonferenz* put it.[50] This statement which recognized and endorsed the expansionist tendencies in evidence throughout Europe was significant evidence of the transformation in attitudes to educational policy in the Federal Republic in the mid-1960s. From being a subject which had

[49] Picht, op. cit., p. 26.
[50] *Kultusministerkonferenz, Pressemitteilung aus Anlaß der 100. Plenarsitzung vom 5/6 März 1964 in Berlin*, p. 3.

evoked very little interest, guaranteed to empty the *Bundestag* when debated, it became an issue of burning topicality.

Roads to Expansion

This consensus that the piecemeal expansion which had taken place during the 1950s had been inadequate and that positive steps needed to be taken to reshape the system in ways that would stimulate a higher output of *Abiturienten* in particular, resulted in a similarity between the policy objectives of the two States that had not been in evidence before. Previously, both had been strongly influenced by economic factors but with quite different implications for the educational system. In the West the success of the economic recovery had argued for a policy of non-intervention allowing piecemeal development in unrelated areas but basically reflecting satisfaction with the *status quo*. In the East there had been from the start a deliberate strategy of change, not least for the reason that the health of the economy appeared to depend on it.

This growing similarity in terms of aims underlines the contrast in the legislative and administrative patterns that characterized the conduct of policy. It was again Picht who made it clear that the cultural federalism whereby all responsibility for educational policy was invested in the *Land* governments was becoming increasingly inappropriate in the face of modern problems. While he accepted that legislation and administration might legitimately be left in the hands of the *Land*, he pointed out that planning and finance could be adequately dealt with only on a national basis. It was not sufficient for individual *Länder* to plan for their own needs unrelated to those of their neighbours but they had a communal obligation to meet the needs of the Federal Republic as a whole. The *Kultusministerkonferenz* was alleged to have shown itself unwilling to cooperate with the Federal government in order to create jointly a 'third level' of responsibility, but rather to have been set up 'as though it were, so to speak, the private club of local rulers who feel the need to meet for discussions from time to time without any obligation to act on them'.[51]

Another point to be reinforced as a result of the controversy was the lack of involvement on the part of politicians in educational affairs. Some attention had been drawn to this in the later 1950s, above all the fact that education seldom featured in election manifestoes—'educational issues are usually dismissed one year before the election even by the parties that first took them up'.[52] The fact that what debates on the subject did take place in the *Bundestag* were generally sparsely attended was now in 1964 seen as evidence of failure on the part of the federal government to realize that educational development was an essential element in the social and economic policy of the entire country. Here again the comparison had been made with France, where a particularly vigorous interest was being shown in educational policy, and where the major debate in November 1963 had been conducted in a packed Assembly. The contrast with the *DDR* can be seen to be equally striking since education was consistently one of the major preoccupations of the Central Committee of the *SED*.

The high attendance at the *Bundestag* debate which followed soon after the publication of Picht's articles indicated a change in this respect and already the time was ripe for steps to be taken to create some sort of machinery for planning on a national scale. Centralization was virtually out of the question for, however good a case could be made out for it on grounds of rationalization of policies, it was extremely unlikely that such a profound change would command sufficient support. If the Federal Republic was to find a way of planning on a national level it had to be one which involved coordination and eschewed *dirigisme*. This presented a much more complex problem than in the *DDR*, where 'democratic centralism' invested the power

[51] Picht, op. cit., p. 403.
[52] Hellmut Becker, *Unsere Gesellschaft bedarf einer anderen Bildung. Das Parlament*, 3/1958, p. 5.

of decision in the central authority and the administrative structure enabled measures to be implemented within a reasonably short time. However, the events of the 1950s had shown that this was not always an advantage and that as a result of the close liaison between politicians and administrators, policy decisions could be pushed through prematurely without adequate awareness of reaction among the public at large. Though whatever emerged in the West would necessarily be more cumbersome it was possible that in the long term it would be more dynamic if it succeeded in turning local interest and initiative to good account.

It can fairly be said that as regards the implications of their differing legislative and administrative structures the contrast between the two States reached its peak in the early 1960s. The controversy which raged during 1964 in the Federal Republic revealed that the preconditions for a planned national policy had not been met. The *DDR* had on the other hand subscribed to planning ever since its creation, and the entire development of policy had been seen as closely related to the series of Economic Plans. By this token it had achieved a great deal in terms of reorganization whereas this had been considered unnecessary in the Federal Republic. But a close examination of the policies followed in the early years of the decade shows that there was less clarity in the *DDR* about long-term objectives than might be supposed. While the contrast was great between the degree to which the necessary conditions had been created in which a planned long-term policy could be adopted, the contrast in actual achievement was not nearly so great.

The introduction of polytechnical education combined with the extension by two years of the school-leaving age had been based on a combination of ideological, social and economic reasoning. The central intention had been to raise the general standard throughout the labour force, producing trained workers who were not shackled to their individual specialist qualifications but had a sufficient foundation of broad general education to enable them to acquire further qualifications as a matter of course. This was seen as an advance on the traditional pattern, surviving in the West, whereby the vocational sector was in the main geared to narrowly based apprenticeships, entered upon after only eight or in some cases nine years of full-time education. But the early attempts to put polytechnical education into practice in the general sense in which it had been conceived gave way in 1963 to a much stronger emphasis on the immediate raising of productivity and the filling of specific gaps in the supply of labour, and in consequence on vocational guidance, which began as early as the sixth class, and vocational training and practical work in production, which began in the eighth.[53] Thus the organization of the vocational training and work experience of the pupils was made very much dependent on the direct needs of the branch of industry or agriculture with which they were brought into contact. This kind of 'professionalization' had precisely those faults which had always been associated with the traditional system, namely that the pattern of training was more in accordance with the immediate needs of specific industries than with long-term considerations or the good of the individuals concerned.

The introduction of this vocational bias running throughout the system was not the kind of measure likely to achieve the aims formulated in 1960, namely to lay the foundations for the acquisition by increasing numbers of workers of higher qualifications demanding a higher general level of theoretical knowledge. In that it revealed a somewhat shortsighted conception of manpower needs, it showed that in the *DDR* full advantage was not being taken of the new framework that had been created. It was not until the strong narrowly vocational emphasis began to recede, particularly in the context of the 1965 Law, that the era of long-term planning for a high output of qualified manpower really began. Thus though it was perhaps less obvious at the time, there was a good deal of

[53] Szaniawski, op. cit., p. 403.

uncertainty about the direction of policy in the early 1960s in the *DDR* as well as in the Federal Republic.

There was however one important difference between the two paths to all-out effort for expansion at the more highly qualified levels. In Picht's indictment perhaps the most telling statistic had been that in order to provide enough teachers it would be necessary for almost all those currently taking the *Abitur* to enter the profession. From this it was deduced that there was a chronic shortage of *Abiturienten* and it was the doubling of their supply that became the watchword of the advocates of reform. The *Abitur* however had remained very strongly academic in character with a linguistic and literary bias, appropriate above all as a propaedeutic training for those intending to enter the academic professions. Whether a policy of expansion of output in this same mould was really the 'blanket' answer to manpower requirements in the economy as a whole, was open to question. Picht certainly did raise the issue of the *zweiter Bildungsweg* and suggest that steps should be taken to end the monopoly of university entrance enjoyed by the *Gymnasium*, and to introduce greater variety into teacher training. But subsequent apostles of expansion, especially Dahrendorf, succeeded in making the quota of *Abiturienten* educated in the orthodox way following the traditional academic curriculum the central issue. This reasoning was based largely on the social grounds of the citizen's right to education but it had little to do with a realistic appraisal of the requirements of the economy.

In the *DDR*, on the other hand, much of the uncertainty of the corresponding period resulted from the problems arising out of the attempt to change the fundamental character of the education leading up to the *Abitur* so that it would correspond to what the economy required. Professionalization was in part at least a reaction against the problems of introducing polytechnical education experienced at the beginning of the decade. What was being attempted however was to break down the barrier between traditional 'general' education and vocational training and in view of the fact that the curriculum had long been dominated by the former, a tendency towards over-compensation in the latter direction was perhaps understandable. Furthermore, the proposed rationalization of the structure of trade qualifications was not as yet completed so that there were still rather more trades in the *DDR* than in the Federal Republic.[54]

When by 1965 the balance had been corrected somewhat, and greater harmony appeared to have been achieved between school organization and curriculum on the one hand, and the estimated long-term requirements of the economy on the other, it is noticeable that the former abhorrence of early differentiation on the basis of academic ability had been abandoned, and that the introduction of specialist classes and schools was consolidated. While this shows a recognition of the fact that total mixed-ability grouping is unlikely to do justice to the specific needs of the very highly gifted, it cannot be equated with the selective structure of the West German system at this time. The latter was geared very much to the requirements of university and the traditional academic professions and in this respect corresponded very closely with the social structure. In the *DDR* while the specialist schools were clearly designed to lead to the *Abitur* and university it should be borne in mind that the structure of university courses was undergoing a change at this time in an attempt to give a different character to them, relating them to specific vocations within a socialist economy. It was therefore claimed that in this respect the academic path they opened up was a new one based solely on the needs of industry or agriculture and for which, incidentally, the charge of perpetuating hereditary class privilege could not arise.

The events of 1965 mark a turning-point after which pertinent comparisons can begin to be made. The 1965 Law in

---

[54] A large reduction in the number of trades in the DDR took place between 1957 when there were 972 and 1964 when there were 658. In the Federal Republic there were 648 in 1960 and 620 in 1965. A. Hegelheimer, *Berufsbildung im Wandel*, Berlin, 1971 (manuscript), p. 3.

the *DDR* fixed the pattern of educational development for the foreseeable future, a pattern very much determined by the findings of the research carried on in the context of long-term planning. In the Federal Republic the creation of the *Bildungsrat*, largely in response to the controversy initiated by Picht, represented a major initiative towards the working out of an overall national policy, again concerned with the long-term perspective.

CHAPTER 6

Planning and its Implications: 1965–70

Approaches to Educational Planning

In the early 1960s the contrast between the approach to educational policy in the two States has been shown to have reached a peak. In the *DDR* the importance of planning had acquired a fresh validity as a result of the more sophisticated methods in research and the increased precision of the information that was quarried. The 1965 Law was formulated in the context of a growing drive to integrate the educational system into a 'comprehensive social system' characterized above all by the harnessing of the scientific and technological revolution to the task of providing for the material needs of society. This implied in practice that the foremost task of the educational system was to provide the necessary manpower for the application of science and the mastering of technological problems. A study of the stage of development reached by 1970 shows how the entire educational system gradually became geared to the output of this kind of manpower.

In the Federal Republic the furore over the alleged inability to meet manpower requirements resulted in successive steps in the direction of central planning through the formation of the *Bildungsrat*. This development can be compared to that which had been taking place for some time in the *DDR* in that it was a response to similar pressures, above all the suggestion that the latent reserves of ability were not being exploited successfully and that as a result economic competitiveness would decline.

In the West the economic argument was coupled more and more with the social one that a long legacy of deprivation of opportunity had to be overcome and that only by so doing would the hitherto unrecognized fund of ability be revealed and made available for use. The same link between the social and economic arguments had been in evidence in the *DDR* in the 1950s but by the later 1960s the emphasis on compensation for social deprivation had receded, whereas the success of the New Economic Policy introduced in 1963 was the paramount objective.

In the *DDR* there was thus a reduction in relevance of the social class issue. From the mid-1960s on it would appear that officially it was considered that the old middle-class monopoly of education had been broken and that a genuine equality of opportunity now prevailed:

With the victory of socialist conditions for production the working class, in alliance with agricultural workers and all others in employment, have created under the leadership of the *SED* the bases for the victory of socialism. . . . All citizens regardless of their outlook, religion, race, nationality or social position enjoy the same rights. The educational privilege of the exploiting classes is broken. As once dreamed of and called for by the best humanist thinkers of the German people, the access to science, culture and technology is open to all. Anyone may develop his abilities in educational institutions or in direct social activity. Thus in the first German *Arbeiter-und Bauernstaat* the new community has grown. The fundamental principle applies: Everything with the people, everything by the people, everything for the people.[1]

Consequently the whole emphasis was now laid on extracting from each individual the maximum contribution to the achievement of economic objectives. From this it followed that two common strands ran through all education, firstly the acquisition of knowledge and skills which could be applied in order to make a direct contribution to the total system, and

[1] *Dokumente zur Geschichte des Schulwesens* . . ., Monumenta Paedagogica VII/2, Berlin, 1969, p. 527.

secondly the development of the commitment to this system. The criterion was usefulness to the State as it was planned to take shape on the basis of socialist principles.

In the Federal Republic, while it is true that the advent of planning reflected a new awareness of the degree to which educational issues overlap with social and economic ones, it was impossible for it to be adopted in the same comprehensive sense as in the *DDR*. It was constitutionally impossible to impose one system on the entire country and despite the growing interest in comprehensive school systems in the political parties, the pace of actual development was slow. It was therefore necessary to find a framework for planning which allowed the individual sectors within the system to adjust to new requirements at their own pace. In approaching the problem via the qualifications structure, the *Bildungsrat* found a way of reconciling conflicting interests without attempting to initiate a reorganization that might prove to be unviable on account of its controversial nature. The notion of an *Abitur I* as a qualification giving admission to an academic course leading to *Abitur II*, equally valid whether acquired in a *Gymnasium*, *Realschule* or *Hauptschule* could potentially provide a guarantee that the chance of an academic education would no longer be denied to those not initially admitted to selective schools. At the same time the *Gymnasium* and the *Realschule*, both extremely proud of their independent identity, could continue to strive for the highest standards they could achieve. The realization of the plan depended on whether sufficient teachers could be found to ensure that it was possible to offer the full *Abitur I* curriculum in all *Hauptschulen*. This was a more formidable problem, but, in view of the overcrowding in all sectors of the system, not one that reorganization along comprehensive lines would have eased.

In essence therefore the planning in the Federal Republic was such as to promote greater opportunity and expansion, but at the same time to leave relatively unscathed individual sectors of the system. Moreover, there was no attempt to change the ideals of such sectors. It could well be, for example, that the aims of the *Gymnasium* could not be reconciled with the economic demands in terms of manpower. If the overriding criterion had been the requirements of the scientific and technological revolution, then almost certainly its curriculum would have had to be adapted. But the fact that little attempt was made to transform the basis of the *Gymnasium* curriculum indicates that it was accepted that the individualistic ideal of self-fulfilment, which had characterized this sector since Humboldt's time, continued to be respected regardless of any pressures deriving from the needs of the economy. In other words it was accepted that the interests of the individual did not necessarily coincide with those of a preconceived notion of the State, and that the development of the latter should in some areas at least be ultimately secondary to the former.

In the *DDR* the reverse was the case. The whole educational system had been reshaped in order to transform the traditional culture into one which was exclusively directed towards the mastery of 'the socialist future'. This educational process therefore meant guiding the individual along paths which would enable him to contribute to this future—as Ulbricht put it:

Our educational institutions today make an essential contribution to the task of training highly qualified specialists and confirmed socialist citizens, and of making it possible for them to fight actively for the victory of socialism and for peace. That however sets all forces in society the task of preparing children and young people today in such a way that they are able and prepared to master the socialist future creatively. . . . The scientific and technological achievements of our Republic, the shaping of the socialist perspective of our social order depend essentially on the quality of knowledge and skill and on the attitude to social class matters which young people acquire today in the various stages of the educational system.[2]

[2] Ibid., p. 729.

Such was the nature of the pursuit of the 'socialist-humanist educational ideal', which was commonly contrasted with the traditional 'classical-humanist' ideal.

Thus, though to some extent the pressures affecting educational policy in the two States were the recognizable ones that derived from the development of industrial society, there remained nonetheless a basic difference in the idealism which invested its aims. Despite the fact that it might not be fully reconcilable with a society dominated by the requirements of optimal technological development, the traditional humanism embodied in the *Gymnasium* curriculum survived in the West. In the *DDR*, on the other hand, there had been an emphatic rejection of a conception of humanism which implied that the ultimate value of education was in the cultivation of the intellect and the refinement of aesthetic appreciation, and that social and economic factors were irrelevant to this pursuit of high culture. Instead, humanism was conceived of as a way of educating the mass of the people beyond a level at which they were merely capable of fulfilling a single function in the process of production, to one at which they had gained sufficient understanding of the process to be able to contribute to the control of it. Humanism was therefore the liberation of the majority from uncomprehending drudgery as opposed to the academic pursuit of high culture on the part of the minority.

Structural and Curricular Developments in the West

This distinction is clearly illustrated in the structural and curricular developments that took place during the period under review. In the Federal Republic the researches continued and the results became more and more accessible to the public so that the general thesis became familiar: that the school system mirrored the class structure, that this lack of opportunity was much worse in some *Länder* than in others, that it was causing a wastage of ability which the country could not afford and that if prompt action was not taken West Germany's leading position in the economic field would be overhauled by rivals who had displayed the flexibility required in order to adapt their systems to meet the rapidly changing demands of technological competition.

In the event, however, neither the general thesis nor the conclusions drawn from it in terms of the structural changes that were desirable in the system attracted overwhelming support. The *Gymnasium* and *Realschule* teachers continued on the whole to view any erosion of their existing status with distaste. Only as regards curriculum reform was the *Philologenverband* interested in re-thinking longstanding practices. In any case this was chiefly concerned with the upper forms—a two-year terminal stage (*gymnasiale Oberstufe*) was suggested in which there would be a flexible pattern of subject options—and did nothing to endanger the tripartite structure and the privileged position of the *Gymnasium*.[3] This position was supported too by many influential voices in the universities, where the retention of the *status quo* was seen as a guarantee of the academic quality of the intake.

The urge to preserve the existing structure did not apply solely to the *Gymnasium*. In industry there was a considerable degree of commitment to retain the other sectors. It has already been noted that in the 1950s industrialists were by and large satisfied with the operation of the system, their main concern being to increase opportunities for education to technician level for those leaving the *Realschule* and the *Volksschule*. The misgivings expressed by the *Ettlinger Kreis* and the '*september gesellschaft*', a group similarly devoted to the discussion of educational policy, were not representative of industry as a whole. This had been evident in the reactions to the *Rahmenplan* of the Council for Industry and Commerce (*Deutscher Industrie- und Handelstag*) and the employers' federation (*Bundesvereinigung*

---

[3] *Deutscher Philologenverband, Rahmen-Vorschlag zur Reform der gymnasialen Oberstufe. Pressemitteilung, 22.11.1968.*

Deutscher Arbeitgeberverbände). Both emphasized the independent role of the *Realschule* as the source from which the middle cadres in industry were filled, and the unity of the *Volksschule* as a preparation for apprenticeship training. The *Rahmenplan* proposal of a *Förderstufe* had been seen as a threat to the supply of good apprentices while the proposals to raise the school-leaving age had been regarded as an intrusion on the vocational sector which had always been under the control of industry.[4]

The thesis of an unexploited pool of ability and the need to double the numbers acquiring the *Abitur* made a certain impact on the general public despite the scepticism in industrial circles. The effect of this was only to harden opinion in such circles against any reorganization of the school system along comprehensive lines. The expansionist policy altering the balance between vocational and general education in favour of the latter was described by a representative of the employers' federation as 'a euphoria that can only be described as educational madness'.[5] Thus the industrial establishment as an interest group tended to complement the efforts of the academic establishment to preserve the vertically structured system. Moreover, the opinions of the employers were all the more authoritative for the fact that on the trade union side interest in fundamental questions regarding the organization of the system was by comparison not greatly developed.[6]

These conservative pressures must be set against the radical viewpoints which were increasingly argued in educational publications. The aspirations of the comprehensive movement were clear:

[4] Cf. *Deutscher Industrie- und Handelstag, Wirtschaft und Bildungsreform, Sonderdruck*, March 1960. In A. O. Schorb, *Für und Wider den Rahmenplan*, Stuttgart, 1960, pp. 155–8.

[5] T. Kemp in *Der Arbeitgeber*. See M. Baethge, *Die Bildungspolitik der unternehmerischen Wirtschaftsverbände. Die deutsche Berufs- und Fachschule*, 6/1969, p. 410.

[6] Cf. F. Nyssen, *Gewerkschaft und Schule. Die deutsche Berufs- und Fachschule*, 6/1969, p. 432.

The continuing discussion of the various aspects of the school reform that is required is increasingly dominated by one type of school: the *Gesamtschule* (comprehensive school). What is meant by the concept of the *Gesamtschule* is a school which merges the existing types of school, not only—as does the grouping of schools on a central site—into a unity as regards amenities and administration, but an educational unity. The vertical structure of the traditional school system is replaced by a horizontal division into *Grundschule*, *Mittelstufe* and *Oberstufe*. *Hauptschule*, *Realschule* and the middle and upper stages of the *Gymnasium* as well as some *Berufsschulen* and *Berufsfachschulen* are integrated into the *Gesamtschule* system and cease to exist as independent types of school. Teachers of all categories work together; pupils of all social classes, talents and interests are to some degree taught together. The instruction is extensively differentiated. The negative selection at fixed stages which is conditioned by the tripartite nature of the traditional system and takes place between the ages of ten and twelve is abandoned: it is replaced by the optimal development of each specific talent and inclination through a combination of core and course instruction, compulsory and optional subjects, large and small groups and instructional programmes of varying length, intensity and methodology. The rigid *Jahrgangsklasse* is gradually dissolved and replaced by a combination of fixed groups for the study of core subjects and flexible groups for particular courses. The wholesale grade-repeating in all subjects disappears. . . .[7]

Of all the arguments in favour of the comprehensive system here outlined the most insistent was the social one of equality of opportunity. The social disadvantagement of the working class was alleged to be greater in the Federal Republic than in a large number of comparably developed countries.

In the course of the preliminaries to the 1969 *Bundestag* elections the *SPD* came out more strongly than hitherto in favour of the *Gesamtschule* as the one type of school which in its structure corresponded most closely with what was desired for society as a whole and which 'offers more than any other

[7] H. Frommberger/H.-G. Rolff, *Pädagogisches Planspiel: Gesamtschule*, Braunschweig, 1969, p. 39.

N

type the chance for the necessary basic education to be given to all future citizens'.[8] The *FDP*, in the model which it called the open school (*die offene Schule*), was even more insistent on the desirability of a horizontally structured system.[9] The *CDU/CSU*, on the other hand, did not envisage the removal of the vertical divisions between different types of school in the belief that the traditional pattern provided the best guarantee of high achievement. The *Gesamtschule* concept was rejected in favour of that of the *Leistungsschule*, a term intended to imply that every school in the system should strive to encourage maximum achievement for all its pupils.[10] But the political programmes at national level remained to some degree matters of academic interest at this stage, since practical policies could still only be initiated by individual *Land* governments and had to take account of a variety of local constraints.

If the recommendations of the *Bildungsrat* were to have a genuine prospect of implementation they had to be independent of the controversy regarding the relative merits of the existing system and the alternative advocated. Furthermore, they had to work towards a bridging of the gulf between general and vocational education which had become increasingly apparent:

The German system of general education has only hesitantly opened its doors to the concerns of the modern world of employment. The schools of general education and the vocational institutions have long stood well apart from one another in terms of organisation and curriculum. Even the *Rahmenplan* of the *Deutscher Ausschuß* tried to structure the two spheres independently of one another. The task of vocational guidance and of vocation-oriented basic education is at present not sufficiently recognised by the *Hauptschule*. Closer links between *Allgemeinbildung* and vocational training in the traditional

---

[8] *SPD. Modell für ein demokratisches Bildungswesen (Entwurf)*, Bonn, 1969, p. 12.

[9] *FDP. Praktische Politik für Deutschland—Das Konzept der FDP*. Programme agreed at *XX Ordentlicher Bundesparteitag*, Nürnberg, 25.6.1969, p. 18.

[10] *Bundesgeschäftsstelle der CDU*, Bonn. *Leitsätze der CDU—Schule und Hochschule von Morgen* ('*Deidesheimer Leitsätze*'),

sense, between the secondary school and the world of employment
have recently been striven for on the side of the general education
system at least partly in the curriculum of the *Realschule* and of the
unorthodox '*F-Gymnasien*', and on the vocational side by the *Berufs-
aufbauschulen* and higher vocational institutions. The *Gymnasium*
has meanwhile remained faithful to its original objectives. Conceived
in direct contrast to the 'world of business', its educational aim was
(and is) not directly related to future employment. But as it wishes
to prepare its pupils for their subsequent studies and thereby for
their subsequent academic profession the *Gymnasium* is also—at least
indirectly—involved in vocational training.[11]

In the separate development of general and vocational education there is little doubt that the latter was given much less
consideration. The Hamburg Agreement did not embrace
vocational education which remained largely the province of
industrial firms and the Chambers of Industry and Commerce.
However, as the general education component of trade training became more important, both for the social reason that
apprentices were more concerned about future career opportunities, and for the economic reason that a more flexibly educated labour force was in theory desirable, the existing arrangements were shown to be inadequate, since fewer and fewer
firms were in a position to meet the more sophisticated demands
of modern training. Moreover, the training of a more flexibly
educated labour force was often not in their immediate interests
which demanded a rapid supply of efficient operatives. Consequently accusations of exploitation of cheap labour were
increasingly heard. The highly organized, articulated training
system of large firms such as Krupps which were on the whole
proof against such accusations were however scarcely feasible
for smaller companies.

During the later 1960s however there was a good deal of
awareness of the problems. In 1966 two separate drafts for a
new law on vocational training were put forward, one by the

[11] *Deutscher Bildungsrat, Zur Neugestaltung der Abschlüsse im Sekundarschulwesen*, Bonn, 1969, p. 40.

SPD and one jointly by the *CDU/CSU* and the *FDP*. These eventually came to fruition in 1969 when a law drafted by a select committee to incorporate elements of both proposals was passed by an overwhelming majority in the *Bundestag*. The major sgnificance of the new law, the *Berufsbildungsgesetz*, lay in the fact that it provided for increased State control which had long been a demand of the trade unions and had been resisted by employers. A key example was the preoccupation with the qualifications of those giving instruction to apprentices, a matter which had never previously been subjected to close scrutiny.[12] In the wider context of educational policy as a whole, however, the law brought no great challenge to the longstanding gulf between general and vocational education. Its main contribution was to set in train measures to compensate for the neglect which the latter area had suffered. The urgency of these was underlined by an inquiry conducted in 1970, which revealed that almost two-fifths of industrial apprentices spent no time in an instructional workshop, and more than half received no theoretical instruction within the firm.[13]

The other part of the dual system of vocational training, the part-time attendance at the *Berufsschule*, was also growing less satisfactory. Information about the state of the *Berufsschulen* was scarce but it was clear that the shortage of teachers was grave. In 1970 it was claimed that about 39 per cent of teaching posts were unoccupied, that only half the pupils were receiving their full complement of instruction, and that often in classes of unmanageable proportions.[14] In the previous year a *Bildungsrat* study of the state of vocational training had added up to a formidable indictment. The training was often incomplete, without adequate theoretical foundation, did not measure up to educational criteria, being neither thought out nor put into practice systematically. The provision for the fostering of individual talent was insufficient, the instructors were inade-

---

[12] *Der Bundesminister für Arbeit und Sozialordnung, Berufsbildungsgesetz.* Section 20, p. 7.

[13] *Der Spiegel*, 18/1970, p. 57.   [14] Ibid., p. 68.

quately qualified and the final examinations showed an unsatisfactory standard of theoretical knowledge. The *Bildungsrat* considered the instruction in the *Berufsschulen* to be 'quantitatively and qualitatively often so inadequate as to jeopardize the prospects of a successful and good apprenticeship'.[15] Thus the developments of the 1960s, above all the expansion of social ambitions, found the system of vocational education ill-adapted to meet changing demands. Events had overtaken what had formerly been a docile sector and one of the foundations of West German economic success. The contrast between the prospects of the apprentice in a small firm and the opportunities open to the *Gymnasium* pupil illustrates once again the formidable nature of the task facing the *Bildungsrat* in attempting to create a unified system fully articulated between these two extremes.

Working on the assumption of ten years' full-time school attendance for all—an objective considered to be attainable by 1975—the Council approached the problem of integrating all the disparate elements into a unified system by way of curriculum and leaving qualifications (Diagram in Appendix VII). One of the greatest barriers to advancement had been that while an intermediate leaving qualification, the *mittlere Reife*, had been awarded at the *Gymnasium* and the *Realschule*, pupils at the *Volksschule* or *Hauptschule* had no corresponding target at the end of their school career. It was now, however, feasible to talk in terms of an intermediate qualification for all pupils at the end of ten years, regardless of what kind of school they attended. The *Bildungsrat* proposed that all secondary schools up to and including the 10th class should be classified under the same designation, *Sekundarstufe I*, and award the same certificate known as *Abitur I*. This proposal was based on the belief that leaving examinations and qualifications constituted the key point of reform particularly in view of their influence on curriculum and teaching methods. The *Hauptschule*

[15] *Deutscher Bildungsrat, Zur Verbesserung der Lehrlingsausbildung*, Bonn, 1969, pp. 14–18.

would therefore no longer be exclusively conceived of as an entrance stage for vocational education but rather the options would be left open.

At all stages [the system] must take account of a wide scale of interests and gifts of young people so that each individual is given every opportunity to reach the stage that he is able and willing to reach. From all levels of qualification school leavers must be given access to existing or newly created places of study and employment in a way which corresponds to individual, economic and social needs.[16]

No irrevocable decision was therefore to be made before the first level, that of *Abitur I*, had been reached.

If this was to be achieved the curriculum to be followed was of crucial importance. The most vulnerable feature of the tripartite division of schools had of course been the fact that it was simultaneously a tripartite division of curricula. For the new *Sekundarstufe I*, the *Bildungsrat* proposed a '*Curriculum I*' which all types of school would follow. This comprised a common core of nine subjects, German, a foreign language, mathematics, science, civics, music, art, religion and physical education. These would be the only subjects studied in school years 5 and 6, the period formerly recommended for the *Förderstufe*. Thereafter additional time would be allotted to optional extra subjects, 5 periods per week in years 7 and 8 and 8 periods in years 9 and 10. An extension of the range of such subjects was suggested, some more obviously directed towards the upper classes of the *Gymnasium*, some towards the traditional vocational sector. In years 9 and 10 in the common core subjects a differentiation was possible whereby the highly gifted and the less able were taught in separate sets. While the curriculum was to be available to all, and on satisfactory completion of it the *Abitur I* would be awarded, it was intended that access to the upper forms of the *Gymnasium* should be conditional on attainment of a specific standard.[17] Thus while opportunity had been

---

[16] *Deutscher Bildungsrat, Zur Neugestaltung . . ., op. cit., p. 43.*
[17] Ibid., pp. 57–62.

greatly enlarged the element of competition had not been eliminated. Its extent would be determined by the number of places available and the standard demanded for entry but the general tenor of the recommendation was that most of those wishing to go on in full-time education would be able to do so.

At the upper secondary level, *Sekundarstufe II*, the need for a rapprochement between the traditionally academic and the more vocationally oriented courses was again taken very seriously. The renewed challenge to the validity of the unitary concept of *Hochschulreife* as embodied in the traditional *Gymnasium* curriculum had come from two sources. Firstly, the *fachgebundene Hochschulreife*, first mentioned officially in the Hamburg Agreement, had gained strength with the growth of the unorthodox '*F-Gymnasien*' from which it was possible to obtain places at university to read social sciences in particular. Secondly, possession of the traditional full *Abitur* no longer guaranteed unrestricted entry and the use of a *numerus clausus* had become quite common in certain subjects, notably medicine, dentistry, chemistry, biology, pharmacy, psychology, physics, mathematics and architecture.[18] It was therefore natural that attention should be paid to the question of whether entrance criteria could continue to be theoretically formulated in an undifferentiated way for candidates in all disciplines.

The new discussion was characterized by a recognition that the concept of *Hochschulreife*, synonymous with *Abitur* and therefore the determinant of curriculum followed, could no longer be defined in terms of traditional 'timeless' norms but would need to correspond to a realistic consensus of the various interests involved. In an attempt to meet this case the *Rektorenkonferenz* produced in 1969 a new version of the *Maturitätskatalog* which tried to reconcile the demand for a greater degree of specialization than hitherto with the conviction of its members that there must remain common requirements that apply to all

[18] *Westdeutsche Rektorenkonferenz, Übersicht über die Zulassungsbeschränkungen an den Wissenschaftlichen Hochschulen für deutsche Studierende im Sommersemester 1969. Anlage 2. RS Nr. 491/69 vom 21.4.1969.*

candidates for entry to university. These were formulated in a more specific way than in the 1958 version of the *Katalog*.[19] Approximately equal weight was to be given to three broadly defined spheres, firstly language and literature, secondly mathematics and natural science and thirdly social science and history. The details included within these categories went some way towards meeting the criticisms that the existing curriculum did not contain a sufficiently representative selection of the most important areas of knowledge. Greater importance had been accorded to social science and natural science, some economics had been included, but the claims of technology had been ignored. The most controversial point was perhaps the retention of the two foreign languages which had consistently been a major obstacle for those whose secondary school career had not begun at a *Gymnasium*.

Beyond this minimum the *Rektorenkonferenz* suggested that specialized requirements should be fulfilled in two or, in exceptional cases, three academic subjects. Though it was made clear that for this, rigorous academic preparation beyond the current average level of studies in the *Oberstufe* was expected, the definitions remained imprecise, as for example 'more intensive penetration into a field of special interest' or 'independent methods of study as understood in a university'. In this can be seen a more constructive attempt to come to terms with the objectives of the Saarbrücken Agreement and draw the *Oberstufe* away from any catechistic inclinations towards a concern to provide a genuine induction into the approach to study that awaited *Abiturienten* at university. But it was also an attempt to preserve the unitary concept of *Hochschulreife* since it was proposed that the *Abitur* awarded on the basis of these two main sets of admission requirements would continue to give the legal right of entry to any faculty. The Conference opposed any measure to qualify the right of entry on a faculty basis on the grounds of its concern to ensure that decisions about

---

[19] H. Scheuerl, *Kriterien der Hochschulreife. Zeitschrift für Pädagogik*, 1/69, pp. 26–35.

direction of study were not taken too early: in its view *Oberstufe* studies were not to be regarded as direct preparation for specific university courses. As regards the expedient of the *numerus clausus*, it urged the provision of emergency funds to enable it to be dispensed with completely.

The *Bildungsrat* proposals regarding the *Oberstufe* curriculum (*Curriculum II*) also followed the pattern of a core of compulsory subjects supplemented by optional courses. The areas of knowledge suggested for the former were language and literature, mathematics, science and technology, and 'history and society'. The main addition to the *Rektorenkonferenz* catalogue was thus technology. A still more significant difference was the reduction of the foreign languages requirement to a minimum of one, a point on which agreement was reached only after some disputation.[20] Equally important was the system of optional subjects which were differentiated into courses which were academically oriented ('S courses') and those likely to be of more direct practical value ('P courses'). It was stressed that this difference was not one of achievement, but of content, and that this was to be made apparent in practice. The intellectual demands would be equally exacting, and though generally they would be different in kind, there would in some cases be a degree of overlap between them. It was especially desired that the optional subjects, their timetabling and the teaching methods used, should contribute towards bridging the gulf between the traditionally academic and the other orientations.[21]

The essence of the *Bildungsrat* proposals lay in the degree of differentiation which they introduced in the *Oberstufe*.

We want in a sense to draw the university into the school. Academics should state clearly what testable measure of knowledge and skills is practically speaking necessary for taking up different lines of study. The *Oberstufe* is being restructured in such a way that there are no longer classes in the old sense but a system of core and course.

[20] *Der Spiegel, Abitur auch für Schlosser?* Interview with Karl Dietrich Erdmann. Undated photocopy of a 1969 issue, p. 50.
[21] *Deutscher Bildungsrat, Zur Neugestaltung . . .,* op. cit., pp. 62–4.

instruction, compulsory and optional subjects, differentiated in accordance with the achievements and inclinations of the individual pupils.[22]

With a differentiation of this kind the *Abitur II* could lead in a number of different directions since the aim was 'to prevent *Hochschulreife* and *Abitur* being synonymous in the future . . . to get away from the whole concept of *Hochschulreife*'.[23] On this issue the *Bildungsrat* was at odds with the *Rektorenkonferenz* which was trying hard to save the unitary concept of the *Hochschulreife*. Yet the credibility of the latter's campaign was undermined by two factors. Firstly, its decisions were not binding on individual members and some of the newer university rectors seemed less likely to defend the traditionalist position. Secondly, in practice, alternative methods of entry by way of the *zweiter Bildungsweg* had become more and more common and in these cases the rigorous requirements of the *Abitur*, for example the second foreign language, were often waived. As it became clear that students could take good degrees without the intensive *Allgemeinbildung* of the *Gymnasium* as a prerequisite, the emphasis of responsibility as regards the stipulation of entrance requirements was moving towards the individual faculty rather than the university as a whole.

Taken as a whole the plans for *Abitur I* and *II* and *Curriculum I* and *II* added up to a model of the education system which was particularly workable in the context of a *Gesamtschule*. Moreover, at the same time as putting forward the new *Abitur* proposals, the *Bildungsrat* issued a companion volume which discussed in detail the principles on which experimental *Gesamtschulen* should be set up. The strength of the plan however remained that it was also workable within the existing system, and was not therefore dependent on a large-scale and controversial political decision for its very survival. It concentrated on the areas in which there was no major dispute between the two main par-

---

[22] *Der Spiegel*. Erdmann interview, op. cit., pp. 49–50.
[23] Ibid., p. 49.

ties, and in so doing was able to produce genuinely constructive proposals while still leaving the question of school types an open one. Potentially the greatest obstacle was lack of funds, but the indications were that in this respect the federal government was prepared to take a larger hand. The creation of a federal ministry seemed likely to be the first of a series of milestones in federal-*Land* cooperation.

The entire work of the *Bildungsrat* in the later 1960s was subsumed within the massive *Strukturplan für das Bildungswesen* of February 1970, the most significant illustration of the interpretation of educational planning in the Federal Republic. To quote from its introductory section:

The declaration contained in the *Strukturplan* is a compromise. The plan is not identical with what each individual member of the Committee would personally have had to say on the subject of reform. Each individual would probably have set out the plan differently, preferred other wordings, placed the emphasis elsewhere. It would contradict the desired provisional nature of the plan if each individual concerned in the public discussion of educational policy were not free to indulge in criticism of the plan which he had a hand in shaping and which is only intended as one step in a continuous development. But an important step certainly, since the compromise which it represents does not lie in a mere mid-point between two diametrically opposed positions but in a new programme for policy for which the responsibility is communal and which is determinedly progressive.[24]

The searching test of the *Strukturplan* was whether it would bring about the changes that the diagnoses of the 1960s had suggested were essential. It could be maintained that the sophisticated pattern and ingenious nomenclature which it proposed were merely a superficial gloss over a situation which might in the event remain very much as it always had been. It might for example seem likely that the *Gymnasium* would not only continue to be the main route to university but also continue to be

[24] *Deutscher Bildungsrat, Strukturplan für das Bildungswesen*, Bonn, 1970, pp. 15–16.

dominated by the middle class. While the *Gymnasium* constantly declared its entrance procedures to be based purely on ability with no account taken of social background, the problem had been greatly illuminated by the research showing the significance of informal education in the distribution of opportunity. With formal schooling beginning at the age of six in the Federal Republic the importance of provision for pre-school education could scarcely be exaggerated in this context. The plan was particularly emphatic that within ten years the age of starting school could be reduced from six to five and Kindergarten places provided for 75 per cent of three- to four-year-olds.[25] In this respect therefore there were very positive proposals for attacking what was undoubtedly one of the chief causes of educational underprivilege and it could be argued that this was a higher priority for expenditure of money and goodwill than the forcible transformation of existing schools.

In any such transformation there was probably a good deal to lose in alienating large sections of the teaching profession. As it was, the *Bildungsrat* had proposed a new structure for teacher training to correspond to the curricular stratification. This rationalization was the principal step proposed towards the solution of the problem of shortage of teachers which had caused so much concern in the early 1960s. The system had not ground to a halt as Picht had predicted but none the less the need for more teachers was now greater than ever if the plan was to be put into effect. The achievement of a genuine improvement of opportunity and of a rise in the supply of well-qualified manpower depended, on the one hand, on the education of the three- to five-year-olds, and on the other, on the expansion of the *Hauptschule* sector so that the target of the *Abitur I* could become a reality for all pupils in *Sekundarstufe I*. This demanded a vast increase in the teaching force on which the success of the plan appeared to rest. In the last analysis, however, the entire operation hinged on the availability of the required finance, the question to which the new *Bund-Länder-*

---

[25] For a summary of these and other findings, see *Die Zeit*, 15.5.1970, p. 16.

Kommission für Bildungsplanung was to address itself in the early 1970s.

Structural and Curricular Developments in the East

In the *DDR* the course of development in the later 1960s was unspectacular by comparison with previous periods. The main thrust was towards revising the school curriculum in accordance with long-term planning and the current interpretation of the needs of the 'scientific and technological revolution'. The awareness that the curriculum was a foremost instrument for determining the future pattern of society is probably the most striking characteristic of policy at this time.

Apart from the introduction of new scientific and technical content there was constant stress on the need for the curriculum to promote ideological conviction in the school population—'the entire material must be seen and consciously used from the standpoint of the Marxist-Leninist *Weltanschauung*, of the tasks in the ideological struggle and of the education of the pupils in the spirit of socialist ethics'.[26] As regards extra-curricular activity there was the familiar insistence on the role of the youth movement, both in encouraging patriotic attitudes and in promoting the desire to work hard in formal school activities.

The politico-ideological education of the school population is an uninterrupted process which must be carried on beyond the confines of formal instruction in the entire extra-curricular time available. . . . Regarding its content, extra-curricular work is determined above all by the instruction and the norms, decisions, tasks and demands of the *FDJ* and the Pioneer organisation. It offers especially favourable possibilities for educating boys and girls into effective happy and disciplined young people. It should contribute above all to the awakening of the thirst for knowledge, intellectual curiosity, love of literature, art and sporting activity and to education for readiness to defend our socialist fatherland.[27]

[26] Monumenta Paedagogica VII/2, op. cit., p. 650.   [27] Ibid., p. 651.

A more strident tone invested a ministerial circular of May 1966 addressed to the youth organizations in the particular context of the preparations for the 50th anniversary of the October Revolution.

Follow the traces of Red October and discover how we, in brotherly union with the Soviet Union, are building socialism in our Republic and protecting peace; how with the friendship treaty USSR-*DDR*, the brotherly relations and the cooperation on an equal footing between our two States are further developed; how the unbreakable German-Soviet friendship arose, how the Great Socialist October Revolution and the building of socialism in the Soviet Union influenced and launched the revolutionary fight of the German working class; how the Soviet people, the Soviet army and at its side the German anti-fascists fought against fascism and destroyed it.[28]

On the evidence of the wording alone it might be thought that these documents reveal a hardening of attitudes at a time when it has been suggested that the ideological atmosphere was becoming less highly charged. This is not however a true contradiction. The new phase known as the 'shaping of the developed system of socialism' was declared to have been ushered in between 1963 and 1965, and there was in the years immediately following a strong consciousness of this, and in particular of the role of commitment among the school population to the realization of a strong Republic; a heightened degree of exhortation is therefore not unexpected and indeed could be regarded as a potentially productive aspect of education as a whole in that it was intended to foster the spirit of the hard-working collective. This is different from the ideological standpoint of the 1950s which was expressed in equally strident terms, but which was accompanied by measures which were later realized to have been manifestly unproductive, whatever their publicity value. Thus in the 1950s there was considerable ideological capital to be gained from proclaiming the total lack of differentiation in the school system, a situation that would be absurd in the

[28] Ibid., p. 680.

context of the steady development of specialist schools in the later 1960s.

As regards the structure of the school system, the developments that followed the 1965 Law were concerned with differentiation. A decree of June 1966 gave notice that the transition to a two-year *erweiterte Oberschule* was to begin in the school year 1967-68. It remained necessary, however, to give potential entrants to this *Abiturstufe*, as it began to be called, special preparation from the end of the eighth year onwards in '*Vorbereitungsklassen*'.[29] Thus though the organizational structure appeared to have a neat pattern of ten years' common compulsory education for all, followed by two further years for those with university aspirations, as far as curriculum was concerned the real pattern remained eight years of common education followed by diverging paths leading to the university and the vocational sectors. This divergence was regarded as transitional and eventually the *Vorbereitungsklassen* were to be merged with the remainder of the 9th and 10th classes of the *Oberschule*, so that entry to the *erweiterte Oberschule* could become a matter of open competition at the end of the compulsory ten-year schooling for all. This was, however, still not the case in 1970 and though there was provision for late promotion from class 10, selection for the *Vorbereitungsklassen* at the end of class 8 (age approximately fourteen) greatly enhanced the prospects of entry to university four years later. The two criteria were academic results and 'proof of commitment to our State through attitude and social activity'.[30] The importance attached to the selection can be gauged by the thoroughness of the procedure adopted.

Each case was considered by a committee consisting of the school head, the subject teachers concerned and representatives of the youth movement, the parents' council, the National Front and the local education authority. This committee had a responsibility to encourage working-class parents who were reluctant to allow their children to go on to the *Abitur*, thereby forgoing two years' earnings and perhaps more.

[29] Ibid., p. 682.   [30] Ibid., p. 684.

For those still unconvinced there remained the compromise whereby the *Abitur* could be taken concurrently with vocational training. The origin of these *Abiturklassen* in 1960 has already been discussed and it will be recalled that the ambitious target was set that by 1965 they would admit 20 per cent of all *Oberschule* leavers. Though no statistics are given for the acquisition of the *Abitur* in this way it appears probable that there was difficulty in reaching the target and that, in the 1960s at any rate, the direct route by way of the *erweiterte Oberschule* remained by far the more popular.[31] It is more credible to attribute this to the recalcitrance of young people in industry and agriculture than to a lessening of the importance accorded to it in official circles since the need for highly qualified manpower continued to be emphasized.

The sphere of vocational education in general became, as might be expected, more and more subject to rationalization and the demands of long-term planning in the years following the 1965 Law. The reorganization of the apprenticeship system first mooted in the early 1960s began to be realized with the introduction of the first '*Grundberufe*' in 1967. The *Grundberuf* was conceived as a multi-purpose trade designed to give workers greater versatility and hence provide greater flexibility and efficiency in production. The sum of knowledge and skills required had been devised anew in accordance with the long-term prognosis of industrial requirements.[32] The process was facilitated by the increasing similarity of various work processes resulting from mechanization and automation. Linked to the development of the *Grundberufe* was the introduction of new basic subjects to be studied by all apprentices with the ten-

---

[31] This is suggested by the fairly close correspondence between numbers obtaining the *Abitur* in *erweiterte Oberschulen* and the statistics of university entry. Ratios of *Abiturienten* to full-time university places awarded were: 1965—19,322 : 16,360. 1966—17,080 : 16,528. 1967—18,090 : 16,413. 1968—21,326 : 20,023. 1969—23,943 : 27,033. *Statistisches Jahrbuch der DDR 1970*, pp. 374, 368.

[32] E. Lass, *Disponible Facharbeiter durch Ausbildung in Grundberufen. Berufsbildung*, 5/1969, p. 229.

year school-leaving qualification. These subjects which included for example 'principles of computer science' and 'principles of electronics' were seen as following logically on the polytechnical education of the *Oberschule* and special significance was attached to their coordination with the school curricula.[33] Developments of the kind just outlined were an outcome of the strong emphasis which in the 1960s was placed on education or vocational training of some specific kind beyond the minimum school-leaving age. In 1968 it was claimed that the number of school leavers not engaged in training was less than 5 per cent.

The year 1968 also saw the culmination of the first of the two major phases of curriculum reform in the introduction of a series of detailed syllabuses (*präzisierte Lehrpläne*). In a report to the *Volkskammer* the Minister of Education described the exercise as a profound transformation, bringing the curriculum into a close relationship with other aspects of the economy and society. The examples quoted were mainly from the field of mathematics and science. In the former case some of the old material had been superseded by new items designed to give a thorough theoretical basis for the understanding of computer science and statistical analysis. To help to accomplish this, the instruction in the *Unterstufe* was greatly intensified—'thus for mathematics teaching the appropriate deductions were made from the fact that in all spheres of social life mathematics is gaining increased significance and that there is an ever-increasing emphasis on mathematical thinking'.[34] In the case of physics it was pointed out that while the content was, as before, essentially drawn from the most important areas of classical physics, already in the beginners' course of class 6 the programme had been expanded by the inclusion of some essential elements of modern electrophysics and by an introduction into the structure of the atom.[35]

[33] Cf. A. Hegelheimer, *Berufsbildung im Wandel* (manuscript), Berlin, 1971, p. 52.   [34] Monumenta Paedagogica . . ., op. cit., p. 841.
[35] M. Honecker, *Ergebnisse der Einführung neuer Lehrpläne und Lehrmethoden an den zehnklassigen allgemeinbildenden polytechnischen Oberschulen. Materialen der 9. Tagung der Volkskammer*, 9/1968, p. 14.

O

In these new curricula the new 'deprofessionalized' concept of polytechnical education also took shape.

Following the trends in the development of science and production, technology and the economy, the general technical and the natural scientific and mathematical foundations are more strongly emphasised in the new syllabuses for polytechnical instruction. This also improves the preconditions for the theoretical underpinning of the productive work of the pupils. In the theoretical instruction, those areas are given preferential treatment which are of significance for many branches of the economy and for many spheres of activity, such as for example mechanical technology and engineering and the economic application of machinery, electro-technology/electronics, economics and technical drawing. During the productive work the pupils should acquire abilities and skills that can be applied in many different ways, above all in the servicing of machines, assembling and dismantling, fault-finding and repair work. A broad poly-technical education of this kind lays a good foundation for subsequent vocational training. . . .[36]

The new *präzisierte Lehrpläne* also illustrate the intention stated in 1966 to use not just civic and moral education but every subject to foster a Marxist-Leninist *Weltanschauung*. The chemistry syllabus for class 7 offers a convenient example.

The instruction in this class is to be used for the politico-ideological education of the pupils. . . . By using the knowledge acquired in the geography course of classes 5 and 7 the pupils are to be made aware of the rapid growth of the chemical industry and the significance of iron ore and steel as the basis for the further development of our economy. The knowledge to be imparted is to be used for education both for patriotism and for friendship with the Soviet Union and the other socialist countries.[37]

A history syllabus lends itself particularly well to political education and here too the opportunities were seized.

In the process of the establishment of capitalism the bourgeoisie and the proletariat consolidated their positions as the main classes of this

[36] Ibid., p. 15.   [37] Monumenta Paedagogica . . ., op. cit., p. 818.

new social order. An unbridgeable opposition was formed between the two classes. The proletariat took up arms in the course of early spontaneous action against capitalist exploitation. It carried on a necessary and just struggle which already indicated the subsequent historical development: the struggle for a socialist ordering of society in which the exploitation of man by man is finally done away with.[38]

Throughout the new curricula there were suggestions for interdisciplinary cooperation, generally speaking with the purpose of strengthening the political and moral components.

By the end of the 1960s the dominant characteristic of *DDR* educational policy was a preoccupation not so much with aims and objectives, which were considered to have been worked out to a sufficient degree to enable predictions to be made for the period up to 1980, as with the practical problems of their realization. This was the *raison d'être* of the second phase of curriculum reform which was well advanced by 1970. Equally, in the matter of the structure of the system there were still shortcomings in the realization of policy. Even in 1970, five years after the law introducing universal ten-year education, it was still found necessary to allow some pupils to leave school after eight years—sometimes estimated at about 20 per cent of the age group[39]—though it was insisted that they continue their general education in a part-time capacity up to the standard of the leaving certificate of the *Oberschule*. In tackling these problems policy seemed likely to take a predictable course based on the prevailing view of 'how the *DDR* will look in the years 1980 and 1985 and what demands this will make on the practice of socialism'.[40]

---

[38] Ibid., p. 815.

[39] O. Anweiler, *Strukturprobleme des allgemeinbildenden Schulwesens in der DDR. Bildung und Erziehung*, 4/1970, pp. 259–60.

[40] *Grundsätze für die Berufsausbildung im einheitlichen sozialistischen Bildungssystem. Materialen der 9. Tagung der Volkskammer*, 10/1968, p. 12.

Assumptions and their Practical Consequences

While the educational systems of the two States did not
diverge so widely in the later 1960s as at earlier stages, the
policies pursued nonetheless provide constant reminders of
their differing underlying assumptions. There are three areas
in which the practical outcomes of these differences can be
particularly clearly portrayed through direct comparisons,
namely the function of the curriculum, the mechanics of
transition from school to university, and the approach to vocational education and training.

(1) THE FUNCTION OF THE CURRICULUM

In the *DDR*, development in this field was characterized by the
determination to move away from the traditional bias towards
languages and the arts:

We recognise the educational value of these aspects of our culture nor
do we wish to lose them in our socialist-humanist ideals. But it is
unmistakably clear that the transformation of science into productive power and the incipent technological revolution of our time
bring with them a shift of emphasis in education in favour of those
subjects which are indispensable for the mastery of these social
processes.[41]

The extensive modifications in the curriculum in the *DDR* in
the later 1960s were designed to realize this new orientation.

Internally the ten-class *Oberschule* was divided into three
stages after 1965. The first of these comprised classes 1-3 and
marked the end of what in the Federal Republic would be a
four-year primary stage devoted overwhelmingly to mather
matics and the mother tongue, together with a certain amount
of instruction in manual skills, gardening, music, art and sport.

[41] S. Baske/M. Engelbert, *Zwei Jahrzehnte Bildungspolitik . . . Dokumente*,
Berlin, 1966, Vol. II, p. 372.

However, the addition of a modern language, Russian, did not come till the fifth year of schooling, the same year in which a modern language, usually English, was introduced in the Federal Republic in the *Gymnasium*, the *Realschule* and some *Hauptschulen*. The first significant difference is that the ten-class *Oberschule* curriculum had three weekly periods of physics in the sixth year whereas no physics was taught at this stage in the *Gymnasium*, *Realschule* or *Hauptschule*. Moreover, in the latter three types of school there was rather less time devoted to mathematics than in the *Oberschule* up to this point. There was thus in the first six years a stronger emphasis on mathematics and science in the *DDR* than in the Federal Republic.[42]

This became considerably more marked in the four years that followed, leading in the case of the *Oberschule* to the ten-year leaving certificate, in the case of the *Gymnasium* and the *Realschule* to the *mittlere Reife*. A general impression of the direction in which they were oriented can be gained by considering certain groups of subjects. In the *DDR* those which might be considered directly relevant to the 'scientific and technological revolution' were mathematics, physics, chemistry, biology and polytechnical education which had three components, 'introduction to socialist production', technical drawing and productive work experience. This group accounted for approximately 52 per cent of the total of the normal curriculum, and, in the case of those taking the additional foreign language with a view to entrance to the *erweiterte Oberschule* and the preparation of the *Abitur*, approximately 48 per cent. The most direct comparison with the latter case would be the mathematics/natural science *Gymnasium*. In this there was no equivalent to polytechnical education, but even if manual skills are included on the strength of their distant relationship to science and technology the corresponding figure is 26 per cent. For the

[42] This and the other comparisons that follow are in the case of the Federal Republic based on the curricula for the *Land* of Lower Saxony. See K. Szameitat/H.-K. Kullmer, *Verzeichnis der weiterführenden Schulen und Hochschulen in den Landern des Bundesgebietes*. Meisenheim am Glan, 1968, pp. 76–80. DDR source: *Vergleichende Pädagogik—Informationen*, 1/1971, pp. 7–40.

Realschule and the *Volksschule*, again including time devoted to manual skills, the proportion was about 38 per cent. The reverse contrast can be seen in the linguistic sphere. In the *Oberschule* German and foreign languages accounted in the normal curriculum for 21 per cent of the total and in the case of those expecting to proceed to the *erweiterte Oberschule* 27 per cent. For the *Realschulen* and *Volksschulen* the corresponding proportion was about 25 per cent and for the mathematics/natural science *Gymnasium* 38 per cent.

When the same comparison is made for the upper secondary level the distinction is more complex. In the *erweiterte Oberschule* 50 per cent of the time was devoted to the scientific group and 31 per cent to the languages group and these approximate proportions applied to almost all pupils taking the *Abitur*. Even for the small number in specialist schools with additional modern language instruction the variations were very slight. In contrast to this unitary pattern of the content of upper secondary education the Federal Republic presented a differentiated picture. In the mathematics/natural science *Gymnasium* the scientific group was allotted 38 per cent of the teaching time and the linguistic group 24 per cent. In the classical and modern languages *Gymnasium* the corresponding proportions were 18 and 46 per cent respectively. In these latter two cases therefore the contrast is still more marked than at the earlier stage as the accompanying table shows (see p. 205).

While it is impossible to undertake a full analysis of the content of the syllabuses it should be pointed out that the immense volume of development carried out after the 1965 Law in the *DDR* was designed to bring the curriculum into a close relationship with the economy and society. Quoting the Minister of Education, Margot Honecker:

Teachers more and more consciously begin their work from the basic assumption that it is the task of our school to play a full part in the struggle to shape the developed social system of socialism. In this we always take our direction from the fundamental principle of our Education Law: the close linking of school with life. . . . In deter-

COMPARISON OF CURRICULA IN THE FEDERAL
AND DEMOCRATIC REPUBLICS

Type of school	Curriculum time as a percentage	
	Maths/ science/ production group of subjects	Linguistic group
DDR		
Oberschule (classes 7–10) normal	52	21
Oberschule (7–10) selected group for subsequent entry to *erweiterte Oberschule*	48	27
Oberschule (7–10) with special modern language instruction	45	30
Erweiterte Oberschule (11–12)normal	52	27
Erweiterte Oberschule (11–12) with special modern language instruction	50	31
Federal Republic		
Realschule (classes 7–10)	38	25
Maths/natural science *Gymnasium* (7–10)	26	38
Maths/natural science *Gymnasium* (11–13)	38	24
Classical or modern languages *Gymnasium* (11–13)	18	46

(Source: see note 42)

mining the content of general education those demands are of
special significance which derive from the scientific and technological revolution. . . .[43]

This implied a marked emphasis on the application of theoretical knowledge, and it was the role of polytechnical education to
create opportunities for the relationship between theory and

[43] Honecker, *Ergebnisse der Einführung . . .*, op. cit., pp. 10–11.

practice to be illustrated and experienced. In the *erweiterte Oberschule*, as already noted, this was to be achieved above all by a kind of creative technology in which pupils were set to solve practical problems in such spheres as electrical engineering, electronics, computer science and industrial chemistry, organized on a joint basis between the schools and the industrial concerns by which they had been 'adopted'.[44] In the corresponding period there was no similarly extensive development of this kind in the Federal Republic. Obviously the practical applications have always featured to some extent in the teaching of mathematics and science, and it would be difficult to measure to what degree the new syllabuses in the *DDR* succeeded in altering the balance between theory and practice. But the institutionalized cooperation between schools and industry was a new element which, coming on top of the polytechnical instruction in the *Oberschule*, reinforced the contrast which has already been demonstrated in the comparison of the total content of the curriculum.

These comparisons combine to illustrate the difference in the approach adopted by the two States to education as a whole and to that of the academically able in particular. In the Democratic Republic the common factors in the curriculum were designed to ensure the formation of a 'socialist intelligentsia' characterized by the ability of each of its members to make a specific contribution to the planned society of the future. Thus Ulbricht:

It is necessary to emphasise once again that the planning of the training and education of scientific cadres must start from this prognosis of development up to 1980. The student who today begins his studies will in about ten years be fully effective in society. For this reason the training is to be developed in accordance with the needs of the future.[45]

The future needs were estimated as requiring an expansion of the numbers of scientists by 250 per cent and of engineers by

[44] Ibid., p. 15.   [45] Monumenta Paedagogica VII/2, op. cit., p. 734.

350 per cent[46] and this above all explains the fact that the curriculum was constructed in such a way that all potential university entrants acquired the necessary knowledge which constituted the precondition for the subsequent study of science or technology.

This unitary approach was not paralleled in the Federal Republic. In all types of *Gymnasium* there was less emphasis on science and technology than in the *DDR*, and particularly so in the languages *Gymnasien*, which accounted for perhaps a third of all potential *Abiturienten*.[47] While in the Federal Republic the need for expansion at the upper secondary level received similar emphasis to that which was evident in the *DDR*, this did not affect the continued survival of a corps of university entrants educated primarily in accordance with the traditional humanistic ideal, which was considered irrelevant to the social and economic preoccupations that largely determined the character of the *erweiterte Oberschule* curriculum. In this respect therefore education continued to be independent of economic planning in the Federal Republic.

(II) THE TRANSITION FROM SCHOOL TO UNIVERSITY

For the *DDR* the rigid organization has already been described whereby the numbers admitted to the various university courses have been determined in accordance with projected manpower needs. This represents a complete transformation of the traditional system, still technically in operation in the Federal Republic, whereby the award of the *Abitur* confers the right to enter university and furthermore to study at any faculty. According to this system the size of the various faculties and the numbers following the various courses are determined by the individual wishes of the prospective students, as opposed to the requirements of the State. Whereas in the *DDR* the entire

[46] Ibid., p. 734.
[47] A. G. Hearnden, *Paths to University: Preparation, Assessment, Selection*, London, 1973, p. 24.

curriculum is geared towards channelling the interests of the individual into directions that are considered productive from the State's point of view, for which the criterion is the findings of long-term projections of manpower needs, in the Federal Republic the system is basically such as to encourage a spontaneous development, with the relationship of this to the needs of society as a whole lying in the hands of the individual's own assessment of supply and demand in the labour market. This contrast between controlled scientific planning of manpower resources in the *DDR* and uncontrolled, less predictable development in the Federal Republic is a logical outcome of the way in which the two systems had diverged by the mid-1960s.

Although the distinction still applied in principle at the end of the decade various pressures had in practice caused limitations to be placed on the free development pattern in the Federal Republic. In the various *Länder* ways had emerged of gaining entry to university by means of a modified school-leaving certificate which restricted the holder to certain types of institution or to specific faculties. Secondly, the pressures of numbers had increased to such an extent that the application of a *numerus clausus* was becoming increasingly common. Thirdly, opportunities were beginning to be created to enter university from employment. As a result of these developments the pressure increased to rationalize the process of entry and this objective can be discerned in the proposals of the *Bildungsrat* to shape the curriculum on the basis of a common core of subjects to be studied by all, supplemented by various options which would give an orientation in the direction of future study. In 1970, however, the task of relating this differentiation at the upper secondary level to the needs of the various sectors of society and the economy and of adjusting the organization of higher education accordingly still lay in the future.

Nor was the common core proposed by the *Bildungsrat* to have anything like the same degree of overall bias in the direction of mathematics, science and technology that marked the curriculum of the *erweiterte Oberschule*, less than one-third of it being devoted to these subjects. *Bildungsrat* curriculum proposals did however envisage that greater attention should be paid to future vocational requirements. Thus it was suggested that while some of the options would be academically oriented in the traditional way, others would have a technical or more directly practical bias. These proposals for the modification of curricula revealed a recognition of the need to adapt the educational system in order to come to terms with what specific sectors of the economy demanded of it. In this respect they constituted a response that had a certain amount in common with the approach in the *DDR*. But they show equally that it was far from being accepted that the demands of the economy as revealed by long-term forecasting were the only criterion to be applied. Side by side with the newer vocationally oriented curricular patterns were to remain the older traditional ones for which vocational considerations were largely irrelevant.

This contrast is further emphasized when the role of the route to university via vocational education and employment is considered. In the *DDR* it was consistent with the refusal to regard the *Abitur* as a purely academic qualification that it should have been made possible to acquire it concurrently with a vocational training. In the 1959 Law it had been envisaged that this would become the normal route to university, and it was characteristic of the obsession with practical experience in industry or agriculture that those who chose the direct route via the *erweiterte Oberschule* should be obliged to spend a year acquiring a trade qualification before they were entitled to enter university. By the end of the decade, however, this somewhat narrow view of vocational education had been abandoned and the preparation for university was interpreted more flexibly, in recognition of developments that had not been foreseen in 1959. The numbers opting for vocational education combined with *Abitur* did not rise as fast as had been anticipated so that full-time attendance at the *erweiterte Oberschule* remained the orthodox route to university. Furthermore the requirement to obtain a trade qualification by spending a year in employment before entry was abandoned towards the end of the 1960s as unrealistic. But the way in which the curriculum had been developed in the later 1960s had guaranteed the inclusion of a large pre-vocational element. Thereby the sharp contrast between general and vocational education had been removed, with the new common curriculum striking what was considered the appropriate balance between mathematics and science on the one hand and the humanities on the other and applying it to all pupils. It was still maintained that as a result of this new balance it was no more difficult to acquire the *Abitur* by way of vocational training, and it may well be that this route to university will gain in popularity in the course of the 1970s.

In the Federal Republic the combination of vocational training with preparation for the *Abitur* was more problematical for two reasons. Firstly, it was generally necessary to acquire the *Abitur* by additional evening study whereas in the *DDR* it was integrated into the vocational training course. Secondly, since the content of the *Abitur* was more strongly biased in the direction of general education, especially literary and linguistic studies, it was inevitably further removed from the kind of work involved in vocational training. In this respect therefore there was not the same degree of integration of the vocational and the general that was found in the *DDR*. Once again the pattern was a fragmented one in which for organizational reasons entrance to university by way of vocational training was rare. On the other hand opportunities in the vocational sector were considerably expanded in the Federal Republic in the 1960s at all levels up to the specialist *Fachschulen* from which it eventually became possible to gain limited access to technical universities. In this respect provision was made to meet the demand for qualified manpower in specific sectors of the economy by a quite different route from that followed by those proceeding to university via the *Abitur* in the normal way. But whatever the pressure of manpower requirements had been, it had not brought about an integration of the general and vocational types of education in the way that this had taken place in the *DDR*.

The *Bildungsrat* planning did not envisage such an integration but continued to subscribe to a policy of differentiation at the upper secondary level whereby those destined for humanities courses at the university followed a curriculum that was markedly literary and linguistic in character, while this bias was less in evidence in the mathematics/natural science *Gymnasium* and largely absent from vocational education. It would be alleged in the *DDR* that this division still reflected the stratification of society, that the humanistic education was still predominantly the preserve of the middle class. There is still truth in this allegation, but the extent to which the thesis of differential opportunities favouring the middle class is applicable to the pattern of career opportunities is a matter for conjecture. It may be that in a society increasingly influenced by scientific and technological developments upward social mobility and avoidance of downward mobility are just as likely, perhaps even more likely, to be promoted by way of the vocational and technical sectors as by way of the traditional path of humanistic education. The *Bildungsrat* planning of the future structure of the educational and qualifications system was built up on the assumption that the general and vocational sides though remaining different in kind could eventually be equated in terms of prestige and desirability. One phenomenon which might bear this out is the degree of early leaving of the *Gymnasium*, the institution of general education, in order to transfer to the vocational sector.[48] But it is also possible that a good many of the more able and versatile young people who could cope easily with the *Gymnasium* curriculum were diverted from consideration

[48] Of the total cohort of 5,383 entering *Gymnasien* in Baden-Württemberg in 1955-56 only 1,236 eventually obtained the *Abitur* in 1964. H. Peisert/R. Dahrendorf, *Der vorzeitige Abgang vom Gymnasium, Schriftenreihe des Kultusministeriums Baden-Württemberg* A1, 1966, pp. 26-7. For the Federal Republic as a whole the rate of early leaving is generally put at about 50 per cent. Unfortunately the pattern of transfer to vocational education does not appear to have been systematically studied as yet.

of career options in applied and technological fields by the humanistic bias of their studies.

The strategy of the educational planning by the *Bildungsrat* can be summed up as it affected two major stages of school education. For the first stage, up to the end of the tenth year of schooling, it was to by-pass the organizational problems of merging different kinds of school by ensuring that in all schools a standard minimum curriculum was offered (*Curriculum I*), leading to a standard leaving certificate (*Abitur I*), which was to give access to the entire range of possibilities at the upper secondary level. Within this framework, reorganization along comprehensive lines could proceed at whatever pace regional and local authorities considered desirable. The novelty of this conception was that the new qualifications system so created would eliminate the situation which had previously obtained whereby choice of school at the age of ten or twelve was simultaneously a choice of type of curriculum, which in turn determined the opportunities that were subsequently available. For the second stage, a pattern was envisaged with a wide range of differentiated opportunities, from the traditionally academic to the specifically vocational. Within this the individual parts were to remain separate but equal, with the degree of commitment to a specific future career left to individual choice.

The first of these stages shared with the *DDR* the objective of making all opportunities open to all pupils beyond the ten-year stage. In the *DDR* however it was considered that any survival of the traditional types of school would inevitably perpetuate the privileged position of the middle class so that only within the framework of a single comprehensive school could the working class acquire the necessary education to achieve a dominant position in society. Aside from the class issue, however, the *Abitur I* of the Federal Republic was in principle similar to the leaving certificate of the ten-year school in the *DDR*. In practice the two would be more generally comparable once the proportion of children spending ten years in full-time education became similar in the two cases. The major contrast at the second stage was that a less heterogeneous choice was offered in the *DDR*. The overriding criterion was usefulness to the economy as preconceived on the basis of long-term planning and consequently a strong emphasis on the humanistic line rather than on science and technology was not possible to the same extent as in the Federal Republic.

The implication of this is that in the Federal Republic there was a greater degree of autonomy allowed to the individual as regards choice of the dominant values in education. While it was possible to follow a course fairly strongly biased in the direction of science and technology it was also possible to opt for one in which science and technology played a very small role. Clearly the supply and demand situation prevailing in the labour market must and did exert pressure to alter the traditional balance but it was a pressure that derived from composite origins not solely governed by the demands of science, technology and production but affected also by the concern in some sectors of the community to preserve humanistic criteria. In the *DDR*, on the other hand, the principle of the unity of education and the economy demanded that ultimately the humanistic criteria must in all cases be subordinate and the significance of the unitary conception of the curriculum, as opposed to the differentiated one in the Federal Republic, is that it obliged the individual to subscribe in practice to educational values decided upon by the State authorities on the basis of the planning of the economy. This conception must necessarily be based on the assumption that the entire school population can ultimately be educated to accept these values: otherwise it can only be construed as a denial in practice of the right and the opportunity to dissent. In this sense therefore as far as full-time education is concerned it must be concluded that in the Federal Republic a greater degree of freedom and autonomy was invested in the individual than was the case in the *DDR*.

One of the justifications for the unitary approach to the organization of the school system and the curriculum in the *DDR* was always that the provision of differentiated opportunities for the more able must be subordinated to the obligation to raise the general standard of education throughout the entire community. This was consistent with the Marxist view, already discussed at length, of the need to educate workers not merely to fulfil a single function in industry or agriculture but to be capable of versatility and mobility. While this was always provided for at the higher levels of the educational system within the limits that have just been analysed, it must also be considered to the extent that it holds good for the less privileged sector. Quite obviously much more progress had been made in ensuring a higher general level of education in the first ten years of school in the *DDR*. Such measures as the reorganization of rural education ensured that a higher proportion reached the level of the ten-year leaving certificate than reached the *mittlere Reife* in the Federal Republic. But it has already been seen to be within the scope of the *Bildungsrat* plan to close the gap, provided that the requisite financial provision was forthcoming.

(III) VOCATIONAL EDUCATION AND TRAINING

In the part-time sector, which absorbs those who leave school directly for employment, similar contrasts can be noted. In the *DDR* the part-time vocational educational system formed an integral part of the total system of economic planning, whereas in the Federal Republic the development lay largely in the hands of various autonomous bodies within the economy. It has already been seen how in the course of two decades of development in the *DDR* various initiatives were taken centrally to adapt the output of trained manpower from the apprenticeship system directly to the needs of the economy, but that at the same time these needs were interpreted as including the requirement that a constant effort should be made to raise the standard of general education, hence the adoption of the aim of universal ten-year schooling before entry to apprenticeship.

In the Federal Republic there was less awareness of the desirability of a higher general level of education for apprentices, a more general readiness to accept minimal school education as adequate for them, and perhaps a greater tendency to exploit their labour, allowing considerations of profit to outweigh the responsibility for providing a more polyvalent education within the branch of industry concerned. Whereas in the *DDR* there was a preoccupation with polytechnical education, in the Federal Republic the bodies concerned with vocational training appeared to be satisfied with a monotechnical pattern.

Whatever the degree of justification for this kind of allegation against the prevailing practices in the Federal Republic, there was in the later 1960s a clear trend towards greater control on the part of the federal government. As a result of the Vocational Law of August 1969 the federal authorities fulfilled the role of coordinator of *Land* policies through a number of specially constituted committees accorded the task of examining policy in a national context. But as in the case of general education there survived a reluctance to infringe the autonomy of the *Länder* or of the Chambers of Commerce and Industry. The degree of centralization stopped a long way short of the practice in the *DDR* where policy was directed by the *Staatliches Amt für Berufsausbildung*, a central government institution for which there was no counterpart in the Federal Republic.

Though the planning machinery was different in structure in the two cases a marked similarity of aims is apparent. In both cases it was seen to be necessary to rationalize the structure of apprenticeship training so that there were fewer but more flexible trade qualifications. In this respect a comparison shows that in the *DDR* the number of trades fell from 972 in 1957 to 305 in 1970 while in the Federal Republic the number fell from 649 in 1955 to 515 in 1970. But there was still a greater conflux of apprentices into a small number of trades in the Federal Republic (70 per cent of the total in 34 trades in 1965) than in the *DDR* (75 per cent of the total concentrated in 65

P

trades in 1966). It would appear however that in neither State was there an obvious proportional growth in the number entering those groups of trades which were considered most important from the point of view of manpower needs.[49] Consequently in both systems there was a need to institute measures to channel apprentices in the required direction.

In the *DDR* this need was interpreted within the context of total economic planning by the creation of the *Grundberufe*. It will be recalled that these represented a new conception in vocational training, a composite trade qualification which, as well as containing a specialism in the old sense, also included knowledge which applies at a basic level to all trades and at a rather more advanced level to the particular group of trades within which the specialism lies. This pyramid-like structure of training corresponded to the conception of 'all-round development' which was intended to characterize the 'socialist personality'. By 1970 26 *Grundberufe* had been introduced.[50] In addition to the advantages to the individual in terms of versatility which a training of this kind gave, it created in theory the precondition for mobility of labour in the rapidly changing situation which had been forecast in the *Grundsätze* of 1960.

In the Federal Republic the lack of a central body to direct the entire development of vocational education inhibited the growth of a wholesale rationalization of this kind. Consequently where similar initiatives were taken it was within the ambit of those individual large firms which had structured their training to offer various self-contained levels of qualification. This '*Stufenausbildung*' did not however amount to a national system as in the *DDR*. Rather it was made up of a number of experimental schemes which as a result of the 1969 Law began to receive encouragement from the Federal Government. The degree to which *Stufenausbildung* would eventually match the *Grundberuf* system in respect of the variety of knowledge and skills built into the training offered, probably depended on the efficacy of the Law. Where the *Grundberuf* guaranteed to all

[49] Hegelheimer, op. cit., pp. 3–6.   [50] Ibid., p. 3.

apprentices the final composite qualification which was applicable to the highest level of skilled work, in the *Stufenausbildung* concept a partial qualification was offered at the various levels so that only some reached the highest level.[51] Inherent in this latter system was the danger that the degree of education offered to apprentices would be determined by the requirements of the company concerned, rather than the needs of the individual apprentice. It was thus in theory open to the longstanding Marxist accusation that capitalism offers only sufficient education to ensure profitability.

The extent to which any such accusation can be justified depends on a series of factors, not least the degree of influence which the new Law in the Federal Republic would have. One traditionally alleged abuse in the apprenticeship system was the failure of firms to ensure the competence of instructors and the Law gave an indication that such instructors would in the future be required to be qualified to give instruction both on the basis of personal qualities and professional ability. It is quite possible that this heralded increased pressure on industry to organize vocational training in the interests of the individual and of the country as a whole, and not merely at the convenience of the individual firm. It was possible that similar intervention would follow in the sphere of content and ultimately bring about a national qualifications structure similar to the one envisaged and already partly realized in the *DDR*.

When the stages of development reached in the two States by 1970 are compared it emerges that noticeably more had happened in the *DDR* than in the Federal Republic. In the vocational sector a direct comparison is more valid than in the case of full-time education leading to the *Abitur* and university, where a clash of values was involved over the degree to which the balance between the various disciplines should be subordinated to economic criteria. In vocational education, which in both cases is obviously directly related to economic issues, the relative interests of the individual concern, the individual

[51] Ibid., pp. 48–50.

employee and the country as a whole can be assessed. At the stage of development reached in 1970 the latter two items appeared to rate more highly in the *DDR* than in the Federal Republic.

CHAPTER 7

Retrospect and Prospect

The 1950s and 'Divergence'

In the occupied Germany of the immediate post-war years it was clear that the role of the educational system was an important one but it was less immediately obvious in what way it should be adapted in order to help promote a change of heart. In the matter of the elusive relationship between education and society it is debatable whether the German school system had been a predominantly negative influence fostering the growth of anti-democratic and militaristic attitudes or a positive one which had striven to encourage humane values but had been gradually and systematically manipulated by the National Socialist regime.

The differing developments in the two States that have been traced in the foregoing chapters have their starting-points in contrasting evaluations of the traditional educational heritage. Educational policy in the West was dominated by the concern to preserve this heritage and in the East by the determination to transform it. Both approaches had obvious inherent risks. Those who advocated preservation or 'restoration' were in danger of clinging to structures that were the product of a different age and were increasingly irrelevant in the face of changing social and economic conditions. Those who were bent on swift radical change were in danger of discounting the importance of the deeply rooted attitudes which permeated the entire system and which could only undergo a constructive transformation through a gradual process of persuasion. These deeply ingrained attitudes were a reality throughout Germany immediately after the war. The teaching profession was of course purged of Nazism with varying degrees of rigour, but even in the Soviet zone where only some 25 per cent of those who had been employed before the war regained their posts, the survival of much of the traditional ethos is evident. This ethos is characterized above all by the prestige of *Gymnasium* education and the commitment to its uncompromising standards of scholarship. The contrast between this kind of provision for the academically inclined minority and the type of education pursued by the remainder was quite stark. For those who did not transfer to the *Gymnasium* or the *Mittelschule* an undemanding programme was the rule leading to apprenticeship from the age of fourteen.

The resulting dualism, going back as it did beyond living memory, played a key role in fashioning attitudes to educational development in both post-war German States. The *Gymnasium* in the West retained its strong, indeed virtually exclusive, orientation to the academic requirements of the *Hochschulreife*. But though in the East it only survived in the form of the four-year *Oberschule*, much of the same exclusiveness remained. Of all the sectors of the system it was the *Oberschule* which was the most resistant to changes envisaged as part of official policy. The concern to retain a measure of priority for the academic standards of the more gifted showed itself repeatedly during the Occupation period and the decade that followed. The 'core and course' system was operated with this end in view so that in practice even after the introduction of the 1946 Law there was a good measure of segregation of the more able after six years and even in some cases after four years of schooling. Though this practice was suppressed in the late 1940s its reintroduction was strongly advocated by the 'revisionists' in the following decade primarily on the grounds that academic standards at the universities were suffering because of inadequate preparation in the schools.

It is difficult to gauge how strong was the general awareness of the social class overtones of the dualism. Many defenders of the *Gymnasium* tradition would have maintained that the criteria were purely intellectual and as such fair to all irrespective of family background. There was little if any documentation of the crucial role which parents played and the degree to which their sins of omission were visited on their children. Some factions of the pre-Nazi Reform movement had of course had close links with socialism but these had never been strong enough to shake the firm foundations on which the *Gymnasium* rested. When the 1946 Law was introduced in the Soviet zone it was the first occasion on which policy had been inspired predominantly by the view from a social as opposed to an academic perspective. But just as in both States the academic teachers retained their preoccupation with the traditional concept of *Allgemeinbildung*, so was it also the case in both that those who had for generations had no contact with it continued to regard it with suspicion or disinterest. The so-called '*Bildungsabstinenz*' of the working class was just as marked a phenomenon to contend with in the *DDR* as in the Federal Republic.

It was the urge to overcome this reluctance to acquire any education beyond the minimum that provided one of the main impulses for policy in the *DDR*. In the Marxist interpretation it was necessary to rectify a sustained exploitation of the working class, whereby they were educated only to the minimum degree necessary to enable them to carry out their allotted task in industry. From being little more than extensions of the machines they attended they were to be transformed into 'fully developed personalities'. The key to the new dignity they were to acquire lay in the versatility that a longer period of education would give them. But, it was agreed, the long years of conditioning could only be combated in an aggressively positive way and hence the policies of the 1950s showed a strong measure of discrimination to this end. It was moreover not just a matter of ensuring that the members of the working class were guaranteed equal opportunity in competition with the middle class but further that they would dominate society as a whole by occupying most of the key positions. Thus from the outset policy in the *DDR* was specifically aimed at changing forcibly the existing order of society. This strong ideological conviction, indeed obsession, created a dynamism that in practice led to a squandering of human resources.

For the corollary to positive discrimination in favour of the working class was denial of opportunity to the middle class and the resulting frustrations caused large numbers of potentially highly qualified people to seek refuge in the West. Consequently the second major objective of educational policy, the guaranteeing of a well-qualified labour force, was made more difficult to achieve as a result of the ideologically inspired measures. Thus though some of the legislation was prompted purely by economic considerations, it seems fair to say that the overriding motives in the 1950s were doctrinaire ones of social ideology. The transformation of the class structure was more important than the maximum exploitation of the talent available.

Whereas the *Bildungsabstinenz* was actively combated in the *DDR* it was viewed in the Federal Republic as a phenomenon which there was no urgent need to do away with. With the restoration of the pre-1933 system the existing social structure was consolidated. The *Gymnasium* continued to be by and large the preserve of the middle class and for the great majority of the general public the type of education that it offered remained remote and mysterious. The educational policy of the 1950s in the Federal Republic, in underwriting this *status quo*, rested on the safe ground of long-established attitudes. For the vast majority the security, the social standing and the good wages guaranteed by the acquisition of a trade qualification constituted the major considerations in selecting a career. The more distant horizons of the *Abitur* and the university were seldom seen as particularly inviting. In social terms the motive behind educational policy was the preservation of the existing order.

A much more influential impulse behind policy, however, was the economic one. The 1950s were the spectacular years of the 'economic miracle' and there is no doubt that one of the main pillars on which the industrial strength of the Federal Republic rested was the efficiently trained labour force. If the system as traditionally organized could meet the needs of industry in this way there was no incentive to change it, perhaps indeed a vested interest in not doing so. And the fact that the economic success brought with it a rapidly rising standard of living at all levels of society was enough to minimize any potential social discontent.

Thus a very marked contrast can be seen between the dynamics of educational policy in the two States. In the Federal Republic various factors operated to ensure that the social perspective was largely ignored. The dominant impulse was an economic one, but passive in the sense that economic interests were best served by retaining the *status quo*. Idealism in educational objectives was confined to the pursuit of *Allgemeinbildung* by the minority. In the *DDR* the social perspective was all-important and caused the adoption of policies that in the short term were scarcely defensible on rational economic grounds. It could be argued, however, that the determination to upset the existing social order would prove beneficial in the longer term when the fluid, dynamic society that was envisaged would be better able to identify and exploit the talent of its members than the existing rigidly stratified one—a case of *reculer pour mieux sauter*.

Of the two States the *DDR* clearly set itself the more difficult task in that an attempt was being made to transform attitudes to the educational system that had existed for generations. The social flavour of policy conflicted to some degree with the traditional regard for academic values. The abortive attempt to abolish the *Oberschule* in 1953 and the subsequent revisionist advocacy of modifications to the comprehensive organization of instruction show how strong was the opposition to a policy that was concerned to equalize opportunity if necessary at the expense of the '*Leistungsprinzip*'. Within the *Oberschule* sector the pursuit of the *Abitur* and the general all-round culture associated

with it remained the major preoccupation. In this way it retained similarities to the *Gymnasium* in the Federal Republic.
The three branches into which it was divided, classical languages, modern languages and mathematics/natural science
corresponded exactly to the Western model. Even the 1959
Law, the culmination of a series of efforts to remove the *Oberschule* from its academic pedestal, was not altogether successful
in this respect.

The far-reaching changes introduced during the 1950s reflect
a very high degree of political interest in education. The fact
that all policy emanated from the Socialist Unity Party ensured
the continuity of an ideological line which made much capital
out of the leeway which the working class had to make up after
generations of underprivilege. For this, improved education
was an indispensable prerequisite. At the same time in the
Five-Year Plans a good deal was said about the relationship
between the educational system and the economy. Thus on
two major counts education was made a foremost issue in
national policy. The political interest was matched by an
enthusiasm in the implementation of policy that was at times
excessive. There were, it is true, shifts of emphasis with changes
of personnel and at one stage the proponents of a moderate line
had become very influential at various levels, but ultimately it
was the unity of hard-line purpose between the politicians and
the administrators that provided the momentum necessary to
hold to the priority of raising the overall standard throughout
the system, even if this meant sacrificing to some degree the
interests of the academically gifted. The same strong momentum was needed to introduce polytechnical instruction throughout the system, in particular the cumbersome *Unterrichtstag in der
Produktion*.

This politically inspired commitment to change was generally
lacking in the Federal Republic. There were notable exceptions
where the Social Democrats held a commanding majority in
Land assemblies and were able to introduce a six-year *Grundschule*, but even in these cases the changes were soon either

reversed or substantially modified. The fate of the reform plans tends to indicate that the consensus in favour of restoration policies was not entirely a passive one, but that where serious modifications to the traditional school system were either threatened or effected it was not difficult to arouse passionate concern for its defence. In support of this view should be mentioned the allegation that some of the reform plans had in any case been realized without any great consultation of public opinion.[1] Elsewhere, however, there was little question of a change in the *status quo*. Politically the only realistic source was the Social Democratic Party but a transformation of the school system was by no means an automatic and consistent item of its policy.

Also working against change was the fact that educational policy at *Land* level was a somewhat parochial affair, inspired more by immediate administrative requirements and occasional rivalry with neighbouring *Länder* than by searching examination of long-term implications. The structure of the school system was not generally speaking a subject on which politicians made momentous pronouncements. It was much more a field that was left to the professional administrators, and as these tended to be drawn from the ranks of those educated at *Gymnasien* and those who had taught in them, it is hardly surprising if the thought of infringing the status of such schools scarcely occurred to them. It will be recalled by comparison that from the very early days of the occupation the Soviets had made a conscious effort to alter this tradition by encouraging the appointment of Communists and Social Democrats sympathetic to radical reform programmes to key administrative posts in the educational service.

At national level education was even less of a political issue than in the *Länder*. Such full debates as were conducted in the *Bundestag* showed that towards the end of the decade some concern was beginning to be felt as to whether the educational

[1] R. Birley, 'Education in the British Zone of Germany', RIIA, *International Affairs*, Vol. XXVI, No. 1, January 1950, p. 42.

system was turning out qualified people in sufficient numbers to maintain the pace of economic advance. Where previously the desire to retain the *status quo* had been reinforced by a degree of revulsion at the egalitarian policies pursued in the *DDR*, the first signs were now appearing that in some respects the latter's performance might be proving uncomfortably challenging. It was, however, a far cry from this to a major rethinking of the educational system. On social grounds it could be ruled out since the *SPD* had by the end of the decade abandoned aggressively left-wing policies after its convincing defeat by the *CDU* in 1957. As to the economic issue, it was felt that the shortage of technically qualified manpower could be made up by increased provision of facilities for technical education aimed at those leaving the *Volksschule* and the *Mittelschule*. Any more far-reaching plan involving the fuller integration of the *Gymnasium* into the system as a whole was not seen as particularly relevant.

The contrast between, on the one hand, a strongly ideological motivation expressed in intense commitment to change in both political and administrative circles, and on the other, a general tendency to sit loose to the whole question of a comprehensively organized educational system, concentrating rather on improvements to different sectors individually on a piecemeal, pragmatic basis is illustrated by a juxtaposition of the two systems that had emerged by the end of the 1950s. The tripartite structure in the Federal Republic was basically the same as it had been in Weimar days. The selective sectors had been enlarged somewhat but for the majority still excluded from them, full-time education ended after the compulsory eight years. In the *DDR* the 1959 legislation had introduced comprehensive ten-year education for all, though there were certain exceptions, and it would be several years before the provisions of the Law could be realized. In terms of organizational 'external' reform, therefore, there was at this time a strong dissimilarity of development in the two States.

The retention of the *status quo* in the Federal Republic did not imply undiluted complacency about education but it had been a significant strand of educational thought that 'external' reform was irrelevant to the problems of the school system and that these could be tackled more constructively by 'internal reform'. The problem that loomed largest was the curriculum of the *Gymnasium*, which an increasing number of pupils were finding unpalatable. It was of course geared strongly to the requirements of the *Abitur*, which necessitated a great deal of pressure to reach high academic standards in a wide range of subjects. The resulting encyclopaedism had long been one of the less acceptable features of the *Gymnasium*, but with sylla-buses tending to expand rather than contract, the pressure, especially on pupils in the upper forms, had increased. Though there were three different types of *Gymnasium*, the broad range of subjects was pursued till the end of the course and in all three the linguistic and literary element was strong.

The reform measures that were introduced were designed to lighten the load and did so. The Saarbrücken Agreement was a remarkably rapid response to recommendations in the *Rahmen-plan* which in turn followed a line of argument that had begun with the *Tübinger Beschlüsse* of 1951, and been further developed in the form of the theory of *exemplarisches Lernen* in the years that followed. What is, in the present context, significant about the modifications made in the *Gymnasium* curriculum is that they did not tamper with its humanistic character to any serious extent. While they did much to lighten the load, they did little to shift the emphasis, so that the *Gymnasium* remained as remote from the applied, the practical, the vocational, as its nineteenth-century ideology had stipulated.

Here again the measures taken in the *DDR* were in sharp contrast in that they were intended to make the curriculum throughout the school system relevant to the requirements of production and to place a premium on the applied, the practical and the vocational. The leitmotiv of the policy of introducing polytechnical education was that the traditional curriculum had been too exclusively theoretical and that much more attention needed to be given to the unity of theory and practice. Though this policy had social significance in that it would help to make education a less remote concept for the working class and thereby encourage longer full-time attendance at school, it was potentially still more important from an economic point of view in channelling the entire school population and, *ipso facto*, the most able sectors of it, towards those fields of study and those careers that were of greatest value in building up the economy. At this stage however the manner of its introduction was precipitate and unrealistic suggesting a similar dominance of ideological verve over rational assessment of the situation to that which had characterized earlier policy initiatives.

At the close of the 1950s, then, a peak was being reached in the divergence of policy between the two States. In the *DDR* it had been a decade of assiduous striving to bring about a transformation of the traditional educational heritage, motivated perdominantly by the social considerations inherent in Marxist ideology, though at the same time maintaining that the measures embarked upon were designed to bring about the solution of economic problems on which this ideology was considered to rest. The Federal Republic had shown itself no less determined in its *resistance* to change, and this polarization of attitudes, fed by mutual repugnance, reflected a more general antagonism between the two States.

Already in 1959 however there were indications that the gulf between the two could not for long remain as wide. The social considerations of policy had dominated the *DDR* to such an extent that in the second half of the decade substantial changes in the social composition at the higher levels of the system could be claimed. It was therefore a fair assumption that these would recede in importance. On the other hand in the Federal Republic the publication of the *Rahmenplan* and the debate which followed it showed that there the social implications of policy could no longer be avoided. The economic needs in terms of manpower were also beginning to be voiced and it seemed plausible that in view of the pace of technological change the system which had served the country effectively in the previous decade was not necessarily well adapted to cope with the problems of the following one. Significantly it was just this kind of consideration that made sense of the policy of introducing polytechnical education throughout the system in the *DDR* even if its actual content and the methods of going about it were consistently in need of refinement. The two systems were bound to converge somewhat during the 1960s if only because it was inconceivable that they could remain quite so polarized.

The 1960s and 'Convergence'

In the early 1960s the chief new element in determining attitudes to educational policy in the Federal Republic was the rapid growth of empirical studies of the system. Gradually these built up a picture of the inadequacies of provision—such as the discrepancies between *Länder* and the degree of underprivilege among certain groups in society—so that a growing awareness was created of shortcomings at a national level. Thus the debate which had begun in the wake of the *Rahmenplan* was periodically refuelled as each fresh battery of evidence came to light.

There were two main strands in the research work. One was the renewed illustration of how closely the structure of the educational system mirrored the social class structure. But whereas in the previous decade the prevailing view had been that this was in the nature of things, corresponding reasonably accurately with the pattern of ability, the new research began to throw light on the environmental factors which suggested that the phenomenon could not merely be attributed to differences of innate ability. The result was a growing agreement in educational circles that social injustice in the system was not uncommon. The second strand was economic. Research studies were also beginning to give a more precise idea of what was required of the educational system in terms of output of qualified manpower and there were indications that the existing structure was ill-equipped to meet a need which was more and more frequently computed in terms of the numbers leaving the *Gymnasium* with the *Abitur*. The calculations suggested that expansion was urgent.

At the same time empirical research was growing in importance in the *DDR*. On the social side the emphasis was somewhat different from the Federal Republic since the main concern was not to promote awareness of the social injustice inherent in the hierarchical structure of the educational and class systems, but to demonstrate how effectively the hierarchy had now been dismantled. In this respect a great deal was made of the proportions drawn from working-class backgrounds at the higher levels of education. On the economic side there was an increasing preoccupation with the more precise forecasting of manpower requirements and identification of the aspects of educational provision where further development was called for. Here there was a genuine similarity to the interest that was developing in the Federal Republic.

When developments in the two States are compared the role of research can be seen as putting forward evidence that could lay claim to a reasonable degree of objectivity and as thereby increasing the readiness on both sides to take it into account as a basis for the formulation of policy. In the Federal Republic objective analysis of the system helped to bring about concern for expansion which a deeply rooted opposition to change had previously inhibited. This meant the stimulation of attempts to break down the former rigid differentiation of the structure. In the *DDR* the ideological commitment to change had overridden objective consideration of the best methods of exploiting available human resources. In this case the contribution of research was to indicate that the necessary supply of highly qualified manpower was not sufficiently well guaranteed by a totally undifferentiated system. Some kind of middle ground was therefore potentially being created.

Essential to the lessening of the polarization of attitudes to education was the new political interest that grew up in the

Federal Republic as a result of the research findings. In the previous decade there had been a sharp contrast between the intense political interest in education in the *DDR* and its failure to feature as a major issue in the Federal Republic. The early 1960s saw only a slow change in this situation until the galvanic impact of Picht's thesis of the 'educational catastrophe'. This was followed by a wave of interest which made the development of the educational system a foremost issue of national social and economic policy.

The social motive came to the fore in the policy proposals of the Social Democrats which from 1964 onwards stressed equalization of opportunity and envisaged a transition from the traditional vertically structured system to a horizontally structured one.[2] The policy of the Liberals was similar, again advocating the breakdown of rigid differentiation. The Christian Democrats on the other hand were reluctant to abandon the traditional structure, taking the view that it need not constitute an obstacle to the provision of fair opportunities for all and would moreover guarantee the preservation of high standards of achievement which was considered an equally high if not a higher priority. The formation of a government by the *SPD* in coalition with the *FDP* in 1969 suggested that a boost might be given to the introduction of a comprehensively organized school system, especially in view of the formation earlier in the same year of a Federal Ministry of Education. However there were no early signs of such a straightforward convergence with the comprehensively organized system of the Democratic Republic. For the future it was an open question, for the present the fact that the *Länder* still held firmly to their cultural autonomy seemed likely to ensure that progress in the introduction of comprehensive schools would be slow. In 1970 the number of such schools planned remained very small indeed.[3]

In the *DDR* the social issue of the breaking down of the class

[2] The first document along these lines was *Bildungspolitische Leitsätze der SPD*, Bonn, 1964.

[3] *Pädagogisches Zentrum, Gesamtschulen Informationsdienst*, 3.70, pp. 26–9.

Q

structure of educational opportunity had been virtually synonymous with the radical reshaping of the system to render impossible any early segregation of privileged groups. By this
criterion it must be concluded that by 1970 not a great deal
had changed in the Federal Republic. By and large the selective
system remained entrenched, with the emphasis in policy
placed on bringing the less favoured sectors, the *Realschule*
and the *Hauptschule*, up to standards of provision that were
comparable to those of the *Gymnasium*. The *Gymnasium* continued
to be dominant and the preponderance of pupils from middle-
class backgrounds that characterized it in the early 1960s was
being reduced only very slowly in the latter half of the decade.
Thus though the research studies had prepared the ground for a
greater spread of opportunity, and the political parties had
taken up the campaign at national level the actual rate of
change 'on the ground' was far from rapid. In this respect
therefore the degree of convergence with the Democratic
Republic was correspondingly low. There was little sign of the
use of the educational system as an instrument for the reordering
of society as had been the case in the *DDR* in the 1950s.

The desire to cling to the *status quo* as regards fundamental
structure, however, does not mean that no positive action
followed the wave of political interest in education that marked
the mid-1960s in the Federal Republic. The most influential
factor in the arousal of this interest had been the publication of
the 'German Educational Catastrophe' and the burden of
Picht's argument in this had been economic rather than social.
To recapitulate, his thesis was that the West German standard
of living was in jeopardy because, in the output of highly qualified manpower on which continued industrial success depended
in an increasingly technological age, the Federal Republic
was being outstripped by the other countries of Europe. The
obvious remedy appeared to be a wholesale expansion designed
to bring about a dramatic rise in the number of *Abiturienten*.
It was moreover quite clear that this could not be achieved
without some degree of planning and in the following year the

Bildungsrat was set up to examine the system and make the appropriate policy recommendations.

The difference between the *Bildungsrat* and its predecessor the *Deutscher Ausschuß* was perhaps above all that whereas the latter had not been greatly concerned to quantify its recommendations and to explore their financial implications, the new council was expected to translate its ideas on the subject of planning into viable governmental measures.[4] Thus it should be emphasized that with the creation of the *Bildungsrat* the Federal Republic was for the first time adopting a favourable, constructive attitude towards overall long-term planning for the educational system. In this respect there is better reason to talk of a growing similarity to the approach in the *DDR* where the long-term planning of the educational system and its output of manpower had always been a feature, but was now fast growing in sophistication. In both cases, moreover, it was the economic advantages of planning that were of paramount interest.

In the Federal Republic the methods adopted by the *Bildungsrat* clearly showed that a radical restructuring of the entire system on comprehensive lines in order that greater equality of opportunity should be introduced and should be seen to be introduced, was not the main preoccupation. It was recognized at the outset that, with the wide range of conflicting pressure groups and vested interests that existed, such a policy was not viable, but would merely be disruptive and debilitating. In approaching the problem instead from the point of view of the qualifications system the *Bildungsrat* attempted to create a structure that was one step beyond the arguments over differentiation and within which the entire variety of possible systems from the uncompromisingly traditional to the radically innovatory could be accommodated. Thus while the *Gymnasium* could continue to be more selective than the *Realschule*, and the *Realschule* more selective than the *Hauptschule*, the same intermediate qualification was to be awarded by all three and was to

[4] F. Edding, 'Educational Planning in Western Germany', *World Yearbook of Education*, London, 1967, p. 101.

give access to whatever type of upper secondary education the pupil wished to pursue. The essence of this proposed policy of creating a comprehensive qualifications system as opposed to a comprehensive school system, was that it was designed to encourage the maximum number to proceed to the *Abitur*, but avoided the issue of whether the *Gymnasium* was continuing to be the preserve of a privileged sector of society. From the academic point of view it had the advantage that the most able would continue to attend the *Gymnasium*, where the tradition of scholarship would ensure that their talents were thoroughly exploited. It had always been a fear in the Federal Republic that the standards of the most able would suffer in any wholesale comprehensive reorganization.

In the Democratic Republic demands for a higher output of qualified manpower had become a commonplace by the 1960s so that both States were by the end of the decade firmly on the path of expansion. The interesting feature of this in the *DDR*, however, was that it had become a good deal more discriminating than previously. It had become clear, no doubt as a result of the activity of the planning commission, that previous calls for expansion had not met the urgent economic need in terms of output of the very highly qualified. It was on these grounds that the various types of specialist classes and specialist schools were introduced in the mid-1960s.

It is sometimes pointed out how with this reintroduction of differentiation the *DDR* had moved away from its extreme position on this issue, just as in the Federal Republic the opposition to the introduction of comprehensive schools had lessened. This is however only partially true. The small percentage represented by the specialist classes and schools in the *DDR* was numerically not comparable with the 35 per cent or so selected for the *Gymnasium* and the *Realschule* in the Federal Republic. Moreover, while in the latter case there is little question that the hierarchy of types of school still reflected to a substantial degree the structure of society as a whole, it would be firmly denied in the *DDR* that the specialist classes or schools were in any way the preserve of one socially privileged group. It is impossible to test this but even if it were true that a degree of privilege was in evidence the small proportion for which the sector catered, some 2 to 3 per cent of the age group—no precise statistics are given—was not sufficient to suggest injustice on a large scale. The undoubted departure from the comprehensive principle, however, is an indication of the readiness to base development on objective analysis of needs rather than on the dictates of social principles.

The later modifications of the school system in the *DDR* indicate how the economic objectives had acquired pride of place. In this respect there is an undoubted similarity with the Federal Republic where the economic importance of the expansion of the system was assuming overriding significance at this time. In both countries it was a major concern to plan educational development accordingly and while this represents a marked degree of convergence of policies in relation to the previous decade, a comparison of the approaches to planning reveals a striking gap between the underlying assumptions. The pressures of industrial competition may have been similar and called for organizational measures—differentiation of various kinds—which were increasingly independent of ideological considerations. Neither the nine-year selective *Gymnasium* nor the thoroughgoing comprehensive principle was completely sacrosanct any longer. But the attitudes to the ultimate purpose of planning and the methods employed to achieve the desired results remained separated by a gap which was fundamentally one of political ideology. The advent of sophisticated educational planning, while in one sense it brought the two countries together in the exercise of the same kinds of expertise, also offers an object lesson on the nature of the gulf between communist and non-communist society.

The comparison made earlier of the mechanics of transition from secondary to higher education provides a striking illustration of this gulf. In the Democratic Republic the distribution of university studies was decided directly on the basis of the planning of national manpower needs and unrelated to the pattern of demand among those qualifying for entry by obtaining the *Abitur*. This represents a complete transformation of the traditional system whereby possession of the *Abitur* conferred the right to enter any faculty the candidate chose, the inviolable individualism conveyed by the term '*Lernfreiheit*'. The *DDR* had therefore passed from the complete absence of planning to its complete implementation. This issue created a profound dilemma for the Federal Republic in the later 1960s. The traditional '*Lernfreiheit*' could no longer be unreservedly acceptable, and it has already been demonstrated how restrictions gradually came to be imposed. Yet it is equally clear that such restrictions were seen as a necessary evil and not acceptable above a necessary minimum.[5] The planning exercise had therefore to stop some way short of laying down arbitrarily the kind of balance to be struck between the humanities, science and technology. This balance could of course be changed by varying the rate of development in different sectors of higher education, but indirect adjustments of this kind are very different from the meticulous planning and reorganization practised in the *DDR*.

Furthermore, an assessment of the value of the most able pupils in terms of their potential contribution to economic needs would be entirely at odds with the educational objectives of the schools of the Federal Republic. It has been amply demonstrated that the *Gymnasium* sector retained throughout the 1960s a marked humanistic bias deriving from a *Bildungsideal* for which economic requirements were irrelevant. Much of the thinking on curriculum development in the later 1960s recognized that this had been a somewhat one-sided emphasis and that more should be done to encourage lines of study which had a more obviously technical or vocational relevance. In this way policy was aimed at building up the existing vocational route to higher education, the *zweiter Bildungsweg*, and at breaking down in the upper forms of the *Gymnasium* too the strict de-

[5] H. Leussink, Federal Minister of Education and Science. Press Conference Report. *Education in Germany*, 1/1970, pp. 7–8.

marcation between the traditionally academic and the more straightforwardly vocational courses at the new level of *Abitur II*. But the various suggestions were all aimed at providing an *alternative* to the traditional *Bildungsideal*, not at replacing it. The choice was still to be with the individual pupil and was guaranteed by the retention of a largely free university entry system, subject only to minimum restrictions.

In the *DDR* on the other hand it was essential to the rejection of the traditional *Bildungsideal* that the entire school curriculum should be oriented towards science and technology. The process of curriculum development to which much more attention was paid in the 1960s than in the Federal Republic reflects deliberate intervention to channel the resources of ability in a direction which coincided with the economic requirements of the State. In the Federal Republic such intervention would have been regarded as a forcible alteration of the natural flow as conditioned by the existing attitudes in society at large. In the *DDR*, however, it was just such existing attitudes that it had been a matter of long-term strategy to change. This planned transformation of the inherited culture through transformation of the curriculum is the key to the role of education in the prevailing political ideology.

For it reveals educational policy as being formulated in order to realize a preconceived notion of society. Education was planned and directed on the basis of long-term forecasting of the development of the 'comprehensive social system'. At the heart of this conception of a comprehensive social system is the identity of social and individual interests. The role of the individual is determined by the requirements of planning and the educational system enlists all available agencies to ensure willing and positive acceptance of this. It has already been seen how the curriculum throughout the system was deliberately oriented towards applied science and technology, how extra-curricular activities were specifically designed to foster this kind of interest and how civic education was intended to nurture a commitment to the end-product of long-term forecasting and economic planning, the comprehensive social system. It has, further, been repeatedly demonstrated how the outside agencies of the youth movement and the parents' associations were mobilized to play their part in inculcating positive attitudes to the development of socialist society. All the strands were drawn together in the effort to create the new culture which was the precondition for the realization of the political ideology of the *DDR*.

In 1970 this transformation of the traditional culture, which was the sum of educational policy measures in the *DDR*, still stood in sharp contrast to the culture that had continued to be transmitted in the Federal Republic. Despite the pressure to raise the output of manpower the *Bildungsideal* had survived. Admittedly the traditional humanism no longer dominated the entire system as it had previously done. The pressure increased for alternative values to be accorded comparable importance and the evidence that this was in fact beginning to happen can be readily seen in the incipient disintegration of the unitary concept of '*Hochschulreife*'. But the contrast with the Democratic Republic is that no one philosophy determined the aims of education, and the comparisons that have been made of curriculum, of the mechanics of access to higher education and of the organization of vocational training show what a wide gap this philosophical difference meant in practice. In the Federal Republic the need to come to terms both with the case for the retention of the traditional *Bildungsideal* and with the subsequent pressures of manpower requirements ensured that the academic career embarked upon continued to be a matter of individual choice. The sum of such choices is a potential influence on the development of society which was inconceivable in the *DDR* where much less autonomy of action was allowed to reside in the individual.

In this vital respect, whatever the apparent convergence in terms of political interest, social awareness or economic necessity, the polarity between the pluralistic and the monistic approaches to the development of society and the role that education should play in this development, remains unmistakable.

The 1970s and New Priorities

The historical perspective of the educational development of the two Germanies has revealed variations of pace and emphasis in policy. The relative sluggishness of development in the Federal Republic which marked the 1950s gave way to a remarkable acceleration in the later 1960s so that by the end of the decade both systems were strongly oriented towards exploiting to a high degree the talent residing in the school population.

In the West, it will be recalled, the yardstick for successful expansion was the proportion of the age group completing a full secondary education—the 'quota' of *Abiturienten*. It therefore becomes interesting to compare the output of the two States in this respect, since in the *DDR* expansion had early on been the watchword of policy (Table, p. 240). Though the statistics available are somewhat incomplete they show quite clearly that in the later 1950s and early 1960s the *DDR* was some way ahead of the West. A peak was reached in 1963 when the rates, calculated as a proportion of the age group, were approximately 11 per cent and a little over 7 per cent respectively. Perhaps significantly this was the year before the publication of the 'German Educational Catastrophe'. By 1967, however, the position had been reversed, the corresponding rate having fallen to a little over 7 per cent in the *DDR* and risen to over 9 per cent in the Federal Republic. Thereafter the rate in the latter showed the faster increase of the two. It is possible that the figures for those taking the *Abitur* by way of vocational education in the *DDR* redressed this balance somewhat, but in view of the reasonably close correspondence between the numbers of *Abiturienten* and the numbers of entrants to full-time university study it seems unlikely that the total picture was altered beyond approximate parity between the two systems. Such a comparison suggests that there is not so obvious a relationship between democratization through the introduction of a comprehensive system and output of potential

Numbers of pupils obtaining the *Abitur* in the *Gymnasium* of the Federal Republic and the *erweiterte Oberschule* of the *DDR*[6]

Year	Federal Republic			Democratic Republic		
	Absolute number	Rate of increase/decrease	Approximate proportion of age group	Absolute number	Rate of increase/decrease	Approximate proportion of age group
1957	42,737	100		22,154	100	
1958	46,742	109·4		19,771	89·3	
1959	51,453	120·4		19,046	86·0	
1960	55,721	130·4	5·9	18,282	82·5	
1961	57,688	135·0	6·2			
1962	58,483	136·8	6·7	20,378	92·0	9·4
1963	59,851	140·0	7·3	16,917	76·4	11·1
1964	55,974	131·0	7·4	15,677	70·8	8·1
1965	48,592	113·7	6·9	19,332	87·3	9·6
1966 I *	51,278	120·0	7·8			
1966 II	44,267	103·6	8·2	17,080	77·1	7·9
1967	63,301	148·1	9·3	18,090	81·7	7·2
1968	73,052	170·9		21,326	96·3	7·6
1969	77,190	180·6		23,943	108·1	

* *Two 'Cohorts' in 1966 owing to reorganization of school year.*

[6] Federal Republic: (1) F.J. Weiss, *Regionale Entwicklung und Verteilung der Abiturientenzahlen 1957 bis 1968. Wirtschaft und Statistik*, 10/1970, p. 597. (Figures for 1969 supplied by Statistisches Bundesamt, Wiesbaden.) (2) *Deutscher Bildungsrat, Zur Neugestaltung der Abschlüsse im Sekundarschulwesen*, p. 23. (Proportion of age group calculated on the basis of figures which include students of Abendgymnasien and Kollegs.)

Democratic Republic: (1) *Statistisches Jahrbuch der Deutschen Demokratischen Republik*, 1962, pp. 106-7; 1970, p. 374. (Figures are for *entrants* for the examination: the failure rate is generally just under 5 per cent.) (2) K.-D. Mende, *Ab-*

university students as is often assumed. In so far as the reasons for change are the economic ones of tapping the unexploited pool of ability in order to raise the output of highly qualified manpower the Federal Republic's policy of retaining the selective *Gymnasium* and *Realschule* would on the face of it appear to be just as successful, if not more successful than the opposite course followed in the *DDR*, namely the creation of an entirely new horizontally structured system. The question of change in the structure of educational systems seems much more a social and ideological one.

As regards social policy it has been amply demonstrated that the overriding motivation in the introduction of the comprehensive school system in the *DDR* in the 1950s was the reversal of the existing social order, so that in the higher echelons the working class would be represented in proportion to its representation in the population as a whole. A detailed look at the statistics given for the social origin of university students shows however that a high representation of the working class was achieved relatively early, reaching a peak figure of 52·7 per cent in 1958. Thereafter there was a steady fall to 38·2 per cent in 1967. Over the same period the proportion drawn from the intelligentsia category rose from 13·8 to 20·4 per cent (see Appendix VI). After 1968 the corresponding statistics were no longer given in the *Statistical Yearbook*. It is impossible to give a precise figure for the size of the intelligentsia in relation to the total population but it would appear to be well under 10 per cent.[7] With regard to future development in the 1970s the scope for speculation is vast, for the figures suggest a decline in the importance accorded to the social aspects of educational policy. There arises the possibility of a new social hierarchy headed by a technocratic élite for which in purely quantitative terms the opportunities for advancement are considerably greater than for the remainder of the population. From time to time there have been indications of a recognition of this danger, reflected in calls for a renewal of the efforts to

[7] Mende, op. cit., pp. 2/88, 153.

discriminate positively in favour of working-class children in order to make the pattern of opportunity correspond to the social composition of the population as a whole. It was, for example, claimed that 'this very principle of regard for the social structure of the population in the promotion of pupils to the *Abiturstufe* is in many *Oberschulen* not adhered to with sufficient rigour.[8] But the possibility must by no means be ruled out that the notion of a self-perpetuating ascendancy of the working class has proved chimeric and that meritocratic criteria may become established in both German States. Of course the Federal Republic would need to advance further along the road to democratization to make such a view tenable but there are indications that this is happening, albeit slowly.[9]

When the prospects for the 1970s are assessed in the light of the economic and social considerations discussed above it begins to be clear that the issue of differentiation which dominated the educational debate in the two previous decades is likely to become less and less prominent. The trends suggest that the really relevant field for comparison is neither the degree of democratization, nor the quantity of *Abiturienten* turned out by the respective systems but the nature of the *Abitur* itself, and still more of the curriculum provided for those not proceeding to this level. It has been amply illustrated how the curriculum in the *DDR* was adapted in order to match the output of the schools to the needs of the economy. The statistics suggest that a policy of this kind did not require a particularly rapid increase in the numbers of *Abiturienten*, such as took place in the Federal Republic. Indeed one of the dangers of the developments in the West has been that the expansion would prove to be unrelated to the vocational opportunities available. And the unfortunate concomitant of the emphasis on the *Abitur*

[8] H. Kahra, E. Rademann, W. Steinke, *Förderung der Arbeiter- und Bauern-kinder unter den Bedingungen der Gestaltung des entwickelten gesellschaftlichen Systems des Sozialismus. Pädagogik*, 11/1970, p. 1020.

[9] For example, in North Rhine Westphalia 19 per cent of pupils entering the *Gymnasium* and 41 per cent of those entering the *Realschule* were from the working class. *Wirtschaft und Berufserziehung*, 7/1970, p. 127.

was the corresponding neglect of the vocational training sector, one which had traditionally been one of Germany's great strengths and which by the end of the 1960s was in a parlous condition.

The problem of dissatisfaction in this sector was clearly too urgent to be resolved in the context of the debate about the introduction of *Gesamtschulen*. Even in a relatively radical *Land* like Hesse with a throughgoing commitment to the introduction of comprehensive education, policy had by the early 1970s developed little further than the introduction of the *Förderstufe* for the 10–12 age group: the further stage of the integration of *Gymnasium*, *Realschule* and *Hauptschule* still lay well in the future. Not least among the deterrents to the wholesale introduction of the *Gesamtschule* and the implementation of the various recommendations in the *Strukturplan* of 1970 was the realization of the high cost involved which followed the studies of projected educational budgets made by the federal body set up for this purpose, the *Bund-Länder-Kommission für Bildungsplanung*.

It is hardly surprising therefore that as far as immediate practical policies in the Federal Republic are concerned, the focus is shifting to the vocational sector, where it is now considered essential to make provision on a comparably generous scale to that previously available for general education. Symptomatic of this new view of priorities was Brandt's statement on future policy to the newly elected *Bundestag* in January 1973. The government, he declared, favoured the reduction of full-length schooling up to *Abitur* level from 13 to 12 years. Furthermore, 'equality of opportunity demands for vocational education the same status as other educational sectors . . . vocational and general education must be more closely integrated'.[10] Clearly one of the foremost problems of the present decade is how this improvement in the quality of vocational education is to be achieved. In this respect the Vocational Education Law of 1969 was a cautious beginning. The issue that

[10] *Das Parlament Nr. 4*, 27.1.1973.

now arises is the redefinition of the respective roles of the industrial and commerical concerns and of the schools in the process. The statement just quoted could justifiably be interpreted as a sober and realistic appraisal of where the new priorities should lie. On the other hand its perfunctory tone could be interpreted as ushering in a period of inactivity, confirming the anticlimactic trend after the longsighted and imaginative proposals of the *Bildungsrat*, the ebbing of the tide that swept education into the forefront of national social and economic policy. The most significant test of the resolution of the new government will be the degree of advance on the Vocational Education Law that is achieved.

In fact, in the West, attention is being focused on a problem which bulked large in the educational debate in the *DDR* in the 1960s and which seems likely to continue to be prominent in policy developments. The interpretation of polytechnical education was still being discussed at length in the early 1970s with particular reference to developments in the Soviet Union.[11] The purpose of this continuing preoccupation was, as previously, to achieve a close fit between the education and training provided and the needs of the economy, at all levels from apprenticeship to *Abitur*. The particular character of this policy derives from the basic tenet of Marxist-Leninist ideology that the economic criteria can be entirely in harmony with criteria for the freedom of the individual. Great importance was attached to 'the prognosis of the development of the system of planning and directing society as well as of the conditions and methods for ensuring the unity between social and individual interests'.[12] These words of Ulbricht rest on the assumption, discussed in the previous chapter, that in a totally planned social system, conflicts between the interests of individuals and those of society scarcely arise.

[11] See for example H. Frankiewicz, *Die polytechnische Bildung als Allgemeinbildung. Pädagogik*, 12/1972, p. 1117, and *Polytechnische Bildung und Verbindung von Unterricht und produktiver Arbeit. Pädagogik*, 1/1973, p. 14.

[12] W. Ulbricht, *Die gesellschaftliche Entwicklung in der DDR bis zur Vollendung des Sozialismus*, Berlin, 1967, p. 95.

It is at this point that the ideological gulf between East and West, as it affects the educational system, is most clearly shown. Such an all-embracing concept is inconceivable in the Federal Republic where free choice of trade or profession is enshrined in the constitution. When a demonstrable imbalance arises between the output of schools and prospects for employment, this cannot easily be corrected by direct governmental action to reduce in size those sectors that are over-producing. There is still a strong feeling that it is the responsibility of the individual to choose his own course of action without interference on the part of the State and to assess for himself what the consequences will be. And for many the criteria for choice in education will continue to be humanistic, irrespective of vocational considerations. Modern conditions do require the balance to be adjusted, but the only viable course is to work towards a situation where provision and prospects in the more directly vocational sectors can compete in attractiveness with those hitherto more favoured sectors concerned with general education. It is in the nature and degree of the intervention on the part of the State to achieve an acceptable balance, that the crucial difference between the approaches to education of the two Germanies will be seen in the future.

APPENDIX I

Curriculum of the top three forms (Oberstufe) *of the three types of* Gymnasium *in West Berlin 1954, i.e. years 11, 12 and 13 of school attendance*

Group of Subjects	TYPE OF GYMNASIUM								
	Classical			Modern Languages			Maths/Nat. Science		
	11	12	13	11	12	13	11	12	13
German, History Geography, Civics	8	8	9	8	8	10	8	8	10
Foreign Languages	12	12	12	12	11	11	7	7	4
Maths, Physics Chemistry, Biology	8	8	5	8	9	5	12	13	12
Music, Art Physical Education	6	6	2	6	6	2	7	6	2
Total number of periods	34	34	28	34	34	28	34	34	28

Source
Senator für Volksbildung, Entwurf eines Bildungsplans für die Oberschule Wissenschaftlichen Zweiges, Berlin, 1954, pp. 1, 4, 8.

R

APPENDIX II

Curriculum of the Oberschule *and* Zehnklassenschule *in the Democratic Republic 1951, i.e. years 9, 10, 11 and 12 of school attendance*

Subject	9 Ten-year school	9 Oberschule A B C	10 Ten-year school	10 Oberschule A B C	11 A B C	12 A B C
German	5	5 5 5	4	4 4 4	4 4 4	4 4 4
Russian	4	4 4 4	4	4 4 4	3 3 3	3 3 3
For. Lang. II	–	5 – 6	–	6 – 4	4 4 4	4 4 4
For. Lang. III	–	– – –	–	– – 4	6 – 8	6 – 8
History	3	3 3 3	3	3 3 3	3 3 3	3 3 3
Civics	1	1 1 1	1	1 1 1	1 1 1	1 1 1
Geography	2	2 2 2	2	2 2 2	1 1 –	1 1 –
Mathematics	5	3 5 3	5	3 5 3	3 5 3	3 5 3
Physics	3	2 3 2	3	2 3 2	2 3 2	2 3 2
Chemistry	2	1 2 1	3	1 3 1	1 3 1	1 3 1
Biology	3	2 3 2	3	2 3 2	2 3 2	2 3 2
Music	1	1 1 1	1	1 1 1	1 1 1	1 1 1
Art	1	1 1 1	1	1 1 1	2 2 2	2 2 2
Phys. Educ.	2	2 2 2	2	2 2 2		
Total	32	32 32 33	32	32 32 34	33 33 34	33 33 34

Transfer possible from ten-year school to branch B of *Oberschule*. Pattern of foreign languages studied:

	A	B	C
Foreign Language II	English, French	English, French Latin	Latin
Foreign Language III	Latin	—	Greek

Source
Amtliche Bestimmungen für allgemeinbildende Schulen, G. 5a 1. *Beilage zu 'die neue Schule'*, 27/1951.

Examples of the curriculum of the Mittelschule *in the Federal Republic 1952, 1956, i.e. years 5–10 of school attendance*

(a) Schleswig-Holstein

Subject	5	6	7	8	9	10
Religion	2	2	2	2	2	2
German	5	5	5	5	5	5
History	1	2	2	2	2	2
Geography	2	2	2	2	2	2
French/Latin	–	–	(4)	(4)	(3)	(3)
English	6	5	4	4	4	4
Maths	4	5	5	5	B 5 G 4	B 5 G 4
Physics, Chemistry	–	–	2	B 3/4 G 2/3	B 3/4 G 2/3	B 3/4 G 2/3
Biology	2	2	2	2	B 2 G 1	B 2 G 1
Art, Handwork Needlework	3	3	3/4	B 3/4 G 4	B 3/4 G 3/4	B 3/4 G 3/4
Music	2	2	1/2	B 1 G 1/2	1/2	1/2
Phys. Educ.	3	3	3	3	3	B 3 G 3
Shorthand	–	–	–	–	(2)	(2)
Typing	–	–	–	–	(2)	(2)
Dom. Science	–	–	–	–	4	4
TOTAL Boys	30	31	32	33	34	34
Girls	30	31	32	33	35	35
Additional Optional Instruction			4	4	5	5

Figures in brackets refer to optional subjects.

Source
Lehrpläne für die Mittelschulen in Schleswig-Holstein, Kiel, Feb. 1952, p. 6.

(b) Lower Saxony							
	5	6	7	8	9	10	Total
A. 'Core' Subjects							
1. Religion	2	2	2	2	2	2	12
2. (a) German							
(b) History	7	8	8	8	8	8	47
(c) Geography	(8)						(48)
(d) Civics							
3. English	6	5	4	4	4	4	27
4. (a) Music							
(b) Art	9	9	8	8	7	7	48
(c) Handwork	(8)						(47)
(d) Sport							
5. (a) Maths							
(b) Biology	6	6	7	7	8	8	42
(c) Physics/Chemistry							
(d) Domestic Science					(+2)	(+2)	
6. Spare period			1	1	1	1	4
TOTAL	30	30	30	30	30	30	180
B. Optional Courses: e.g.							
French	–	–	4	4	4	4	16
Shorthand/Typing	–	–	–	2	2	2	6

Source
Richtlinien für den Unterricht an Mittelschulen im Lande Niedersachsen, Hannover, 17. Oktober 1956, pp. 7, 8.

APPENDIX IV

Curriculum of the Zehnklassenschule *in the Democratic Republic 1955–56, i.e. years 1–10 of school attendance*

Subject	1	2	3	4	5	6	7	8	9	10
German	8	12	14	12	8	7	6	6	5	5
Environment	–	–	–	4	–	–	–	–	–	–
Russian	–	–	–	–	4	4	4	4	3	3
History	–	–	–	–	2	2	3	3	2	2
Civics	–	–	–	–	–	–	1	1	–	–
Geography	–	–	–	–	2	2	2	2	2	2
Maths	5	5	6	6	5	5	5	5	5	5
Biology	–	–	–	–	2	2	2	2	3	3
Physics	–	–	–	–	–	2	2	2	3	3
Chemistry	–	–	–	–	–	–	2	2	2	3
Needlework (Girls)	–	1	1	1	1	1	1	1	–	–
Handwork	–	–	–	–	–	–	–	–	3	3
Tech. Drawing	–	–	–	–	–	–	–	–	–	1
Stenography	–	–	–	–	–	–	–	–	1	1
Music	1	1	1	1	1	1	1	1	1	–
Art	1	1	1	1	1	1	1	1	1	–
Phys. Educ.	2	2	2	2	2	2	2	2	2	2

Classes 1–8: *Anweisung über die Stundentafel der allgemeinbildenden Schulen für das Schuljahr 1955–56. Vom 11. August 1955.* In *Verfügungen und Mitteilungen des Ministeriums für Volksbildung,* Nr. 19/1955, p. 181. Classes 9, 10: *Anweisung über die Stundentafel für die 9. und 10. Klasse der Zehnklassenschulen. Vom 12 Juli 1955.* In *Verfügungen und Mitteilungen des Ministeriums für Volksbildung,* Nr. 16/1955, p. 152.

APPENDIX V

Curriculum of the top three forms (Oberstufe) *of the three types of* Gymnasium, *North Rhine Westphalia 1961, years 11–13 of school attendance*

Group of subjects	Classical			Modern Languages			Maths/Nat. Science		
	11	12	13	11	12	13	11	12	13
Religious Education	2	2	2	2	2	2	2	2	2
German, History Geography, Civics	8	8	8	8	8	8	8	8	8
Foreign Languages	12	10	9	12	10	9	7	3	4
Maths, Physics, Chemistry, Biology	8	6*	7*	8	6*	7*	12	13*	12*
Music, Art Physical Education	6	4	4	6	4	4	6	4	4

* In years 12 and 13 Philosophy is offered as an alternative to Science, 3 periods in each case.

Source
Amtsblatt des Kultusministers Nordrhein—Westfalen, 4/1961, p. 75.

APPENDIX VI

Social Origins of Students in Higher Education in the Democratic Republic

Category	1954	55	56	57	58	59	60	61	62	63	64	65	66	67
1. Industrial workers	47·5	48·9	50·4	51·4	52·7	51·4	50·3	50·3	48·7	44·9	42·2	40·6	39·1	38·2
2. Clerical workers	23·8	22·3	21·0	19·9	19·2	19·0	19·2	19·4	20·5	22·0	23·1	24·0	23·5	23·5
3. Agricultural workers	5·7	5·6	5·6	5·7	5·5	5·5	4·2	5·3	5·5	6·3	6·3	6·7	7·2	7·8
4. Intelligentsia	12·0	12·9	13·6	13·8	13·8	14·9	15·6	15·4	15·9	17·0	18·5	18·7	19·7	20·4
5. Self-employed	11·0	10·3	9·4	9·2	8·8	9·2	8·0	6·2	6·3	5·9	6·4	6·7	6·9	7·1
6. Others							2·7	3·4	3·1	3·9	3·5	3·3	3·6	3·0

German designations as follows: 1. *Arbeiter*; 2. *Angestellte*; 3. *Mitglieder von Produktions-genossenschaften*; 4. *Intelligenz*; 5. *Selbstständige Erwerbstätige*; 6. *Sonstige*.

Sources

1954–59 (Global figures not broken down by 'direct' and 'indirect' study) *Statistisches Jahrbuch der DDR*, 1959, p. 141. Thereafter *Statistisches Jahrbuch*, 1960–61 p. 141, 1962 p. 125, 1963 p. 425, 1964 p. 453, 1965 p. 465, 1966 p. 477, 1967 p. 479, 1968 p. 473. After 1968 the item was excluded from the Yearbook.

APPENDIX VII

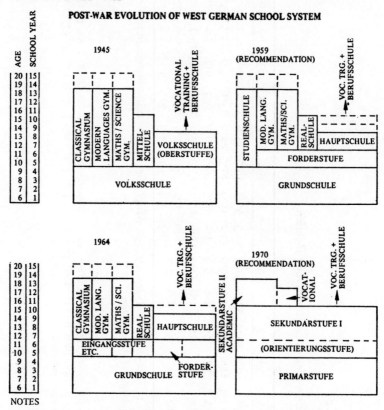

POST-WAR EVOLUTION OF WEST GERMAN SCHOOL SYSTEM

NOTES

1. Diagrams do not attempt to represent proportions of school population in different types of institution.

2. Federal structure allows for variations; diagrams give approximate representation of situation obtaining in most of country.

3. 1945: 13th school year (9th *Gymnasium* year), abolished by Nazis, progressively restored during period of Allied Occupation.

4. 1959: *Rahmenplan* scheme was purely a recommendation with no obligation on *Länder* to implement it.

5. 1964: Hamburg Agreement on inter-*Land* standardisation shows reaction in majority of cases to *Rahmenplan:* two year observation stage before *Gymnasium* not accepted but incorporated after *Gymnasium* entry under various names e.g. *Eingangsstufe.*

6. 1970: *Bildungsrat* recommendation for structure seen from perspective of acquisition of qualifications:
10 years to *Abitur I* – access to any form of upper secondary education
12 years to *'Fachschulreife'* – access to technician training
13 years to *Abitur II* – university entry

Reproduced from Comparative Education, *Volume 9, Number 1, March 1973*

APPENDIX VIII

POST-WAR EVOLUTION OF EAST GERMAN SCHOOL SYSTEM

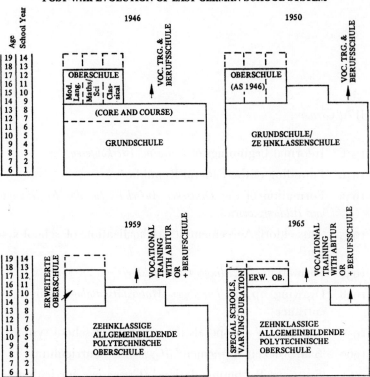

NOTES

1. Diagrams do not attempt to represent proportions of school population in different types of institution.

2. 1945: situation as for West Germany.

3. 1946: differentiated curriculum in top two classes of new *Grundschule*.

4. 1950: top two classes of *Zehnklassenschule* were generally added to an existing *Grundschule*.

5. 1959, 1965: progressive raising of minimum full-time schooling to ten years but still not fully realised.

Reproduced from Comparative Education, *Volume 9, Number 1, March 1973*

S

CHRONOLOGICAL LIST OF EVENTS

West Germany

1946 Informal beginnings of *Kultusministerkonferenz*
1949 Founding of the Federal Republic
1953 Formation of the *Deutscher Ausschuss für das Erziehungs- und Bildungswesen*
1955 'Düsseldorf Agreement' (standardization of school system)
1957 Formation of '*Ettlinger Gesprächskreis*'
1958 Drawing up of '*Tutzinger Maturitätskatalog*' (university entrance)
1959 '*Rahmenplan*' (proposals for structure of school system)
1960 'Saarbrücken Agreement' (*Gymnasium* curriculum)
1961 'Stuttgart Recommendations' (*Gymnasium* curriculum)
1964 Georg Picht: *Die deutsche Bildungskatastrophe*.
      'Hamburg Agreement' (standardization of school system)
1965 Formation of *Deutscher Bildungsrat*
1969 *Berufsbildungsgesetz* (vocational education law)
      Creation of Federal Ministry of Education
1970 *Strukturplan* (proposals of *Bildungsrat* regarding school system)
      Creation of *Bund-Länder-Kommission für Bildungsplanung*

CHRONOLOGICAL LIST OF EVENTS

East Germany

1946   *Gesetz zur Demokratisierung der deutschen Schule* ('1946 Law')

1949   Founding of the Democratic Republic

1950   First Five-Year Plan
       Introduction of the *Zehnklassenschule*

1952   Second *Parteikonferenz* of *SED*—'*Aufbau des Sozialismus*'

1953   Proposed introduction of the '*Elfklassenschule*'

1955   Second Five-Year Plan

1958   *Schulkonferenz* of *SED*—denunciation of 'revisionism'

1959   *Gesetz über die sozialistische Entwicklung des Schulwesens* ('1959 Law')

1960   Seven-Year Plan
       Grundsätze zur weiteren Entwicklung des Systems der Berufsbildung (principles of vocational education)

1963   VI *Parteitag* of *SED*—'*Umfassender Aufbau des Sozialismus*'

1964   *Grundsätze für die Gestaltung des einheitlichen sozialistischen Bildungssystems* (principles of general educational system)

1965   *Gesetz über das einheitliche sozialistische Bildungssystem* '(1965 Law')

1967   Introduction of first *Grundberufe*

1971/2 Completion of introduction of extensively reorganized curriculum and syllabuses in *Oberschule* and *erweiterte Oberschule*

GLOSSARY

Abendgymnasium   *Gymnasium* for part-time evening study
Abitur   leaving certificate of *Gymnasium*
Abiturient   pupil in final year of study at *Gymnasium*
Abiturstufe   stage of school system leading to *Abitur*
Abkommen   agreement
allgemeinbildend   providing a general education
Allgemeinbildung/allgemeine Bildung   general education in the
    Humboldt tradition
altsprachlich   concerned with classical languages
Amt   office, Ministry
Arbeiter- und Bauernstaat   State run by the industrial and
    agricultural working class
Arbeitsgemeinschaft Deutsche Höhere Schule   federation of academic
    subject teachers' associations
Arbeitsschule   'activity school' as pioneered by Georg Kerschen-
    steiner
Aufbaugymnasium Gymnasium   with shortened course for late
    beginners
Aufbauzug   promotion stream for more able pupils in *Volks-
    schule/Hauptschule*
Aufklärung   enlightenment
Ausbildung   training
Berufsaufbauschule   vocational school for pupils leaving *Haupt-
    schule* and *Realschule*, but offering courses at a higher level
    than the *Berufsschule*, both part-time and full-time
Berufsausbildung   vocational training
Berufsbild   trade profile
Berufsbildungsgesetz law concerning vocational education
    (Federal Republic 1969)

Berufsschule   vocational school for part-time study, usually in conjunction with apprenticeship

Beschluß   decision

Betriebsberufsschule   vocational school housed within a large industrial concern (*DDR*)

Bildung   education, particularly in the sense of acquisition of knowledge and refinement of aesthetic appreciation (cf. *Erziehung*)

Bildungsabstinenz   reluctance to pursue education beyond the statutory minimum

Bildungsdefizit   educational deficit

Bildungsdichte   geographical concentration of educational provision

Bildungsideal   educational ideal

Bildungskatastrophe   educational catastrophe

Bildungsplanung   educational planning

Bildungspolitik   educational policy

Bildungspolitische Leitsätze   Guidelines for Educational Policy (*SPD* 1964)

Bildungsrat   Education Council

Bildungsreserven   unused reserves of intellectual ability residing in the school population

Bund entschiedener Schulreformer   League of Radical School Reformers

Bundestag   Federal parliament of Federal Republic

Bürgerrecht   citizen's right

CDU (Christlich Demokratische Union)   Christian Democratic Party

CSU (Christlich Soziale Union)   Bavarian wing of *CDU*

DDR (Deutsche Demokratische Republik)   Democratic Republic of Germany (East Germany)

Deutsche Lehrerzeitung   German teachers' newspaper (*DDR*)

Deutsche Oberschule   type of secondary school created in the 1920s, later much favoured by the Nazis

Deutscher Ausschuß   German Committee (for Education)

Deutsches Pädagogisches Zentralinstitut   (now *Deutsche Akademie*

der Pädagogischen Wissenschaften) Central Institute for Educational Research (*DDR*)

Durchlässigkeit   liberal provision of opportunities for transfer between different types of school

einheitlich   unitary

Einheitsschule   general term for comprehensive school or comprehensive school system, mostly used in the *DDR*

Elfklassenschule   type of comprehensive school proposed in the *DDR* in 1953

Elternrecht   parents' right of choice, especially in matters relating to religious education

entwickelt   developed

Entwicklung   development

erweiterte Oberschule   upper secondary school (*DDR*)

Erziehung   education, in the general sense of upbringing (cf. *Bildung*)

Erziehungsbeihilfe   financial grant towards cost of education

exemplarisches Lernen   method of learning based on paradigmatic choice

Facharbeiterbrief   skilled worker qualification

Fachschule   higher vocational school

FDJ (*Freie Deutsche Jugend*) Youth Movement, senior branch (*DDR*)

FDP (*Freie Demokratische Partei*) Free Democratic Party (Liberal Party of Federal Republic)

F-Gvmnasium   *Gymnasium* not offering the orthodox range of academic subjects

Förderstufe   proposed two-year observation and guidance stage between primary and secondary school (*Rahmenplan* 1959)

Freier Deutscher Gewerkschaftsbund   trade union organization (*DDR*)

Fürstenschule   historical term for grammar school

gebildet   educated in the sense of 'cultured'

Gelehrtenschule   historical term for grammar school

Gemeinde   parish

Gemeinschaft   community

Gemeinschaftskunde civic education

Gemeinschaftsschule community school

Gesamtschule comprehensive school (Federal Republic)

Gesellschaft society

Gesetz law

Gewerkschaft trade union

Gleichberechtigung granting of equal rights

Göttinger Beschlüsse resolutions agreed upon at a conference in Göttingen (1964)

Grundberuf general trade, incorporating a number of formerly separate trades

Grundgesetz Basic Law, constitution of Federal Republic

Grundlehrgang basic course of instruction

Grundsätze basic principles

Grundschule primary school

Gymnasium grammar school (academic secondary school)

Hauptschule new kind of secondary school, a development of the upper classes of the *Volksschule*

Hochschulreife fitness for university study: (a) *allgemeine Hochschulreife* attested by full *Abitur*, traditionally giving right of access to any faculty; (b) *fachgebundene Hochschulreife*, attested by reduced *Abitur*, access being restricted to certain faculties

höhere Schule general term for the academic secondary school in the Federal Republic

Ingenieurschule middle-level school of engineering

Jahrgangsklasse cohort, i.e. class of pupils, generally kept together for all instruction throughout their school career

Klosterschule historical term for grammar school

Kreis (as in *Ettlinger Kreis*) discussion group; (2) local administrative district

Kulturkunde study of (German) culture

Kultusministerkonferenz Standing Conference of *Land* Ministers of Education (Federal Republic)

Land constituent State of Federal Republic

Landerziehungsheim independent boarding school, sited in rural surroundings

Landschulreglement   decree of Frederick the Great concerning elementary education

Landwirtschaft   agriculture

Lateinschule   historical term for grammar school

Lehrer   teacher

Lehrerzeitung   teachers' newspaper

Lehrplan   curriculum

Leistungsprinzip   achievement principle

Lernfreiheit   freedom of students to move from one university to another in the course of their studies

'Lernschule'   school oriented overwhelmingly towards factual learning and not greatly concerned with fostering inquiring attitudes

Maturitätskatalog   catalogue of academic requirements for university entrance

Mittelpunktschule   central school serving a number of rural communities (Federal Republic)

Mittelschule   intermediate school

Mittelstufe   intermediate stage of a school system

mittlere Reife   intermediate qualification/leaving certificate

Monatsheft   monthly journal

naturwissenschaftlich   concerned with natural sciences

Neues Deutschland   New Germany, *SED* Party newspaper

neusprachlich   concerned with modern languages

Oberschule   secondary school; the term is sometimes used as an alternative to *Gymnasium* in the Federal Republic; in the main, however, used in the *DDR* first to denote the four-year upper secondary school introduced in 1946, subsequently as the name for the comprehensive school introduced in 1959

Oberstufe   upper stage; generally used with reference to upper classes of *Volksschule* or *Gymnasium*

Parteikonferenz   minor Party conference (*DDR*)

Parteitag   major Party conference (*DDR*)

Philologenverband   association of *Gymnasium* teachers

Pioniere   see *Verband* . . .

Politbüro   policy-making organ of *SED*

polytechnisch   polytechnical

polytechnisches Kabinett   recreation room for promotion of polytechnical education

präzisiert   detailed

Produktionstag   see *Unterrichtstag* ...

Rahmenplan   Outline Plan for the school system, Federal Republic 1959

Rahmenvereinbarung   Outline Agreement on curriculum, Federal Republic 1960

Realien   subjects considered modern in relation to the classics, namely modern languages and natural science

Realschule   intermediate school, synonymous with *Mittelschule*

Reformpädagogik   educational theories of the pre-Nazi reform movement

Regierungsbezirk   administrative district

Rektorenkonferenz   Standing Conference of University Rectors (Federal Republic)

Ritterakademie   school for children of Court nobility in seventeenth and eighteenth centuries

Schulpolitik   educational policy specifically affecting the school system

Schulwesen   school system

SED (Sozialistische Einheitspartei Deutschlands) governing Socialist Party of *DDR*

'*Simultanschule*'   multi-denominational school

sozialistisch   socialist

SPD (Sozialdemokratische Partei Deutschlands)   Social Democratic Party in the Federal Republic

staatlich   of the State

Stadtschule   medieval 'city school'

Strukturplan   structural plan for the educational system, Federal Republic 1970

Studienschule   proposed designation for academic secondary school with classics-biased curriculum (*Rahmenplan* 1959)

Stufenausbildung   rationalized system of vocational education (Federal Republic)

Tübinger Beschlüsse   resolutions of a conference in Tübingen 1951

Turnerschaft   society for the furtherance of the gymnastic movement in the nineteenth century

Turnvater   leader of the *Turnerschaft*

Unterrichtstag in der Produktion   one school day per week spent in industrial or agricultural production

Unterstufe   primary stage of a school system

Verband der Jungen Pioniere   Youth Movement, junior branch

Verdienter Lehrer des Volkes   'honoured teacher of the people', a civic decoration

Vielwisserei   undiscriminating accumulation of factual knowledge

Volkskammer   *DDR* parliament

Volksschule   elementary school

Vorbereitungsklasse   preparatory class

Vorschule   fee-paying primary school

Wandervögel   lit. birds of passage; used in the sense of ramblers or hikers to denote members of the Youth Movement of the early twentieth century

Weltanschauung   ideological outlook

Zehnklassenschule   intermediate school (*DDR*), at one stage also known as *Mittelschule*

zehnklassig   having ten classes or grades

Zentralschule   central school serving a number of rural communities (*DDR*), cf. *Mittelpunktschule*

zweiter Bildungsweg   alternative route to higher education via vocational training and part-time study

SELECTED BIBLIOGRAPHY OF
WORKS IN ENGLISH

Alexander, T. and Parker, B., *The New Education in the German Republic*. New York, 1929.

Balfour, M., *West Germany*. London, 1968.

Bereday, G. Z. F., *Comparative Method in Education*. New York, 1964.

Childs, D., *East Germany*. London, 1969.

Dahrendorf, R., *Society and Democracy in Germany*. London, 1968.

Führ, C./Halls, W. D. (eds.), *Educational Reform in the Federal Republic of Germany*. Hamburg, 1970.

Gimbel, J., *A German Community under American Occupation*. Stanford, 1961.

Grant, N., *Society Schools and Progress in Eastern Europe*. Oxford, 1969.

Grant, N., *Soviet Education*. London, 1964.

Hans, N., *Comparative Education*. London, 1949.

Helmreich, E. C., *Religious Education in German Schools*. Harvard, 1959.

Holmes, B., *Problems in Education, A Comparative Approach*. London, 1965.

King, E. J. (ed.), *Communist Education*. London, 1963.

King, E. J., *Comparative Studies and Educational Decision*. London, 1962.

Kitzinger, U., *German Electoral Politics*. Oxford, 1960.

Knappen, M., *And Call It Peace*. Chicago, 1947.

Kohn, H., *The Mind of Germany*. London, 1961.

Laqueur, W. Z., *Young Germany*. London, 1962.

Lawson, R. F., *The Reform of the West German School System*. Ann Arbor, 1965.

Leonhard, W., *Child of the Revolution*. London, 1957.

Mallinson, V., *An Introduction to the Study of Comparative Education*. London, 1957.

Mann, E., *School for Barbarians*. London, 1939.

Paulsen, F., *German Education, Past and Present*. London, 1908.

Rust, V. D., *German Interest in Foreign Education since World War I*. Ann Arbor, 1965.

Samuel, R. H./Hinton Thomas R., *Education and Society in Modern Germany*. London, 1949.

Shafer, S. M., *Postwar American Influence in the West German Volksschule*. Ann Arbor, 1964.

Simons, D., *Georg Kerschensteiner*. London, 1966.

Warren, R. L., *Education in Rebhausen*. New York, 1967.

Williams, G., *Apprenticeship in Europe*. London, 1963.

Willis, F. R., *The French in Germany 1945–1949*. Stanford, 1962.

Zink, H., *The United States in Germany*. Princeton, 1957.

Index